# CITY PEOPLE

# CITY PEOPLE

## The Rise of Modern City Culture
## in Nineteenth-Century America

GUNTHER BARTH

OXFORD UNIVERSITY PRESS
Oxford   New York   Toronto   Melbourne

Oxford University Press

Oxford   London   Glasgow
New York   Toronto   Melbourne
Nairobi   Dar es Salaam   Cape Town
Kuala Lumpur   Singapore   Hong Kong   Tokyo
Delhi   Bombay   Calcutta   Madras   Karachi

and associate companies in
Beirut   Berlin   Ibadan   Mexico City

Copyright © 1980 by Oxford University Press, Inc.
First published by Oxford University Press, New York, 1980
First issued as an Oxford University Press paperback, 1982

Library of Congress Cataloging in Publication Data

Barth, Gunther Paul.
   City people.

   Bibliography: p.
   Includes index.
     1. Cities and towns—United States—Growth—
History—19th century.   2. Urbanization—United
States—History—19th century.   I. Title.
HT123.B297     307.7′6′0973     80-10875
   ISBN 0-19-502753-1
   ISBN 0-19-503194-6 pbk.

Printing (last digit): 9 8 7 6 5 4 3

Printed in the United States of America

To Our Children

# ACKNOWLEDGMENTS

I am deeply grateful for the assistance my work received from many sources.

I benefited from the support of the Committee on Research, the Humanities Research Fellowship Program, and the Department of History of the University of California at Berkeley. The custodians of libraries and archives aided my research, specifically the librarians of the various collections on the Berkeley campus, of the Bancroft Library, and of the Interlibrary Loan Department of the General Library.

My search for direction profited from conversations with Berkeley colleagues, particularly Thomas G. Barnes, Woodrow W. Borah, Robert Brentano, James H. Kettner, Leo Lowenthal, and Robert L. Middlekauff. Richard M. Abrams and William B. Slottman patiently and sympathetically shared with me their knowledge of history. My students furnished insight and inspiration. The Amerika Institut of the University of Munich provided a sudden opportunity to present my views on the cultural dimensions of the American city, and I am indebted to F. G. Friedmann for that stimulating experience. As in other endeavors Sheldon Meyer of Oxford University Press freely gave help and support.

Various contributions improved the book. John Browning gave me a copy of his paper about vaudeville's economic organization. Moses Rischin furnished the clue for the baseball article in the New York *Forward;* Chana Kronfeld helped with its Yiddish. I appreciated the good will of Joan Van Brasch, Beth Collins, Sheila Saxby, and Peter Warfield, who typed portions of the manuscript. Linda Schieber located pictures in New York, and Carol McKibben did so in Berkeley. Richard M. Abrams, John M. Findlay, James H. Kettner, Roger W. Lotchin, and Robert L. Middlekauff read and discussed the text, and their comments enriched my understanding of the nineteenth century. As so often I have benefited from Rawson L. Wood's incisive logic and practical wisdom. The rigorous as well as understanding editorial work of Stephanie Golden at Oxford University Press made the final stage of the undertaking an inspiring experience.

A few friends eased the task continuously. As research assistant Catherine M. Scholten gathered materials, shared the exploration of concepts, and edited a draft of the manuscript. Willis L. Winter, Jr., again dealt with the manuscript with that compassion and sagacity that he had mustered on previous occasions for similar editorial tasks.

Ellen W. Barth shouldered my chores at home and discussed and edited drafts. Her mind and heart made this enterprise, like earlier ventures, a part of our marriage. The result I dedicate to our children, Christine and Giselle, Dominic and Gilbert, to make up for the time I was not with them.

G. B.

*Berkeley, Calif.*
*April 1980*

# CONTENTS

# CITY PEOPLE

# INTRODUCTION

The words of a fellow-traveler inspired me as I walked the banks of the urban culture that channeled the flood of life in nineteenth-century American cities. In 1839 Henry Wadsworth Longfellow urged scholar and poet to live in the dark, gray city close to the river of life "bearing along so many gallant hearts, so many wrecks of humanity."

Throughout the ages big cities have fascinated people because they concentrate many ways of life, displaying splendor and misery on a stage for the entire world. In nineteenth-century America the drama of the scene increased when intensified urbanization and rapid industrialization exposed people to modern life.

In an atmosphere of expanding personal freedom and individual opportunity, nineteenth-century cities severed the old ties of men and women with the countryside, setting them adrift in a maelstrom of people radically different from themselves. The widening gap between past and present heightened the residents' anxiety about the meaning of an existence framed by tenement and factory. In this novel environment, amid the tumultuous encounter of everybody with everyone, people sought new ways of life to strengthen their commitment to a common humanity.

People understood themselves better once the growing complexity of the new setting forced them to look around at others. After groping for a sense of direction in their encounters with failure and success, men and women found answers to mutual prob-

3

lems of urban life, and these accommodations created new patterns
of getting along with each other. Their accomplishment was a distinctly modern and American urban culture.

I have traced the outlines of the new culture in the framework of
the modern city, an intellectual construct put together with empir-
ical evidence taken from the record of life in big cities in nineteenth-century America. The building blocks of the concept came
primarily from New York, Boston, Philadelphia, Chicago, St.
Louis, and San Francisco. Combined, they epitomize the features
of a type of city that rose in the 1830's and faded away in the
1910's, give or take a decade or so on either side to account for the
fact that this cultural process had no obvious beginning or end.

The "modern city" constitutes a rapidly expanding urban world
in a uniquely American context, characterized by striking physical
and human contrasts. Like all concepts it is an abstraction that has
no separate historical existence. It comes to life through the accounts of people who experienced its features in the metropolitan
centers of the United States. The construct makes it possible to
group together related evidence from cities all over the continent
and to delineate the cultural elements of a complex development
sometimes obscured in the turbulence of daily life.

In the modern city the residents' cultural diversity and heterogeneous make-up enabled them to create ways of life out of new
social and economic institutions and to employ the technology of
communication and the corporate organizations of business to un-
derwrite the extension of their urban culture across the continent.

City people forged the new culture from the elements that characterized their world. They used the apartment house, metropolitan press, department store, ball park, and vaudeville house to
cope with the problems created by a rapidly expanding urban setting. Old urbanites, newcomers from the countryside, and immigrants from abroad relied on these novel social and economic
devices in their search for privacy, identity, and happiness. They
also depended on them to provide women with a place in the modern city and to establish bonds between diverse groups of people.

In view of their role in modern city culture, the apartment house, metropolitan press, department store, ball park, and vaudeville house occupy the center of this study. Unlike church and school, they came into existence with the modern city, and their development mirrored faithfully the struggle of city people with change and chance. These new institutions also contributed more directly and extensively to the emergence of modern city culture than did the factory and political machine.

The ability of many groups of people to create new cultural forms indicates the city's potential as a durable form of social organization. Out of a variety of urban experiences emerged cultural expressions answering basic needs constantly laid bare by a changing environment. The modern city lived up to its promise of offering a better life than great numbers of men and women had known before.

In our century new urban practices have grown out of the heritage of modern city culture, perpetuating the age-old lure of the good life that the city holds out. At the same time the contrast between the magnificence of high-rise buildings and crumbling housing projects raises visions of the end of the city as a meaningful social order.

In a world doubting the value of urban life and facing the threat of ecological blight, an account of the creation of modern city culture by motley groups of people in nineteenth-century America supports the speculation that men and women will find ways to fulfill their expectations within the urban context of an automobile technology that shattered the adjustments to urban problems which city people had achieved.

In that perspective modern city culture gains lasting significance. Its success indicates that the shortcomings of urban life are less an intrinsic defect of the city and more a reflection of the fact that people's search for the better life leads as often to greed as to selflessness, which affects country as well as city existence. Reflecting on the experience of city people will uphold faith in some form of the city as the dominant way of life.

# I

# MODERN CITY CULTURE

Although she knew the scene by heart, the contrasts between the people always startled Jane Addams. The world of her Hull House, bisected by the six miles of Halsted Street that ran from the stockyards in the south to the shipyards in the north, clashed with the fashionable downtown and exclusive residential sections of Chicago. Urban diversities engulfed her daily life, accompanying "the withdrawal of the more prosperous Irish and Germans" from the area "and the slow substitution of Russian Jews, Italians, and Greeks." The striking variations of life etched into the cityscape seemed to persist long after she had first described the street "lined with shops of butchers and grocers, with dingy and gorgeous saloons, and pretentious establishments for the sale of ready-made clothing."

Several ethnic neighborhoods surrounded Hull House, sections of a rapidly growing city that had swallowed the suburb in which the residence once stood. Old World conflicts continued to divide their inheritors in the New World, and Jane Addams recalled her surprise at the arrest of a Greek boy who had threatened to hang a young Turk, having been "stirred by some vague notion of carrying on a traditional warfare, and adding another page to the heroic annals of Greek history."

Jane Addams referred to that divided world as "the modern city," a phrase members of her generation began using in the 1890's to denote a large city straining under the impact of inten-

7

sified urbanization and industrialization.[1] In the context of the history of urbanization, the rise of the modern city was a phenomenon of the nineteenth century; but by the time people actually recognized the new urban phenomenon they had been so busily living, the twentieth century was already shaping the world. Within a few decades the automobile destroyed the distinct downtown focus of modern-city life and gave suburbia a separate identity. However, despite this spatial fragmentation, people continued to label their new forms of urban life "the modern city," equating "modern" generally with the present.

Divisions of a different order than twentieth-century spatial fragmentation characterized the modern city as a stage of American urban development and marked its decades of hectic growth after the 1820's. Most noticeably, the rifts resulted from the cultural diversity of the inhabitants. A novel degree of personal freedom heightened the ferment. Then, too, the age-old interplay of social rivalry, economic conflict, and political differences also separated urban people.

In the span of a few decades, waves of migrants from the countryside and abroad had inundated the remnants of the distinct American community, which, some observers assumed, had once formed the city's core. In its place emerged a "queer conglomerate mass of heterogeneous elements," as Jacob Riis called the "mixed crowd" in tracing the patterns of mutual rejection in the succession of various ethnic groups streaming into the modern city. "The once unwelcome Irishman has been followed in turn by the Italian, the Russian Jew, and the Chinaman," he said, "and has himself taken a hand at opposition, quite as bitter and quite as ineffectual, against these later hordes. Wherever these have gone, they have crowded him out, possessing the block, the street, the ward with their denser swarms."[2]

Even a casual glance at a neighborhood's types of housing revealed some of the contrasts. Homes provided clues for a quick guess as to the social status and ethnic origin of the people who lived in them. The morning after Theodore Dreiser arrived from

Chicago in "the great city of St. Louis," in 1892, life began "manifesting itself through this city," he recalled in his autobiography. The very first time he saw the gardens and the mansions of the very rich, the grandeur of their "newly manufactured exclusiveness" staggered him. Dumbfounded, he stared at the "great gray or white or brownstone affairs" with "immense carriage houses, parked and flowered lawns." The city's variety of styles and layouts taxed his senses until he discovered the monotony of "long streets of middle-class families, all alike, all with white doorsteps or windowsills and tiny front yards."

Gradually the existence of the poor sections, hidden behind "long throbbing wholesale streets, crowded with successful companies," penetrated the young reporter's mind. Along the waterfront he found a mill area, "backed up by wretched tenements, as poor and grimy and dingy" as he had ever seen. During his wanderings all sorts of streets opened themselves up to him. His search revealed many kinds of people, "Jewish, Negro, and run-down American," and the mass of humanity making up the "plain slum."

These kaleidoscopic scenes reinforced impressions of the relationship between houses and people gathered in Chicago where Dreiser had found his way into newspaper work. There the daily walk to his job had taken him from Halsted Street east to the river, through streets "lined with vile dens and tumbledown yellow and gray frame houses." Behind their rickety or grimy windows, he imagined "slovenly, rancorous, unsolved and possibly unsolvable misery and degeneracy," adding up to "whole streets of degraded, dejected, miserable souls."[3] John Sloan expanded Dreiser's verbal sketches with his etchings of streets and people that captured the contrasts of the modern city as they appeared in New York. Inspired by Hogarth and Daumier, the artist discovered in 1904 that he "saw the life of the city really for the first time" when he walked through its streets.[4]

David Graham Phillips recognized the divided quality of the cityscape in the early 1890's when he leaned against the fence of New York's Herald Square as a young reporter, "watching a great city under full swing." He had been in the city several months and had noticed the gross differences between Hester Street teeming with peddlers and customers and Wall Street crowded with clerks and messengers. He also knew the tide of shoppers sweeping along both sidewalks of Fourteenth Street and the rush of commuters leaving ferry slots and railroad stations. At the crossing of Sixth Avenue and Broadway, he recognized for the first time the subtle contribution of chorus girls, two-bit actresses, and general "about town people" to the image of a street. Their seedy appearance gave Sixth Avenue a certain dinginess in his eyes that the street could not shake off even at its intersection with the metropolitan Broadway.[5]

The crowded downtown streets brought into focus the contrasts diffused over residential districts associated variously with haughty exclusiveness, stern respectability, shabby gentility, outright misery, and brazen indolence. The streets presented a constantly surging mass of humanity. Struck by the elementary vitality of New York's major thoroughfares in 1856, George Templeton Strong, a great diarist of nineteenth-century urban America, recorded an "orgasm of locomotion."[6] In 1871 an Austrian aristocrat saw Broadway as "the principle of mobility, . . . a royal road leading to everything," with "a floating population large enough to give the impression of that agitation and preoccupation and that provisional state of things which is the characteristic of all the great American cities."[7] This steady movement of people obscured the truly floating and shiftless city population, which a probing camera or graphic pen at times found collected in stale-beer dives.[8]

The enormous energies of the bustling crowds lent motion to the cityscape itself. On the facades of businesses colorful advertising banners, swinging in the breeze, mimicked the movement of people in the street. The more deliberate motion of huge streamers strung from one side of the street to the other orchestrated the rhythm of the daily race. The webs of telegraph and telephone wires, suspended in a forest of poles, measured the speed of sailing clouds.

From time to time, the turmoil froze in congestion. Only the hideous mixture of smells and the varying level of noises continued to assault nose and ear. Traffic snarls offered a momentary rest for the eye, swiftly to surrender once more to the cries for impetuous movement. With renewed intensity, pedestrians hustled along to overtake carriages, horses again pursued trolleys, while the clanking elevated lines renewed their efforts to extend motion and speed into a new dimension.

These "passengers in masses," to quote Edgar Allan Poe's phrase from "The Man of the Crowd," when closely watched presented "innumerable varieties of figure, dress, air, gait, visage and expression of countenance."[9] The sounds of English and foreign speech in the din of the streets packed with people multiplied the contrasts already apparent in the material and the style of people's clothing and in their bearing. The clamor defied the idea of the universality of English as "America's Mightiest Inheritance" extolled by Walt Whitman in 1856. The "mystical rhapsody" of his poetry sought to absorb the fantastic contradictions of the street scenes, which he registered on his walks through the city, but the visual conflicts usually silenced most observers.[10]

Varying styles of behavior also revealed differences—from a casual remark indicating the extent of someone's education to the ways of walking that distinguished various trades from each other. On a Sunday or Sabbath, or any religious holiday, the demeanor of passersby distinguished the faithful from the indifferent. His own contact with crowds led a famous orator and Universalist clergyman, discoursing on humanity in the city in 1854, to identify "the diversities of human conditions" as "the first lesson of the street."[11]

Thus the "moving panorama of human life" on the main streets of big American cities adsorbed country folk despite their outlandish appearance.[12] Though their behavior demonstrated their ignorance of city ways, this only temporarily kept them outside the rather flexible bonds of urbanity that quickly assured adsorption but left absorption to the future. Acceptance came as a matter of

course because the city generally ignored most distinctions, indiscriminately embracing the sage and the fool, the good and the
wicked, the rich and the poor. Under these circumstances, a col-
umnist for the San Francisco *Overland Monthly* averred in 1883,
hayseeds and greenhorns coming into the city felt as if they were
part of the crowd, just watching "the building of Babel."[13]

Before city ways had a chance to bridge the gap between
country and urban folk, the differences produced tension that tore
some people apart. Couples experienced the conflict in particular,
when man and woman met again after a period of separation during which one of them had come to the United States. In the
1890's, Abraham Cahan's vignette of two people searching for each
other in an immigration station exposed the depth of the dilemma.

The husband tried to spot his wife among the newcomers who
had just disembarked. For three years he had made his way alone
in the American modern city, while she and their child stayed
behind in the East European *shtetl*. "Freshly shaven and clipped,"
looking like a "*regely* Yankee," Yekl finally recognized his wife in
her "brown jacket and skirt of grotesque cut" among the crowds of
passengers. A "voluminous wig of pitchblack hue" that Gitl wore in
honor of the Sabbath and the great event "added at least five years
to her looks." Smartly "dressed in his best clothes and ball shoes,"
Yekl looked younger than usual, but the days at sea had bronzed
his wife's face, "which combined with her prominent cheek bones,
inky little eyes, and, above all, the smooth black wig, to lend her
resemblance to a squaw."

Yekl's heart "sunk at the sight of his wife's uncouth and un-
American appearance." Gitl suppressed concern about her husband's shaved beard, worrying what it signified about his religious
devotion. Their words and kisses "imparted the taste of mutual
estrangement to both." Only when Yekl approached his boy, with
his wife appealing in his behalf to the frightened child, did he feel
for a moment the grip of the old country. "Presently, however, the
illusion took wing and here he was, Jake the Yankee, with this
bonnetless, wigged, dowdyish little greenhorn by his side."[14]

Long before Jews arriving from Eastern Europe in the 1890's had to learn to cope with the variety of customs in the American modern city, newcomers from the city's hinterland had encountered clashes between modes of life. In the 1820's people just off the nearby farms marked the onset of a long procession. The experience was repeated so frequently that at the beginning of the twentieth century writers of pulp romances could speak glibly about a heroine's movement from "the quiet of her mountain village" to "the great metropolis," as if the actual circumstances of the migration did not seem to matter any longer.[15]

Girls and women came from the small towns and isolated homesteads of rural America to get away from the doldrums of household and farm chores. Increasingly they found their way into the sales force and the office help of the big city, leaving the field of domestic work to immigrant women. At the end of the nineteenth century, they looked to the city "as a sort of Mecca for all in search of opportunity," as one observer noted.[16] The symposium "The Girl Who Comes to the City," which *Harper's Bazaar* ran in its columns during 1908, suggested certain similarities that characterized women's widely different experiences.

Although most of them arrived with little training for the jobs available, they quickly turned to newspaper advertisements and employment bureaus for information about work opportunities. Many sought to add to school learning some sort of instruction that would increase their bargaining position in the job market. Their low income forced all of them to live frugally, one emphasizing that she always wore black to keep her laundry bills small, another recalling that she walked to and from work to save carfare. Hunger and loneliness dominated the hardships they suffered, but in retrospect most of them thought their initial years in the bewildering city to have been worthwhile.[17]

Although the elegance of the urbanite appeared superficial to many critical eyes, most women assiduously sought the stirring smartness of the big city, striving to shake off the provincialism that separated country people from cosmopolitans. "The overwhelming tendency of modern life is toward the cities," Joseph Kirkland stressed in an article about Chicago in the early 1890's, "and it almost seems as if they would have to be walled about" in order to keep men and women in the country "to provide food for all."[18]

The early-comers from the farms of the city's hinterland had the benefit of the English language, a common cultural heritage, and exposure to American institutions to ease their adjustment. In the opening phase of the migration, the urbanites' growing need for household help, factory workers, office clerks, salespeople, and shop assistants made the migrants welcome. Riverboats and railroads steadily brought the modern city within reach of farming folk in more distant regions. When these people also responded to the growing ease of movement that made some of them part of a new work force, they carried the dress, speech,, etiquette, and outlook of the countryside with them into the city.

Out of the differences between newcomers and urbanites grew stereotypes that nourished condescension and resentment. Tom Corey, the scion of an old Boston family in William Dean Howells's *Rise of Silas Lapham*, felt that if "he hadn't passed a winter in Texas" he might have found his fellow New Englander Silas Lapham "rather too much." The genteel Coreys considered the self-made Lapham as an intruder, since he had been born in the sticks of Vermont so close to the Canadian border that he "came very near being an adoptive citizen."[19]

The distinctions between migrants from the countryside and small towns and old urbanites faded when waves of immigrants from abroad inundated the modern city. In the late 1840's, torrents of Irish Catholic immigrants obscured the steady trickle of people from England and Scotland. The Irish disrupted the bond created by the English language with the divisive element of religion. The language barrier as a source of discord affected first the immigrants from German and Scandinavian countries. Even so, these groups still fitted vaguely into the loose framework of an Anglo-Saxon nation that some English-speaking people saw rising in North America, the fusion of "the peoples of the world . . . run into an English mould."[20]

Head-on collisions of different life-styles ensued when immigrants from southern and eastern Europe surged into the United States in the waning decades of the nineteenth century. Italians, Greeks, Hungarians, Serbs, Croats, Czechs, Moravians, Poles, and Russians contrasted vividly with their new surroundings as well as with each other. The groups of Jews among them found that the city already sheltered other Jews who differed in origin, custom, and social status. The haunting photograph by Jacob Riis of one of the newcomers taking his Sabbath meal in a coal cellar in the early 1890's demonstrated to outsiders that adherence to religious practices was a possible bond among the members of the varied phases of Jewish immigration. Most older inhabitants of the modern city, unfamiliar with the ways of all the new immigrants, saw only a sea of strange faces, babbling in alien tongues and framed by freakish clothes, flooding their streets. Walking through these multitudes now was really "like a voyage round the globe," as a guide had already said it was in 1869.[21]

The contrasts among the people of the modern city, accentuated by the discordant features of ethnicity and race, loomed largest in the case of newcomers of Asian and African origin. In a world in which most people were strangers, the Chinese seemed the strangest, in appearance, speech, and customs. Their age-old cultural heritage stressed loyalty to their families in distant China, so that, in order to earn money for the support of their extended families, many Chinese laborers in the United States were indentured to Chinese merchants who had provided their transportation across the Pacific. The resulting living and working conditions dispersed early exalted visions of citizens of the oldest and the newest empires meeting in harmony in the American modern city as the expression of a new humanity. Crowded into a few city blocks by American hostility and Chinese clannishness, their teeming, squalid quarters seemed to challenge American beliefs more than did other ghettos. Unable to fathom the exploitation that set Chinese against Chinese under the guise of benevolence, many Americans thought that a country dedicated to ending all slavery should not allow the city to shelter men living voluntarily in bondage.

Blacks, who as slaves in the United States had been exposed to the language, customs, and religion of their masters, envisioned the northern city as an island of freedom in a sea of oppression. Their faith in the existence of that by-product of urban life indicated the depths of their sufferings in slavery. However, their hopes for a better life exaggerated the amount of freedom that the modern city could provide for black people in nineteenth-century America. In the face of racial discrimination and economic exploitation, they sought to realize their dreams of human dignity and economic opportunity by pursuing the chance for a breath of freer air. "Colored people will congregate in the large towns and cities," Frederick Douglass predicted in a letter to Harriet Beecher Stowe in 1853, "and they will endure any amount of hardship and privation."[22] Relatively few black people were able to make the move in the nineteenth century, yet their presence further enriched the range of humanity there, adding differences to a manifestly diverse population.

Other factors exaggerated the contrasts. Throughout its history, any big city has inspired visions of the free life. The American modern city, however, actually generated a novel degree of personal freedom that allowed great numbers of people to live as individuals more fully than before. The chances for building a new life rested primarily on the possibility of responding immediately to the myriad opportunities to better one's lot. These openings in the loose fabric of society, which differed according to an individual's perception, ability, and luck, appeared seemingly everywhere.

In particular, they accounted for the enormous attraction of the American modern city for the European poor. Its freedom formed a striking contrast to the conditions in Europe, where law and custom still bound most people to specific stations in life. There, most men and women saw the course of their lives shaped at birth, by the occupation of their parents, the social status of their families, or the nobility of their ancestry.

To be sure, race and ethnic hostilities and sex discrimination excluded groups of people from sharing fully the opportunities of the American modern city. But at least for most white males, the obstacles to personal advance and individual happiness were far less oppressive than the complacent workings of a hierarchic order of society that in many European states seemed to be keeping the mass of people forever in their place.

Imperial Germany, which in common with other Central European countries, considered the category human being to begin with the aristocrat, demonstrated its limited understanding of the urges of the common man in parliamentary debate in 1889. During a discussion of social legislation in the Reichstag, Chancellor Otto von Bismarck related his experience with some of *his* people who had left his estate in Pomerania to live in Berlin. "Housing and treatment, all that is hardly as good as at home," he had argued with his former tenants. They readily agreed, but the Chancellor finally detected the reason for the move when the farm workers blushingly told him that "a place where they could sit outdoors, just listen to a band, and drink their beer" could be found only in Berlin. [23]

The Chancellor had discovered human impulses that expressed themselves openly in the American modern city. There freedom rested on an extension of political democracy into many spheres of life. The existence of choices between political candidates, at times questioned by critics of American municipal government who regarded many officials as placemen of urban bosses, meant more than possible participation by eligible citizens in the political processes. As demonstrated by loyal followers assuring the strength of political machines, sharing any form of political life stirred hopes that the chance to act freely in one area would lead to a steady expansion of the entire realm of liberty.

The day-by-day operation of that democracy of the urban machine opened up avenues for getting ahead in life. With the boss allocating some of the spoils of the office and influence to his followers, it provided access to economic opportunities to people who at times could not vote or did not care to, but under other circum-

stances might be in the position or inclined to cast their ballots.
The fusion of politics and economics affected the social sphere, too.
In the modern city, "where human relationship is not taken account of by big business, by the schools, by commercial amusements, or by any of the dominant institutions," the political machine represented a benevolent institution, reformers explained in
1914, "social during the man's ordinary life, benevolent in his time
of trouble." [24]

The pulse of urban life beat irregularly but strongly. Limited
legal restraints left little too high to be aspired to, and little too low
to be done. The urge to get ahead in life fostered an attitude that
considered anything permissible that assured gain and regarded all
activities that the law did not actually punish as acceptable. The
accompanying social fluidity made life in the modern city more
desirable for most people than the world they had left behind.
Even if their conditions or their status did not measurably change,
they could hope that chances for betterment existed because
others had improved themselves.

The freedom fostered by the American big city quickly broke
down the exclusiveness of many professions and crafts. During
economic booms, when labor was scarce, men and women applied
for jobs on the spur of the moment, inspired by advertisements as
well as rumors about openings, or just following their hunches.
Work books, labor contracts, and apprenticeship papers received
slight attention, as did other routines of the European labor structure that kept workers in bondage. If the need for hands was great
enough it even curbed the racial, ethnic, or sex biases of prospec-
tive bosses. Lean years, when products and labor glutted the market, limited workers' choices, deprived them of work, and forced
them into unaccustomed activities, adding yet another element of
change to the flux of the modern city.

Compared with the working conditions in the countries they
came from, many residents found and lost jobs with bewildering
ease. The visible effects of momentary affluence or starvation reflected the uncertainty of employment. In weeks of full employ-

ment, new curtains appeared on parlor windows to replace those worn thin by the scrubbing and rubbing in cold water during lean years. Appearances made people, the hustling crowds learned, and women and children entered the work force in large numbers to assure a steady income to keep up a family front. In turn, this labor earned each family member a measure of independence that put additional strains on family ties.

When there was time free from work, people took their leisure in the same unstructured way in which they struggled for their daily bread. Each chose activities that suited him or her best, as informally as they did everything else. They relaxed talking on streets or rooftops, drinking in bars or kitchens, and walking or playing in parks. No sequence of fixed traditional pageants, but rather the rhythm of work, shaped the calendar of holidays. People celebrated their individualized feasts the way they fell, whenever an opportunity offered itself. The structured course of metropolitan life, primarily regulated by time clocks, streetcar schedules, and factory whistles, ensured that they would have a multitude of responses to work and leisure.

The familiar effects of social, economic, and political divisions appeared in versions symptomatic of the modern city. For example, a new social distinction reinforced the biological division between young and old. The momentum of rapidly growing cities placed a premium on youthful energy and drive; while at the same time respect for old age diminished, because a smooth, matter-of-fact transition to old age as another phase of life no longer existed. The metropolitan setting was out of touch with the agricultural world that each year experienced anew planting, ripening, and harvesting as part of a harmonious cycle. In the unending rush for the new, older people were pushed aside like older buildings that disappeared to make way for new ones long before they showed signs of age or had outlived their usefulness.

Urban life, as an artificial construct of human energy and imagination, ignored the natural rhythms of birth and death, youth and decay. People's biological aging, which contradicted the defiance of age actualized in the constant updating of the cityscape, came to be viewed as a social concept. This device allowed men and women to feel as young as was necessary to remain in step with their whirling surroundings. "Young America," mid-century America's catchword for politicians challenging the complex problems of a nation dividing, also referred to the youthful exuberance of urbanites preoccupied with building their world. Since people continued to age biologically as they always had, the effect of the new social convention was to widen the gulf between young and old. The city world, out of touch with natural growth and decay, now identified old age as an existence separate from ordinary living.

Another aspect of the conflict between young and old was the confrontation between old families and nouveaux riches. The newness of the modern city and the rapid increase of the population prevented the development of a patriciate. A few families had kept their links with the city through several generations, but that kind of distinction meant little in the face of the power of the enormous wealth with which the newly rich battered their way to eminence. The tenets of American democracy had done away with the aristocratic titles that ranked people in Europe. But in this professedly egalitarian society the modern city accepted a hierarchy in which money was the badge of distinction.

"Money is the habitual measure of all things," an English visitor to America emphasized in the 1860's, "the only secure power, the only real distinction." [25] The possibility of unrestrained pursuit of riches opened up many opportunities for seeking distinction, since this did not depend on family background or princely favor, as it did in Europe. The direct links between money and status heightened the incentive to gain and demonstrate wealth and power. Furthermore, the captive audience of thousands of spectators in an urban environment created many opportunities to display one's wealth, from charity to self-indulgence. This attraction of the modern city also brought to the scene those newly rich who had amassed their fortunes elsewhere. The struggle to be on top of the heap, or to share the summit, created splendid rivalries among the affluent and lengthened the distances that separated the rich from each other and from the poor.

The sheer numbers of scrambling people not only accelerated the rush for riches but also broke the links of paternalism and discredited the argument that the rich were merely the stewards of poor people's so-called share in the wealth. The recognition of the humanity of the poor that had once constituted the conventional reward for their subservient behavior now appeared as pure condescension. Moreover, there was little room in the great free-for-all to exercise deference. Whoever made it to the top first intended to stay there as long as possible; anyone seeing his opportunity was expected to take it. In any case the legions of poor, who swirled hopelessly in the eddies of the mainstream of seemingly unlimited material progress, made any rich man who tried to justify his wealth by paternalistic rhetoric look like a crafty thief who had found a philosophy in the bargain.

The great inequalities between rich and poor caused unrest and riots, which Joel Tyler Headley considered an index of ongoing "changes in tone and temper" of a great city in 1873.[26] Indeed, riots marked the modern city. In 1886, the stormy year of especially intense industrial conflict, the contrasts were expressed so violently as almost to erase the distinction between strikes and anarchy. For a leader of the Social Gospel Movement the struggle raised the plain question, "Is It Peace or War."[27]

Although at times a clash between the haves and the have-nots seemed imminent, the line between them was not immutable, and that flexibility balanced the rocking social boat. People resented the trappings of distinction that made the frontier between the two social camps so noticeable, yet they clung to these marks because they indicated the next goal on the way up or marked the rung already reached on the social ladder. This involvement showed that people expected movement, up or down.

An intense and ever-changing diversity of people characterized the American modern city. This feature distinguished it from other

end list of examples of diversity

big cities in the Western world, even though some of them also doubled in population and adsorbed many strangers. Most of these newcomers hoped to better their individual lot in life, too. However, the migrations of Eastern Europeans into Vienna or Berlin or of Italians into London never approximated the dimensions of the human mix and flux of the American modern city. The poor of the American modern city were not fashioned by a shared historical experience into uniform building blocks for the urban proletariat that some social philosophers saw emerging in European cities. Most of the American poor cared enough for the opportunities in their new surroundings to prefer the promises of a free life to any call for solidarity.

Although heterogeneity gave the modern city its distinctly American character, one group of residents considered that this cultural diversity threatened what they perceived as "American ways." Some reformers saw diversity as endangering the political vision of an educated, homogeneous society of yeoman farmers, the backbone of American democracy. Although city-dwellers themselves, they had been raised in small towns and rural settings, and their views of democracy clung to a rather remote past in which it had been hoped that the political life of the young nation could be linked to its farmers as the embodiment of public virtues. These men and women strove diligently to create a civic morale that would perpetuate aspects of this ideal, even though it had disintegrated almost at its inception under the impact of industrialization and urbanization.

At times, urbanization and industrialization seemed to these reformers the roots of all evil. From their perspective the one destroyed the dignity of people, the other the dignity of their labor. To them the new forms of urban life that both supported, such as reading a newspaper on Sundays or spending a salary on clothes, were just one more sign of the erosion of thrift and piety, prudence and self-reliance, those attributes of rural life that they considered the basis of the nation's social integrity, economic stability, and political wisdom. As a remedy they turned to education in political behavior to bring, belatedly, attributes of the yeoman into the city. They hoped to Americanize all residents through the political process. In his life history, an Italian tailor reduced the "big work to build the future" to these steps: "to learn the English, to become the citizen, to take part in the political life."[28] While these reformers strove to eradicate the divisive and clashing features of various groups (tolerating cultural diversity in the form of handicraft skills and home recipes that faced extinction in an industrial age of power looms and canned foods), they failed to substitute any elements of a new identity that people could latch on to as part of their new urban existence.

Most people accepted the heterogeneity of their world as an integral component of their lives. No single culture dominated their activities outside their living quarters. To give and take of daily chores, the mingling of people in the crowded streets, in parks and theaters, shops and factories, exposed them to a multitude of different influences. Over the years these encounters eroded old loyalties. From the chaos emerged the experience of living with the various elements of a new, diverse culture. This awareness of others produced an urban identity that stamped members of heterogeneous groups generally as city people. The process led to the development of more comprehensive social values. Slowly, something like a common frame of mind emerged out of the actions of thousands of people, as amid conflicting attitudes and diverse modes of living and working the residents of the modern city came to share certain perceptions and behaviors.

Shared feelings about their common urban life and the recognition of mutual concerns lent vitality to the emergent modern city culture. That culture constituted a response to major problems of metropolitan existence as perceived by large groups of people: the lack of identity and the need for communication; women's urge to partake in big-city life and men's search for leisure as part of the urban existence; and everyone's hope to be recognized as individual in a crowd. Consequently, the expressions of the culture in the form of the metropolitan press and the department store, the ball-

park and the vaudeville house, reached beyond conventional mani-
festations of transplanted European culture, epitomized in painting
and sculpture, literature and music, and other artifacts of seemingly absolute value. The new cultural expressions sought answers
to the problems of a world being perpetually modified by the interaction of crowds of diverse people concentrated in a limited
area.

The current of urban life stirred people into constant activity. It
also left little opportunity for unrestrained adulation of traditional
cultural expressions; these withered without the fertile soil of a
common heritage. Each day stimulated variations of modern city
culture to answer the need of that moment, from the expansion of
news coverage in daily papers to the introduction of a faster ball
speeding up the action of baseball. The new practices pushed into
the background other usages that suddenly seemed irrelevant.

These constantly changing cultural responses to suit novel demands baffled European visitors. Rooted securely in a world ruled
by a pantheon of great masters, Europeans saw culture as a timeless affair, expressed in a great painting, an imposing edifice, or a
powerful symphony. But culture "lives in America from day to
day," as one of them perceived during his tour through the United
States in 1876.[29]

The traditional forms and modes of culture also lost ground because they had not been marked by the dynamic life of the modern
city. Although these time-honored artifacts represented responses
to the age-old search for the good and the beautiful, they also bore
the trademarks of the glorious ages of the past, rather remote from
the turbulent metropolis. In contradistinction, the forms of modern city culture rested on "the deepest and broadest" experience
of city people, constantly updated in their encounter with the
problems of the urban scene. This collective experience Hutchins
Hapgood considered a source of the "most genuine culture possible" in his *Types from City Streets* of 1910.[30]

City people coined their cultural forms out of the new social and
economic institutions forged in the modern city. Fortified by their

cultural diversity, they devised answers to their most pressing urban problems. In the apartment house they adapted private space to a spatially divided city. They received from the metropolitan press the pieces of an urban identity and a language for communicating with each other. The department store assured women a place in city life, and they in turn made downtown the center of urban elegance. In the ball park men were exposed to the meaning of rules in the modern city and to that basic form of urban leisure, watching others do things. The vaudeville house brought a sense of common humanity to diverse people, who emerged from the experience with social skills and cultural values that helped them cope with the intricacies of metropolitan life.

In their encounters with modern city culture, the residents of other American cities and towns recognized its value to themselves in dealing with everyday urban problems. At the same time, the dynamics of modern city life contributed to the expansion of that culture beyond the confines of metropolitan centers until it permeated all cities and towns across the continent.

From the 1870's on, advances in economic organization and in communication increased the effectiveness of the activities of certain citizens in emerging urban societies throughout the country, who had been attempting to inaugurate in the new settings a style and tone of life characteristic of great cities. This metropolism, the tendency to foster behavior typical of large urban centers regardless of the vast expanse of nature separating a new town from the older cities in the East, acquired a corporate dimension in the closing decades of the nineteenth century.

Above all, nationwide economic organization increased the financial gains obtained from such cultural exports. A communications network of newspaper chains and wire services stimulated demand by expounding the benefits of modern city culture to the entire country. These factors added size and momentum to schemes previously undertaken on a much smaller scale.

The corporate stage of metropolism had truly continental dimensions. The department store became the retailer for a national market. Big-league baseball provided the basis for a national spectator sport. Vaudeville circuits carried the lessons of modern city culture from ocean to ocean. These gigantic enterprises produced forms of wealth that contrasted with the type of reward reaped earlier by solitary entrepreneurs who combined the export of culture with the hunt for a private fortune. One such was George Gordon, who in 1854 almost singlehandedly laid out a San Francisco park after a residential square of his native London, and with the profits from his real estate scheme started a sugar factory that inspired a poet's barb: "First man then sugar he refined."[31]

In December 1848, Sidney George Fisher, Philadelphia gentleman and diarist, had noticed the dawn of this awesome process during a trip through upstate New York. In every little village he found well-filled stores selling urban artifacts and goods, an entire culture on the Hudson River and the Erie Canal exported from New York City. "Fifty years ago the whole country was a pathless forest," he marveled, while pointing at analogous developments, "hundreds of miles further west, in Ohio & Illinois, in Michigan & Iowa," which carried big-city ways across the continent.[32]

The appeal of modern city culture increased its rate of expansion, thus hastening the emergence of a uniform urban civilization stretching from the Atlantic to the Pacific. The "foreign immigration and the restless spirit of the native population have reduced all our cities to a common level of chaotic sameness," an American living abroad discovered when he saw his native land again in 1881.[33] "The city," the editor of *Harper's Bazaar* emphasized in 1908, "does not mean New York alone" or "the half-dozen big cities of the United States." When his magazine called on women to contribute their experience to a symposium "The Girl Who Comes to the City," he assumed that despite obvious differences between Boston or Chicago, St. Louis or San Francisco, the basic conditions of urban life existed "the land over," in "any city over twenty thousand people."[34] Sameness had risen out of diversity.

Modern city culture stretching across the continent provided a distinctly American answer to the problems of urban life. City people utilized economic and social solutions to the problems of the big city for cultural purposes. Initially, they relied on some solutions growing out of their cultural diversity for the task of ordering urban space into districts of residence and districts of work.

*[Handwritten notes:]*

1. many people lived in crowded tenements because they couldn't afford better
2. plans to organize cities failed
3. parks became very important
4. buildings started getting higher and more people lived in apartments
5. poor lived close to job until horsecar and cablecar then electric streetcar came and people could more easily more toward suburbs

# II

# DIVIDED SPACE

Delightful moments lightened William Dean Howells's horsecar commute to Boston. "Happy to cling with one foot to the rear platform-steps," he looked "out over the shoulder next to him into fairy-land." The sight of river and bay, meadows and uplands, gave way to the Bunker Hill Monument, "soaring preeminent among the emulous foundry-chimneys," and then to rooftops rising "one above another on the city's three hills, grouping themselves about the State House, and surmounted by its India-rubber dome."

However, the views rarely compensated for the "passions and sufferings" of the "spoiled children of comfort" in the crowded streetcar, "indecorously huddled and jammed together, without regard to age and sex" and "reduced below the level of the most uncomfortable nations of the Old World." The horror existed, Howells reflected, "not only in Boston, but in New York, Philadelphia, Baltimore, St. Louis, Chicago, and Cincinnati," where "the same victims are thus daily sacrificed." In his existence as a commuter, he detected "our weakness as a public" in suffering the indignities and hardships of a hideous experience day in, day out.[1]

Howells's reaction obscured city people's dependence on systems of transportation to ameliorate the isolation of suburbs and residential districts. Streetcars linked various sectors of a divided world, predominantly the place of residence and the place of work. It was technological innovations, from horsecar to subway, rather than architectural forms, that unified the space of the modern city.

28

Moreover, they complemented the apartment house as the new unit of private space.

This role of public transit grew out of the division of real estate into areas rather strictly segregated by function—one way of structuring the suddenly expanding, large and diverse city. The economics of land value doomed traditional devices for giving the cityscape an exterior unity and shaped the arrangement of space in the modern city. The rapid rate of urbanization precluded a slow ordering of the landscape over a period of gradual expansion and made it difficult to deal with urban space as a totality.

However, forces shaping the modern city—commerce and manufacturing and people's pursuit of wealth in line with their social aspirations, cultural values, and psychic needs—created some regularity in the spatial chaos through land values that fluctuated with a certain degree of predictability. As long as topography permitted, city growth took place in all directions from a downtown business district, but favored those areas specifically suited for warehouses, factories, or residences. Distinct districts sprung up around these subcenters, which might overlap or interlock, but always depended on each other.

Banks and offices occupied the main business center, together with various enterprises serving these sources of financial and administrative control. Their functions and the people they attracted in turn brought newspaper plants and the department stores that gave the business district its downtown atmosphere. Retail shops and wholesale houses located along traffic lines that reached out from the city center to the residences of their customers. At intersections, clusters of stores gave rise to shopping areas that reflected the shifting values of the parcels of real estate caused by their changing function. The location of residences—in midtown enclaves, on the outskirts of the city, or at the fringes of industrial sections—indicated the social status of their inhabitants. Despite the conflicting influences determining land values, from individual caprice blocking the use of a lot to political manipulation of real estate, an early historian of the phenomenon found a "striking unifor-

mity" in the process: self-interest compelled individuals to obey
"economic laws."[2]

The structuring of urban space along changing functions and
shifting real estate values was greatly facilitated by a surveying system that divided land into plain rectangular strips. Without concern for topography or aesthetics, this gridiron plan produced
straight streets intersecting at right angles. The system appealed to
city residents' preference for rational solutions and scientific methods, as the gridiron had done in other times and places. A practical
approach to the age-old task of ordering urban space, the method
simplified surveying and facilitated speculation. It absorbed sudden as well as protracted growth because the rectangular layout of
the streets extended far beyond the actual city, making possible
the sale and resale of lots in advance of settlement, and stimulating
the promotion of undeveloped areas. The price that the grid ex-
acted in ugliness appeared small in a strange world where monotony also sugested familiarity.

Philadelphia first demonstrated the utility of checkerboard
streets in the English colonies of North America. New York City
added to the gridiron system its luster as the great metropolis of
the United States at the beginning of the nineteenth century. Its
commissioners, appointed to re-order the cityscape, in their report
of 1811 opted for "rectilinear and rectangular streets," on the
ground of "plain and simple reflections." They saw a city "composed principally of the habitations of men" and regarded "strait
sided and strait angled houses . . . the most cheap to build and
the most convenient to live in."[3]

More than the need for housing, the commercial and manufacturing interests that sustained the rise of the modern city were
well served by the gridiron system. It accommodated a distinctly
modern attitude towards city building that considered nothing per-
manently fixed but the individual parcels of real estate. These lots
enjoyed a life of their own, unrelated to any more general schemes
of ordering the cityscape of the type that during these decades
shaped European capitals such as Munich, Berlin, London,

Vienna, and, above all, Paris according to royal or imperial designs. Taken singly or in city blocks, the lots carried into city building the spirit and practices of a democracy fostering equal opportunity for those of its members who had the money to enjoy it.

These small parcels of real estate enabled people to make maximum use of property for purposes which changed with their interests. They made city building and re-building an obsession. "All is moving and removing, organizing and disorganizing, building up and tearing down," one traveler commented in 1849, describing what Walt Whitman had called "The pull-down-and-build-over-again-spirit" a few years earlier.[4] New York "is never the same city for a dozen years altogether," stated *Harper's Monthly* in 1856, identifying one reason why it "is notoriously the largest and the least loved of any of our great cities." Anyone born there forty years ago "finds nothing, absolutely nothing, of the New York he knew," the editor emphasized.[5]

The exuberant spirit of change which pervaded all bodies, things, and places thrived on the checkerboard system of streets that directed many enterprises into the rational penetration and financial exploration of the vast urban environment. Real estate as big business backed the grid with the heavy weight of capital and the conservative strength of property. Its speculative market and the construction industry flourished on and sustained this division of the city. The strength of these influences triumphed even in moments when extraordinary circumstances suggested an opportunity to overcome the gridiron design.

At the time of the San Francisco earthquake and fire of 1906, a plan to re-order a city and a disaster destroying its core almost coincided. In response to an invitation from a group of San Franciscans, the Chicago architect and city planner Daniel H. Burnham had begun in 1904 to draft a plan for their city that envisioned boulevards radiating from a civic center and streets following the contours of hills crowned by parks. However, the city rose again after the earthquake and fire with little regard for the Burnham Plan of the San Francisco Improvement Association.

Long before this, however, the freedom of life in the United States had doomed most attempts to order public space by arranging it according to principles derived from aesthetic considerations, historical examples, or religious beliefs. Deliberately planned urban space, beyond the division into rectangular parcels, appeared rarely, and the examples of Savannah, Washington, D.C., and Salt Lake City stood out boldly. The residents of the modern city, who took Paris as their model of stylish life whenever possible, nevertheless disregarded the practical implications for ordering urban space suggested by the re-making of the French capital under Napoleon III. They recognized neither prince, priest, nor planner as guide. Some of them, however, dismayed by the chaotic scenes that the free use of space produced, did advocate relying on architectural styles to superimpose an exterior visual harmony on the cityscape.

Among them the Neo-Gothic style found various advocates, inspired during the 1830's and 1840's by the Neo-Gothic architecture used to revitalize the Church of England and to complete the Cologne cathedral as a symbol of national unity in a Germany divided into many states. Admirers of the Neo-Gothic considered architectural ideas and actual buildings based on medieval Gothic models particularly suited for their purposes. As expressions of a distinctly urban as well as Christian style, imposing Neo-Gothic structures seemed to answer not only the city's need but also the churches' search for identification with institutionalized Christianity in a setting where churches were beginning to lose their place as central social institutions.

In the 1840's, the Cambridge Camden Society, a dominantly Anglican group working to revive the medieval English parish church as part of the Oxford Movement of reform within the Church of England, expanded its activities to the United States. It related the trend toward the Neo-Gothic, which involved moralistic objections to the commercialization of society and the mechanization of production, to ecclesiastical and theological concerns. The body of thought created by the Society concerning the

study of church buildings and its functions and arts came to be
called "ecclesiology" and the members "ecclesiologists."

A New York Ecclesiological Society briefly dedicated itself at
mid-century to the spread of ideas about church reform and Neo-
Gothic architecture. With that backing, the Gothic Revival left its
mark primarily on church buildings, but also motivated the practitioners of secular architecture to think about the influence of their
profession on society and about the relation between a building's
function and its appearance.[6] As a result, 60 percent of the house
designs published in *Godey's Lady's Book* between 1846 and 1851
showed the mystique of the Neo-Gothic.[7]

The influence of the Gothic Revival as a distinct nineteenth-century style lingered, predominantly in the form of churches, aca-
demic buildings, and townhouses. New York's Gothic landmarks
ranged from Trinity Church, built between 1840 and 1846, to the
Woolworth Building, the cathedral of business erected between
1911 and 1913, and included the lofty spire of Grace Church, the
massive structure of St. Patrick's Cathedral, and the masonry
towers of the Brooklyn Bridge.[8] Although the Neo-Gothic stimulated theological thought and religious devotion, it lacked the vitality to order the modern city. Its architecture failed to produce visual harmony because the original style had been forged by the
pattern of life, labor, and worship of the medieval city, which no
longer existed.

The culture of the modern city was based on the residents' distinct commercialism. Such a city could surely claim "a superior
standing" and call for appropriate architectural expressions, as the
report of the building committee of the New York Board of Alder-
men reasoned in 1803, in justifying the extensive use of marble for
three of the new city hall fronts.[9] At mid-century, aware that a
building represented "the exterior of society," in a phrase popularized by Yale president Timothy Dwight, many city people came to
think that the Palazzo style best served their aspirations.[10]

The Palazzo style, named after the public and private palaces
that had been built in Italian cities during the Renaissance, at-

tracted attention because it was at once practical and impressive. It mattered little to businessmen whether the inspiration came from Italian, French, English, or German sources, as long as the building looked stately. But in addition, and in contrast to the temple of the Greek Revival, the palazzo provided well-lighted space at low cost, particularly in combination with iron construction, in a design unit that could be repeated if necessary.[11]

Appearance and economy explained the popularity of the palazzo as the commercial style. Although it lived on until the builders of the largest business projects of the 1880's turned to the skyscraper, the palazzo mode never dominated other styles to the extent that it could overcome the visual diversity of the urban landscape. It was unsuited to a world seething with seemingly unlimited liberties and boundless opportunities, which defied the old ideas of public order that in an earlier phase of American urban life had expressed republican virtues through Classical architecture.

Only through its mode of dividing space did the modern city achieve structural unity. The gridiron system reduced vast tracts of land to manageable segments of real estate. These lots could be joined into units that answered the needs of a warehouse, a factory, a train depot, or an apartment house complex. They satisfied the divergent interests of builders and speculators, residents and politicians, who could pursue their goals free of a ruler's demand for a specific kind of urban order or a social ideal expressed in a dominant style of architecture. By this process the city was organized into distinct areas of work, residence, and leisure.

Space for leisure, in a predominantly work-oriented urban society, appeared in the form of the municipal park. The park arose from the interaction of a variety of influences, as varied as the urban scene itself, as a result of which the building of a park came to be seen as a suitable way to satisfy specific interests and at the same time serve the city as a whole. The broad support for the park briefly linked for that mutual purpose groups which opposed each other on issues of city life, until wrangling about the uses of the park, once achieved, reactivated their conflicts.

Temporarily, money and art, politics and aesthetics worked together. Businessmen considering the rise of real estate values in a neighborhood or the flow of visitors riding streetcars joined company with visionaries who regarded a park as a work of art that produced primarily aesthetic and psychic benefits. Petty politicians, attuned to speculation in land and franchises, regarded a park project as a source of labor for faithful voters temporarily out of work in depression years. Since outsiders, that is those who did not share in the graft, viewed some official expenditures as signs of municipal corruption, local politicians welcomed the broad support for spending public money on parks. They were undoubtedly delighted by such comments as the San Francisco *Real Estate Circular*'s observation in 1873 that "no public money has been more economically or usefully expended" than on Golden Gate Park.[12] Lastly, urban reformers presented areas of grass, trees, and lakes as the lungs of the city that would breathe fresh air into a congested, disease-ridden social organism. Their concern with hygiene matched the yearnings of other urbanites for relief from the gridiron's "deadly uniformity of mean ugliness" that Edith Wharton recalled from her New York childhood.[13]

Besides these obvious hopes attached to the municipal park, a kind of public conscience concerned about the quality of urban life in general directed a broad range of supporters to it. Cosmopolites among them had been inspired by the English example and had followed the European agitation for public gardens after the Napoleonic wars. They noticed the conversation between traveler and editor in landscape architect Andrew Jackson Downing's *Horticulturist* about the French and Germans who despite their politics seemed greater practical "republicans" than Americans because their cities had parks and gardens "provided at public cost, maintained at public expense, and enjoyed daily and hourly by all classes of persons."[14]

They also shared the sense of urgency voiced by the poet-editor William Cullen Bryant, who warned in 1844 that "commerce is devouring inch by inch" New York's harbor, shore, and land, and that "if we would rescue any part of it for health and recreation it must be done now."[15] In the parks of landscape architect Frederick Law Olmsted, who emerged as the towering figure of the municipal park movement in the United States, they saw instruments of reform providing relief from drudgery for thousands and fostering communal bonds between diverse groups of people.

Park proponents came into conflict not only with each other but also with groups of gymnasts and pedagogues, and proponents of zoological gardens, patriotic displays, and merry-go-rounds, who wanted to determine the uses of the park as soon as the transplanted trees showed their first fresh green. With the growing importance of the park in city life and its increasing use by large numbers of people, there appeared a "strong tendency" to convert it "into a great, perpetual metropolitan Fair Ground" that disturbed those who saw it as a work of art, "framed upon a single, noble motive," as well as those who regarded it as a device to convert their fellowmen to their own concepts of leisure.[16] In the long run, all supporters of the municipal park found their original ideas amended by the sheer number of people who responded to a public space in the modern city that suggested country scenery to their city imaginations.

The attempt to conjure up rural vistas in the modern city set the municipal park apart from other public spaces that had existed in American towns since the beginning of colonization. The design demanded more land than a common or a market, while the need for a park came to be felt at a stage of urban development that reduced drastically the amount of open space, concentrated large numbers of people in a limited area, and severed most residents' ties with the countryside. These characteristics of the modern city may have accounted for the feeling that something new was afoot. Irrespective of analogous trends in European countries, Frederick Law Olmsted viewed the movement for municipal parks in the United States as an independent development, spontaneously engendered by the "Genius of Civilization."[17] Most residents, the crowds of people untouched by rhetoric and unconcerned about origins or precedents, just cared for the grass and the trees that seemed to bring them in touch with nature for a few leisure hours.

Before the modern city began building parks, the remnants of nature on the urban scene had diminished steadily. Streets and buildings cut gradually into the green spaces of popular pleasure gardens, where on a pleasant day visitors could eat and drink or promenade past a few trees, some beds of flowers, and other guests of the establishment. They destroyed the country-like atmosphere that clung to these places, until only names attached to restaurants or theaters recalled former bucolic settings.

Rural cemeteries, which sprang up in the neighborhood of large cities in the 1830's, not only assured mourners' communion with nature but also attracted large numbers of visitors who liked greenery and open space. The dedication poem for the opening of Mount Auburn Cemetery in 1831 alluded to the gardens of Eden and Gethsemane—"To the first garden's doom we bend, / And bless the promise of the last"—introducing a fresh tone into burial literature that paralleled the rediscovery of nature in the urban environment through the municipal park.[18]

The enormous appeal of that first great "Garden of Graves," which had been founded by the Massachusetts Horticultural Society in the vicinity of Boston to accommodate the crop that large cities raised bountifully, produced other spacious cemeteries.[19] In 1849, Andrew Jackson Downing described the ten-year-old Greenwood Cemetery in Brooklyn as "grand, dignified, and park-like," estimating that many of the 60,000 people who visited it during the summer came solely to enjoy trees and lawns.[20]

The initiative of a few citizens determined to embellish the drab cityscape with horticulture and rural scenes or to succeed in business as nurserymen created botanical and public gardens, where the scientific atmosphere of conservatories and greenhouses gave a special legitimacy to moments of leisure devoted to the enjoyment of nature. Essential urban services, such as waterworks, also provided a focus for public parks, as the grounds of Fairmount Park in Philadelphia, with pumping stations along the Schuylkill River, demonstrated.

Without any pretense of paying respect to the dead, of devotion to science, or of serving a practical purpose, the design of New York's Central Park, the first great municipal park of the nineteenth century, boldly carried the search for harmony with nature into the core of a mid-century world that gave the undertaking its poignancy. One "great purpose of the park," as asserted by Frederick Law Olmsted and Calvert Vaux in their prize-winning plan of 1858, was "to supply to the hundreds of thousands of tired workers, who have no opportunity to spend their summers in the country, a specimen of God's handiwork."[21] Nature and culture seemed to join in the modern city, too.

"Apart from considerations of sanitary economy," a public-spirited physician and one of the first reviewers of the history of parks and public grounds in the United States argued in 1869, "public parks may be regarded as an unerring index in the advance of a people in civilization and refinement."[22] However, the landscape architects also considered the presence of the masses of people who made up the modern city a major obstacle in the pursuit of the fusion of city and nature. Their breathtaking vistas re-introduced nature into the urban landscape by keeping the surrounding city and its residents out of sight, behind shields of foliage.

Among all the manipulations of the environment in the modern city, the municipal park alone preserved public spaces for leisure, free from commercialism or pietism, in an order predominantly oriented toward work. In their attempts to assure its uses in socially acceptable ways, the designers relied on people's timeless respect for earth, trees, and water to bring forth their better nature in their communion with nature. In an age that encouraged the plunder of natural resources, they reinforced appropriate public behavior with guards who kept people on walks, lest they injure young trees and plants. However, there could not have been con-

cern that they would spoil the grass of Central Park, an English
visitor speculated in the 1860's, "for during a considerable part of
the summer the whole surface of the ground is thoroughly
parched."

The "freedom of action and healthful recreation" which that observer missed was also missed by thousands of men and women
who yearned for the kind of relaxation that suited them as individuals.[23] The crowds' pressure reduced all visions about the uses of
parks to a perpetual struggle to protect shrubbery, trees, and
flowers and curb public expressions of leisure that violated the
age's sense of decency. The freedom of the modern city limited the
role of the municipal park as an instrument of social planning; but
the attempt it represented to structure a part of the environment
for the common good inspired a new concern for a measure of
urban planning.

Although hopes for Olmsted's planned rural environment in the
big city that had been attached to Central Park in the 1850's
perished in the New York of the 1870's, the park movement in
other cities benefited from the inspiration. Its supporters signifi-
cantly broadened their concept of forms of relaxation to include
diverse groups of people in "*neighborly* receptive recreations" that
departed from the lofty vision of the rural park and substituted for
it the practical urban playground.[24] They recognized that activities
on playgrounds in various neighborhoods adhered to local codes of
behavior and that there was room for diverse forms of leisure in a
city of heterogeneous people. Their awareness of the significance
of leisure in an urban society grew into systematic efforts to build
various recreation facilities "to meet the numerous interests of the
neighboring community rather than to fulfill in the highest measure any single want of the whole city."[25]

In the 1880's, Boston developed the "first local recreation
ground," with a running track, field houses, sports equipment, and
trained attendants.[26] At the beginning of the twentieth century,
the neighborhood park, a city block or two between factories and
tenements, relied more on facilities for exercise and play and less

on pastoral scenes to provide opportunities for leisure. Grass gave
way to sand, on fields and in boxes, and to water-filled pools, instead of lakes, to make people clean and healthy by enticing them
to wade and swim.[27]

The multiple uses of playgrounds paralleled the expansion of
planners' thinking from individual parks to networks of interrelated
parks, and from single boulevards to belts of parkways that girdled
the whole metropolis. At the beginning of the twentieth century,
Boston and Chicago furnished striking examples of this changed
approach, which "instead of superimposing one oasis of beauty" on
a big city aimed at changing the aspect of its entire life.[28] In con-
verting parks into "a series of country clubs for the poorer people,"
the *Architectural Record* stressed in 1908, "no city in America
has . . . spent money more freely and more consistently" than
Chicago.[29]

The concern for public space awakened by the municipal park
hardly improved the condition of the streets, which until the appearance of the automobile remained a "study in filth and frustration."[30] However, the park movement's concern for the quality of
urban life in general did draw attention to the significance of private space. This new awareness put the steadily growing suburbs
in a new light.

In the spring of 1858, roaming through the "remote regions of
Southern Brooklyn," George Templeton Strong suddenly realized
that a great city had been built there within his memory. "The
compact miles of monotonous, ephemeral houses" which he over-
looked from the Greenwood Cemetery ridge impressed him as a
"great reef half bare at low tide and dense with barnacles," each
"throwing out its prehensile cilii into the great sea." His zoological
analogy gave emphasis to his concluding comment: "Each is a
*home*, . . . with better fortune or worse, good investments or bad,
credit or disrepute, progress up or down, . . . an epitome of
human life within each shabby domicile."[31]

For those who could afford it, the search for a home in the modern city ended in the domesticity of the suburb, Frederick Law

Olmsted concluded in his report on Chicago's Riverside area in 1868.[32] The move to the suburbs was motivated by a longing for the pleasant aspects of nature, as well as rising land values in the built-up areas and improved transportation between outskirts and downtown. These considerations encouraged some people to escape the excessive rents destroying single-family homes in the city and to acquire a small house in the suburbs. Such a move, in the view of a Boston reformer, also promoted "the independence of character and life."[33] In 1874, the promotional tract of a Cincinnati railroad enunciated a more marketable combination when it promised businessmen who bought a suburban home "health and longevity" as well as "economy in living."[34]

The soaring-cost of real estate steadily reduced the amount of private space each person could call his or her own in the big city, while the new transit systems continued to tie land that was as yet distinctly rural to the urban world. These factors also led land speculators and real estate developers to survey fields, meadows, and woods and blueprint streets and boulevards onto them in advance of actual settlement. They created landscape, neither rural nor urban, where some people seemed to enjoy both city and country lives without experiencing the rigors of the latter. The natural hazards had long vanished, and most suburbanites saw nothing of them after they had learned, like the Suburban Sage, "to avoid the only patch of underbrush within a mile."[35]

Suburban sprawl accompanying the earlier stages of urbanization became a characteristic of the modern city. It was intensified by industrial growth, population pressure, new modes of transport, and a nostalgia for rural life. Some of the earliest suburbs appeared in the 1820's, but they were soon absorbed by municipalities that measured progress in terms of increased acreage and population. Annexations and consolidations not only increased the number of residents quickly, but also turned the modern city into a political entity of awesome dimensions.

The three largest American cities of the nineteenth century led the way. In 1854, Philadelphia expanded from 2 to 129 square miles by absorbing independent suburbs. Chicago acquired its largest addition of 133 square miles in 1889. The most dramatic adjustment of boundaries took place in 1898 when New York City added Brooklyn, Queens, Staten Island, and part of the Bronx to Manhattan.[36] Throughout the nineteenth century every large city shared these expansion booms, which cut short the development of independent foci of urban life on the periphery, reinforced the economic links which tied suburbanites to the modern city, and presaged the rise of new suburbs.

Most people, however, lived where their economic circumstances located them, in the residential districts of the modern city, "as it nearly always costs more time, effort and money to live well in the suburbs than in town," a social worker emphasized in 1909.[37] "Moderately well off" in the estimate of the rich, but definitely rich in the eyes of the poor, many members of the middle class took over houses at the edge of the central business sector, vacated by owners who had moved their families to the periphery of town or into the suburbs to get away from encroaching warehouses, office buildings, and small factories. They subdivided the old residences and rented single rooms or entire floors to lodgers, or ran boarding houses outright. By 1856, the custom was so widespread in New York that Walt Whitman accepted the estimate of "judicious and extensively informed observers" who assumed that seven out of ten dwellings were used that way. Counting permanent hotel boarders into this group, Whitman thought that almost three-quarters of the middle- and upper-class inhabitants of New York did what the little girl so aptly described when asked where her parents lived: "They don't *live;* they BOARD."[38]

"Like death, no class is exempt from . . . this universal *barrack* system," the author of an early comprehensive treatment of boarding-house life stressed in 1857. His lurid accounts of the many varieties of the institution drove home again and again his point that the boarding house did not and could not substitute for a home. However, he also considered it useless to rail against the "inherently mischievous" features of "our anomalous social state" as long as it was next to impossible to find a suitable dwelling in the big city for those who wanted to live at once "privately, decently, and economically."[39] In the 1870's, the Reverend Henry Morgan, as part of his crusade to purify Boston, sketched the horrid conditions of streets with "miles on miles of lodging-houses instead of homes."[40]

Among the big American cities of the nineteenth century, only Philadelphia managed to retain the image of a "City of Homes." In 1880 one Philadelphian counted "a dwelling-house for every six inhabitants."[41] The city, at times castigated for the "doleful architecture" of these houses, took pride in loan associations that, in the form of savings banks, financed their construction.[42] In 1900, with about five people to a home, it faced housing issues different from those of New York or Chicago. However, Philadelphia exhibited problems of population concentration in the form of the rear dwelling, a small house built singly or in rows in back of the front house and characterized by social workers "as the horizontal rather than the vertical tenement."[43]

Poor people, who in the eyes of many residents neither "lived" nor "boarded," formed the most visible tenantry of the modern city. In a setting that priced traditional homes out of the reach of almost everyone, they were also at the mercy of "many mercenary landlords," as the classic report about their housing put it in 1903, "who only contrive in what manner they can stow the greatest number of human beings into the smallest space."[44] The previous year, discussing Chicago housing, Jane Addams had emphasized that if the average tenement-house density in three districts investigated were spread throughout the city, "we could house within our borders 23,000,000 people."[45]

The landlords speculated on poor people's need for shelter and their helplessness in the face of exploitation. Frequently immigrants themselves, aware of the thoughts, fears, and customs of their immigrant tenants, they obtained long-term leases on houses from owners who preferred to receive income without the burden of property management. For quick profits the landlords pursued a policy that immediately made the houses overcrowded, filthy, and dilapidated. They divided the tenements, as these structures generally came to be called at mid-century, into as many small units as their greed could contrive and paid no attention to the conditions of the buildings or the tenants as long as they received the rent on time.[46]

Many concerns for the quality of private space vanished amid poor people's clamor for housing. The tenants who rented on a weekly or monthly basis small rooms, which one observer of conditions in New York described in 1844 as closets, often sublet space in their rooms to raise the rent, which was due in advance.[47] Waves of reform and waves of immigration clashed, so that the improvements in tenement living produced by one group were almost immediately obliterated when another flood of newcomers inundated the city seeking shelter and thus reactivating the pernicious cycle.

The ups and downs of one model tenement, New York's Big Flat, built six stories tall on six city lots as the Workmen's Home by philanthropists in 1855, epitomized the experimentation that attempted to improve housing in the second half of the nineteenth-century. Workingmen and their families, with and without boarders, almost immediately crowded all available space, from the cellars to the attics, from the hallways to the closets. In the hope that supervision would improve the conditions, the philanthropists converted the building into a well-organized home for workingwomen in the 1860's, with room for about 500 boarders in sixty dormitories and twenty apartments. That experiment failed when women avoided the home because they disliked both the disreputable neighborhood and the filth and stench of decrepit tenements and small factories nearby. When private owners took over in the 1870's, they restored the apartments and increased the number of them, and the Big Flat lost all claim to be a model tenement, with lodgers moving in again with the families and trespassers living again in the hallways. Each solution alleviated only temporarily the problems of sanitation, overcrowding, or trespassing in the face of the enormous demand for a decent place to live. Ultimately, failure crowned decades of struggle when the building was demolished in 1888–89 to make way for a carriage factory.[48]

The housing misery of the modern city directed many in search of private space to the apartment, which emerged at mid-century. This improvement in living conditions answered some of the needs of people who had previously tried to make a home in a boarding house. It also furnished an alternative to the social stigma of tenement-house living and an opportunity to better one's status.

Most people who experienced the change would have smiled in disbelief at the reaction of a fastidious person when first encountering apartment living. Newland Archer was startled by the "unexpected vista of a bedroom" that he saw from the sitting room of the family matriarch in Edith Wharton's Age of Innocence. The life of the aging Mrs. Manson Mingott was beyond reproach in the New York of the 1870's, and she could risk moving her bedroom to the first floor to avoid climbing stairs. However, the foreignness of the setup brought to Archer's mind scenes in French fiction and "architectural incentives to immorality such as the simple American had never dreamed of. That was how women with lovers lived in the wicked old societies, in apartments with all the rooms on one floor, and all the indecent propinquities that their novels described."[49]

The apartment house, universal in Paris and common in most other big European cities, was exotic in the American modern city of the late 1860's. Many residents still imagined acquiring for their families a brownstone in a sidestreet, where uniform fronts disguised narrow homes that stood "like books on a shelf," Charlotte Perkins Gilman thought.[50] Although in 1894 Charles Augustus Sala regarded a house in London, which had doubled its population to five million inhabitants during his half-century of chronicling urban life, as "a far more advantageous dwelling, as well as infinitely more comfortable than a flat," city growth—particularly skyrocketing real estate prices and cumbersome commutes—prevented fulfillment of the Anglo-American ideal of the single-family residence and eliminated reservations about the "French Flats," as apartments were popularly known.[51]

The development of the apartment house started in the 1830's when intensified urbanization began driving large numbers of residents into boarding houses and tenements. In 1833, poor New York families crowded into a tenement on Water Street, the first house built exclusively for tenant families of which I. N. Phelps Stokes—architect, housing reformer, and historian *par excellence* of Manhattan's iconography—had a record; in 1855 well-to-do families experimented with sharing the so-called Spanish Row on Fifth Avenue.[52] Paris provided the models for the Stuyvesant Apartments built in 1869, the first structure erected in New York City as an apartment house for several families. The Parisian precedent legitimized making the modern city a world of apartments. Added respectability came from the social status of Rutherford Stuyvesant, who financed the venture, and the Paris training of Richard Morris Hunt, the first American student of the École des Beaux-Arts, who designed it.[53] These credentials helped turn a subversive way of living into the dominant form of urban housing.

Land usage, building methods, and social conventions altered the Parisian heritage of the apartment in such a way that it only briefly remained a "French Flat." In France, the size of the lots and the habit of building for generations had encouraged the erection of big, solid houses and the family practice of living in flats. In America, the small family house, an ideal often pursued so recklessly that the structure barely outlasted the life of its builder, accounted for narrow lots and flimsy, cheap construction. The heritage of these practices, together with the outmoded idea of private space in the form of a single-family residence, the acquisitive instinct of builders, the social insecurity of middle-class tenants, and the actual dimensions of building lots created problems for the apartment house emerging in the modern city.

In the view of members of a leading New York firm of architects and builders of apartment houses in the 1890's, "even Yankee ingenuity could not devise several complete apartments all on one

level and properly lighted and ventilated on a space intended for a
. . . single house." In addition, the light lath-and-plaster construction of these houses could not stand up to the wear and tear of several families, nor provide protection from noise, odor, or vermin,
or safety in case of fire.[54]

The social freedom of the modern city bred insecurity that in
turn influenced the nature of the emerging apartment complexes.
The absence of recognized dividing lines between people produced houses that, unlike Parisian buildings, did not shelter residents from different walks of life. In a French apartment house the
relationships between the residents reflected long exposure to
clearly defined social divisions. Artisans occupied the upper stories
of houses; the lower floors were reserved for aristocrats. If such
neighbors chanced to meet on the stairs, neither had to think
about how to act because their behavior had been molded by earlier generations.

The free atmosphere of the American modern city brought distinct classes of apartment houses into existence, because the social
flux that attracted people of different origin also prevented easy
contact between various groups. Mobile people thriving on the opportunities of the modern city as well as suffering the social in-
securities that made up-and-down movement possible, sought to
buttress their newly gained position through the kind of housing
they rented. Residents of the same status flocked together under
the same roof to reinforce their mutual resentment of all claims
others made to social superiority and strove "through an excessive
exclusiveness, to guard their dearly cherished state of exaltation."[55] Residential districts reflecting that exclusiveness appeared
as the most convenient way to assure a resident's enjoyment of his
private space.

Ordinary builders of apartment houses had other immediate,
tangible profits in mind. They speculated that the rich felt the
housing pinch, too, and they built their new ventures first in fashionable quarters. These structures were leased long before they
were completed. Their high rent placed them out of the reach of

people with moderate income, but their owners were looking for an immediate high return on their investment because they assumed there would be so many apartments in a short time that rents would drop below a rate they considered profitable.

Another negative influence was the method of financing and constructing, which interfered with erecting an apartment house that looked like a building designed to shelter families in search for homes in the modern city and not like a Moorish castle, a Romanesque city hall, or a baroque palace. If apartment buildings were designed for middle-class families, the speculative builders, living off borrowed money and facing the high costs of loans, land, and construction in their risky but determined pursuit of money, built cheaply to make quick profits and got away with it because people needed housing. The builders then frequently clung to an "architecture" of terra-cotta ornament just elaborate enough to spoil the impression of simple domesticity that housing reformers hoped to achieve, and the flimsy materials they used to produce ornate facades scarred the cityscape.

At the beginning of the twentieth century, a commentator on Chicago apartment houses felt that in Midwestern cities lower land prices and lower structures resulted in more attractive buildings than "the thousands of six and seven-story apartment houses erected in Manhattan during the past fifteen years" that "have only tended to make it look either ugly, commonplace or trivial."[56] However, most people did not care about the aesthetics of the apartment house. For them the apartment offered a new concept of home; it was not merely "a substitute for the house," as it was called in 1903 by a leading architect who still saw the flat in relation to the single-family house.[57]

The emerging apartment house reduced one of the great dilemmas of big-city living, the search for a suitable place for a family to live. Many families had moved every six months or year desperately seeking decent living quarters. In 1882, a journalist's vignette portrayed one resident's tension from ceaseless thinking about where and how he and his family would live. Stopping at any dwelling marked "To Let" to find out when, for how long, and for how much it could be had, had become second nature to him, even in his busiest moments. The sketch described him as "seldom settled anywhere," simply "staying in such a street, at such a number," until he moved again. That was "his custom and curse." For months and years "he had been waiting for a better, or less bad, order of things," but periodical promises of it had never yet been redeemed. Finally, trying to become resigned to the inevitable, the story envisioned him buying a lot in a cemetery, comforting himself "with the reflection that, once a tenant there, he need not move—that he has at last secured a home."[58]

The apartment house slowly alleviated such problems. However, "no one would be so foolish to imagine," commented *Scribner's*, expressing the pessimism of the seasoned urbanite in 1873, "that the general introduction of apartment houses would straightway inaugurate a domestic and social millennium."[59] The way in which apartment houses spread across the city reflected constant experimentation with new ways of living. Each setting was modified by the lay of the land, the need for flats, the availability of capital, the resourcefulness of speculators, and the aspirations of the tenants. On occasion, an area of the city went from open land to rows of apartments in one leap. Elsewhere a gradual transition involved closely spaced, free-standing residences and row houses as intermediate stages. The height of the buildings and the size of the apartments also varied widely. In New York City the size ranged upward from one room with one bath, and ultimately reached a fifty-four-room triplex with sixteen baths, built in 1926 at 1107 Fifth Avenue because the owner of a townhouse agreed to sell her site only if the builder would duplicate her residence on top of the new apartment structure.

Other extremes indicated the range of experimentation and of human nature. From 1882 until 1915, New York's narrowest apartment house stood on the northwest corner of Eighty-second Street and Lexington Avenue. It was 102 feet long and 5 feet wide, put up by the owner of the lot presumably to spite the builder of the adjacent apartment house who had been willing to pay only one-fifth of the $5,000 he wanted. The rooms, strung out like railroad cars, required special furniture, and in the spiral staircase and narrow halls two people could not pass. However, until his death in 1897, the owner found space in his apartment for his coffin, built from the lumber of a tree he had chosen in 1854.[60]

Apartments became more readily available when they were built in less attractive neighborhoods, which they then upgraded. A number of families housed independently under one roof made a locality more respectable and tolerable than one family alone could, reducing the effect of objectionable features. In 1882, *Harper's Magazine* reported scores of apartment houses going up in New York near saloons, stables, tenements, and rookeries, "occupied by refined, fastidious people" who would never have thought of living in such a neighborhood as a single family.[61] The clusters of apartment houses scattered through the city formed the cores of residential districts.

Some of the changes in housing entered into the opening chapters of *A Hazard of New Fortunes*, which William Dean Howells wrote in New York in 1889, "in a fine, old-fashioned apartment house, which once had been a family house." The Marches suffered disappointments in their search for a home in New York that were deepened by fresh memories of their Boston house. They listened to agents, explored neighborhoods in coupés, and were lured by advertisements "to numbers of huge apartment-houses chiefly distinguishable from tenement-houses by the absence of fire-escapes from their facades." They discovered that smell provided a distinction between gentility and shabbiness when a picturesque street invariably made its strongest appeal to their noses, and they developed dormant character traits in conversations with building superintendents while looking at expensive apartments and lying glibly when rejecting them "for one reason or another which had nothing to do with the rent."

Inflexibly, or so it seemed to the Marches, the New York ideal of a flat was seven rooms and a bath—or sometimes eight, counting the bath as one room and any room with a window to the open air, a court, or a shaft as a room with daylight. They considered houses, too, but all within their means were small; further, "the fact that none of them was to rent kept Mrs. March true to her ideal of a flat" and induced Mr. March to try living his "Anglo-Saxon home," as he knew it from the "Anglo-Saxon house," in the "Franco-American flat."[62]

The emergence of the apartment house in the modern city of the 1860's marked the waning of housing concepts that dated back to the rebuilding of rural England during the reigns of Elizabeth and the first Stuarts. In the middle of the sixteenth century, many English people still lived in the cramped quarters of the late Middle Ages, often eating, working, and sleeping in a one-room cottage. Gradual changes brought additional rooms and stories and a general division between living and sleeping space, so that by the 1650's "the typical farmer's house had three to six rooms, rising to eight and ten among the bigger yeomen."[63]

English colonists in North America carried this rural mode of housing, oriented around the privacy of a spacious dwelling, into their growing towns. While urban laborers never managed to live that way, affluent people clung to the ideal as long as they could and burdened their cities with a troublesome heritage. At the beginning of the nineteenth century, New Yorkers divided their city blocks into small lots of 25 by 100 feet, sufficient at that time for a moderate house with rooms lighted from the street and yard. They thus created a unit of land ownership that by the end of the nineteenth century had become "the worst curse which ever afflicted any great community" because a narrow, high-rising building now crowded every inch of the small space.[64]

In the modern city the apartment constituted a basic unit of urban life that once again could expose the whole family to what Howells called "the moral effect of housekeeping."[65] Parents and children sat down for dinner at "their" table, instead of eating à la carte in a restaurant or table d'hôte in a boarding house, like one of Henry James's Bostonians, who "got her supper at a boarding-table about two blocks off."[66] The group around the table in the kitchen or dining room of the apartment was a single family unit, a fact reflected in the smallness of the room. It gave a feeling of home, in contrast to the boarding house, where one of Frank R. Stockton's heroines "never felt at home except when she was out."[67]

Occupants quickly embraced the improved conveniences of the apartment, which with running cold and hot water, steam heat, elevators, separate toilets, electric light, fire exits, and more privacy made their lives safer and healthier. Technological advances and apartment living complemented one another. The innovations made accepting the new life-style easier, and the flats demonstrated the advantages of the innovations. Both lightened the daily drudgery of women in the home. In the face of the alternative of suburban housing, they produced yet another argument in favor of apartment living: it freed the energy and time particularly of middle-class women, who were surrounded by opportunities to utilize their freedom. Although in 1870 Manhattan had consisted of single-family homes, boarding houses, and tenements, in 1900, when only ten single-family houses were built, apartment houses dominated the island.[68]

The interaction of the new household technology with the new mode of living stimulated a brief series of experiments with various styles of apartment-house living. Fashionable "apartment hotels" had communal dining rooms instead of private kitchens, while in others family cooks worked in a downstairs kitchen and servants sent the meals into the apartments in dumb-waiters. The need for privacy went unanswered in most of these cases, and the experiments continued until the self-sufficient family flat in a well-managed apartment house became the desirable form.

As an essential urban institution the apartment house had a number of economic advantages. It was an intensive and functional way of living that permitted the concentration of people in most areas of the big city, boosted land values almost everywhere, stimulated building construction, and augmented the power of capital to provide services. It created new jobs and enabled people to benefit more directly from the jobs their great numbers called into being. Tenants' needs for services ranging from garbage collection to elevators created groups of employees attached to an apartment house, from manager to janitor.

The daily retreat of residents—adults returning from work and children from school—into the many stories of the apartment house adjusted people to the vertical growth of the big city, a dimension of urban life that guests and clerks in high-rising hotels and offices had already begun exploring. The movement into vertical space also brought freedom from the vexation of keeping up a house and grounds. The labor-saving devices linked to apartment living shortened domestic work, while other innovations—such as electric light, which came into many homes via the apartment— quite literally lengthened everyone's day. With several families living under one roof, the burden of cooperation enforced by necessity was slight compared with the amount of convenience and comfort the apartment offered relative to boarding-house or tenement life, or to searching for a brownstone rental.

The spread of apartment houses enhanced the job mobility city life offered by enabling people to find basically equal living conditions wherever new jobs appeared. Such a new flat, in another part of the city, in many cases was removed from the ground by several flights of stairs. The vertical expansion of attractive living units increased the area of urban space that could be structured by the individual.

The isolationist features of modern city life, fostered by the division of urban space, were partially offset by the emerging systems of urban transit. Assuring the viability of separate business, factory, and residential districts, innovations in urban transport linked the sectors of the modern city. The horse-drawn omnibus appeared in Paris in 1819, in New York in 1827, and in London in 1829.[69] Although New York had experimented with the first horse-drawn streetcars in 1832, the national streetcar vogue did not occur until the late 1850's. The pioneer lines of Boston began operation in 1856, and those in Philadelphia, Baltimore, Chicago,

Cincinnati, Pittsburgh, and St. Louis in 1859 and 1860. In the latter year, horse-drawn streetcars also began to run in San Francisco, and soon San Franciscans learned to rank the "modern horse
car" as one of the "most indispensable conditions of modern metropolitan growth." [70]

The horsecars, however, did not provide vast numbers of laborers with a chance to leave their congested living quarters. To
be sure, they were faster, cheaper, and more convenient than the
older horse-drawn omnibuses, which lacked the tracks that set
aside a segment of urban space for the horsecars. Still, the horsecars were too slow and their fares too high to start men who
worked ten hours a day for one or two dollars thinking about living
elsewhere than in their crowded tenements. "At whatever cost of
comfort and health, and even of money," the prize essay of the
American Economic Association for 1892 argued, "the workman
will live near his work, and unless the factories are moved to the
suburbs, he will continue to reside in the most crowded portion of
our cities." [71]

Subsequent innovations in urban transit further improved communication among the city's districts. Street railways, cable cars,
elevated railroads, and electric trolleys replaced the horsecars.
These new forms allowed more affluent residents to live further
from the business district, making a daily commute part of their
urban existence and taking a step further the deconcentration, signaled by the movement of these people into suburbia, that had already characterized the "largest American cities before the introduction of the electric streetcar in the 1890's." [72]

Technologically, the electric trolley eliminated most of the draw-
backs of the horsecar and the cable car. It was more sanitary than
the former, and safer and faster than both. Horses fouled the
streets, and their droppings released the tetanus bacterium that
endangered public health. The animals also represented a major
investment that could be wiped out by an epidemic such as the
Great Epizootic of 1872, which killed 2,250 horses in Philadelphia
within three weeks. Cable cars produced hazards, too, above all on

the curves, which had to be taken at top speed, frequently fouling grips in loose cable strands and sending the car out of control. These threats disappeared when the electric car appeared on the urban scene.

The electric trolley "was one of the most rapidly accepted innovations in the history of technology."[73] Between 1894 and 1897 it eliminated cable cars from most cities. In 1890, about 70 percent of street railways relied on horses or mules; by 1902, 97 percent used electricity. But the regularly scheduled runs of the trolley frequently stalled in the congestion of downtown traffic. Long strings of cars often lined up on the tracks of the crowded downtown streets that fed into the core of a ten-, twenty-, or thirty-story city. At times the only breaks in the chain of stalled streetcars occurred at cross streets, where stages, drays, and the antiquated horsecar of a cross-town connection struggling to get through the barrier heightened the confusion.

In general, the new systems of transportation served the immediate need of the modern city by facilitating communication between its various districts, even though most companies extended lines only as far as their competition forced them or their profits encouraged them to do. It was primarily the routes running out of the central business district that produced enough demand to justify investment in an electric line.

The potential of efficient transportation for placing better residential areas into the reach of working people received slight attention from companies ensnarled in battles over franchises. However, the presence of the suburbs functioned as a kind of psychological safety valve. The Boston suburbs that grew with the help of the streetcar between 1870 and 1900 served to assure aspiring poor families "that should they earn enough money they too could possess the comforts and symbols of success."[74]

Exploiting transportation needs within the modern city appealed to speculators and investors more than building into uncharted suburbia because, broadly speaking, it required less capital and represented fewer risks. Although there were streetcar lines serv-

ing suburbs, these systems were not extensively developed, because the outlying areas lacked the concentration of people on
which public transport thrived; as yet suburbia was unexplored as
an alternate mode of living by the great number of residents. The
crowds of passengers in the city itself did not strain the limits of
the technology as much as did the unfocused demand for stops,
stations, and services in suburbia before the automobile increased
individual mobility.

As far as city people were concerned, convenient access to a
streetcar line was more important than the speed of travel. The
tracks, fanning out from the city center in several directions,
aimed at touching as many clusters of apartments and tenements
with as many stops as possible. The resulting delays reduced the
rate of progress, but getting off and on a tram as close to home as
possible was considered worth the longer trip. Without straining
technology or reducing profits, the streetcar assured the function-
ing of the divided world of the modern city.

Rapid transit, the next development, involved the adaptation of
the streetcar to the transportation needs of even greater numbers
of people who were in a hurry. In 1897, Chicago saw the first multiple streetcar unit. Electric trains quickly replaced existing steam
elevated lines. Beginning with the Boston subway in 1898, Boston,
New York, and Philadelphia built underground rapid-transit systems until the Panic of 1907 stopped private construction of lines.

Rapid-transit technology surpassed the streetcar in speed and
safety, but it was less flexible in its routes and demanded larger investments. Although it could carry more passengers, only the geographic, demographic, and commercial characteristics of New
York, Boston, Philadelphia, and Chicago generated the level of
traffic that could sustain these lines as additional links between
well-defined business, residential, and factory districts.[75] There,
during the morning and evening rush hours, as these segments of
the day came to be called in the late 1890's, when a "modern steel
building twenty to thirty stories high and housing thousands in
place of hundreds under one roof" absorbed or discharged its

workers, "the concentration of people in the trains and cars is like the packing of sardines in a box."[76]

In the modern city, forms of public transport unified the divided urban space. They linked residence, place of work, shopping areas, and centers of entertainment, and kept suburbs an integral part of the modern city. No matter how far away people lived, the streetcar tracks radiating from the city center tied them to the downtown business district. Despite the absence of systematic planning and the inability of traditional architectural forms to shape the cityscape, public transport gave it a functional unity. That unity lasted until the automobile freed residents from tracks, increased their lateral mobility, and broke their dependence on the trolley to travel between residence and districts of work, shopping, or amusement. The freedom of movement the automobile produced undermined the unity achieved by streetcars and eventually made suburbs independent entities.

While the streetcar assured physical contact between individual residents and their cityscape in a divided world, another new instrument of mass communication, the metropolitan press, fostered emotional bonds among residents.

# III
# METROPOLITAN PRESS

In August 1831, a young man who looked and acted like a country bumpkin landed in New York City, after a twenty-hour boat ride from Albany. With ten dollars in his pocket, he wore most of his worldly possessions on his back, in the form of plain summer clothes, so that someone could have mistaken him for a printer's apprentice escaping from a country newspaper. From the boat deck he had watched suburbs slowly give way to rows of stone houses cut by gullies of streets and shaded by forests of masts near the river. The port and the metropolis fascinated him, and the thought of the thousands they sheltered and employed awed him because he had never seen a city of even twenty thousand until the day before. Anxiously he began hunting for a job in this city of two hundred thousand people, where no one knew him as a regular journeyman printer and where he "knew no human being within two hundred miles."[1]

Many residents of the modern city shared the essence of Horace Greeley's experience. However, while he made a name for himself as the editor of a well-known newspaper whom Liberal Republicans and Democrats chose as presidential candidate in 1872, most people remained exposed to the isolation and frustration created by the metropolis. Yearning for contacts with each other and their world, they obtained some awareness of the bonds of city life from a new form of journalism, the metropolitan press, which reduced anxiety and solitude by revealing their common humanity and identifying their pursuit of money as the common denominator of urban life.

Between the 1830's and the 1890's, gradual changes in the content and format of the American newspaper produced the metropolitan press. Intimately connected with the complexity of life in the modern city, the new type of newspaper depended on the freedom of the press in developing new journalistic techniques to attract masses of readers. Technological advances in printing, managing, and circulating, the use of the press as a road to fortune, and a shift in public values that replaced the minister with the editor as the conscience of the community all contributed to the rise of the metropolitan press.

The introduction of the telegraph, the expansion of the railroad network, and the reduction of postage rates aided in the emergence of an efficiently organized, well-equipped industry. In the span of two generations, the economic power of the modern city converted the newspaper, formerly a stodgy mercantile sheet or a straggling political journal, into another form of big business. By the time of the Census of 1880, the rate of growth of the news industry seemed unparalleled "in any other country of the world" and hardly equaled by "any other phase of industrial development in the United States."[2]

From another perspective, the burgeoning newspaper industry represented the response of one instrument of communication to a new market created by the longing of urban masses for identity. The metropolitan press pioneered journalistic practices that satisfied people's need for information about the bewildering place they found themselves in, the other inhabitants, and themselves. It spoke of their hope and despair, honesty and corruption, success and failure, and virtue and sin, in a world that let a few dreams come true by shattering many. It captured the greatest news story of the nineteenth century—modern city life—and this differentiated the truly metropolitan press from the many newspapers that appeared urban merely because they were published in a large city.

The nineteenth century attached rather vague meanings to the phrase "metropolitan press," but one of the outstanding news-gatherers of the new journalism equated it with "modern" newspapers, and his usage points in the right direction.[3] At times, "metropolitan press" designated all newspapers and journals of a big city, and in the voluminous exposé literature of life in the wicked city the term was employed in that way.[4] Occasionally, the word "metropolitan" just described a successful newspaper published in a large city.[5]

Other terms used to refer to big newspapers ignored the crucial interaction between journalism and life in the modern city, and simply described one or another aspect of the press that attracted attention at a given time under specific circumstances. In the 1830's when newly started papers began selling for a penny in search of an urban audience, journalists called them "penny papers." In the 1890's, newspapers that relied on odious sensationalism for victory in their circulation wars were labeled the "yellow press." In our century, writers have either repeated these narrow designations or spoken broadly about a "new," "modern," or "popular" journalism.[6]

Only taken all together, and in conjunction with certain social and economic factors, do all these terms suggest adequately the role of the metropolitan press in the modern city. The residents' need for information, together with technological advances and managerial innovations, produced a new form of journalism between the 1830's and 1890's. During these decades newspapers became newspapers in the true sense of the word, bringing daily the latest information about events and people in the form of news reports and human interest stories to masses of readers who bought the papers and constituted their primary support. With extended coverage of urban affairs, they increased in size, expanding advertisements and adding Sunday editions, sports sections, women's pages, and other features to hold readers and increase their numbers. This development added to urban communication a distinct dimension which, in historical perspective, appears as a stage between the street gossip and back-fence talk of the inhabitants of smaller towns and the chatter generated by a society saturated with telephones.

The rapid increase in the population, its heterogeneous nature, and the steady extension of the city into the countryside invalidated daily gossip and personal experience as sources of information in the modern city. People as eager to gather news as sponges to absorb water actually reduced its flow to a trickle. They could talk to the few who bothered to listen, but only those people stopped who anticipated that what they heard would be significant. The heightened tempo of life just swept most people along, like the Boston physicians who considered no one "bound to waste his time in awaiting his dilatory colleague." But the crowds knew no common frame of reference and lacked the intellectual discipline a group of professional people could impose upon the behavior of its members to make sure they all waited at least five minutes for each other.[7] The differences that separated large groups restricted the appeal and circulation of a bit of information which, without an obvious relevance, lacked value; further, most urbanites began valuing their time more than idle talk.

The sheer physical dimensions of the modern city also made gossip and experience no longer sufficient as sources of knowledge. The spires of the churches, the porticoes of the theaters, the rooftops of passenger depots, the chimneys of factories, the lobbies of hotels, and the windows of department stores promised a better life for those seeking one. Wharves, warehouses, and markets held out a vast range of opportunities to each resident. The fluid geography of the city, in which buildings, viaducts, and bridges gave way to new ones before they had aged, increased the residents' longing to see in black and white what the city had in store for them.

The message from the environment was clear. "He who is without a newspaper," P. T. Barnum emphasized in *The Art of Money Getting,* "is cut off from his species."[8] The rising circulation figures of large city papers demonstrated that many people recognized the importance of the new journalism to their lives. The report of the Census of 1880 summarized a major reason for the spectacular growth of the metropolitan press in the detached language of an official statement: the conditions of daily life, it said, required "some general medium of communication between man and man."[9] People's constant search for information about all aspects of the modern city produced the outstanding characteristic of the metropolitan press—its use of news reporting to present the facts of urban life.

Newspaper reports began to cover many aspects of the modern city. They took up the intimate affairs of people, poor as well as rich. News items about the fluctuations of the stock market, the outcome of a speculative scheme, and the output of a factory related the performance of the economy to the residents' desire for a better life. Reporters assigned to city hall connected the use of technological innovations to cope with the physical needs of the rapidly growing city and the actions of politicians to the interests of masses of people, irrespective of the interests of a political party. The newspaper, now a mirror of urban affairs, featured events from the stage and the sports arena that gave leisure legitimacy in a work-oriented world.

The residents' search for knowledge about their world blended with their quest for identity. In the modern city, law, custom, and tradition lacked the authority to assign people to a station in life, but newspaper stories about neighbors, work, and leisure helped residents identify themselves. Being informed was a substitute for the visible ordering of people by appearance or location that in earlier centuries had allowed throngs of strangers to live city lives.

Newcomers to the modern city, migrants from the countryside and immigrants from abroad, knew they differed, but in a world composed of differences they missed clear standards of citizenship. The migrants found their rural, small-town conventions of diminished importance in the city. Immigrants, ignorant in the ways of becoming citizens, turned to the metropolitan press for answers. In 1885, the New York *World* symbolically stressed the obligation to provide guidance when it collected from its readers the money for the pedestal of the Statue of Liberty, which no one else felt motivated to furnish.[10]

Migrants and immigrants realized that prosperity could overcome many obstacles to acceptance. The nouveaux riches demonstrated this daily, and newcomers looked to the papers for success stories that would reveal the secrets of success and assure them that their hopes for a share in the riches would indeed be rewarded. In a world riddled by divisions and inequalities, they accepted money as the criterion that measured achievement.

Despite the social imbalance between rich and poor, the recognition of the rule of money assured equality in the pursuit of wealth, though with significant qualifications. Most women, blacks, and Indians remained outside the pale of the nineteenth-century American economy, but for many citizens and immigrants, white and male, the path to a fortune seemed open. That made money, in the columns of newspapers that became big business, a democratic feature.

Stories about successful urban lives provided information about freedom of choice among life-styles. Readers needed to know about the new forms of economic activities and political behavior, of housing, food, dress, leisure, and etiquette that residents of the modern city pioneered, because their acceptance as city people depended upon the successful adoption of these innovations. They found in news reports, human interest stories, and advertisements information about styles that indicated their rank in the procession they had joined.

The plain English of large newspapers, "devoted more to the news of the New than of the Old World" in the words of immigrant Joseph Pulitzer, helped people increase their command of the language by reading news reports about the life most of them hoped to live.[11] Few poor questioned the importance of English for getting ahead in life, as Abraham Cahan's Jake demonstrated to his fellow workers in a New York sweatshop in the 1890's. With knowledge culled from the daily newspapers he explained to his audience the fine points of boxing and the fighting styles of champions, and when one of his listeners admonished him that there were other things in life that could only be obtained by studying with a teacher and reading books, Jake passionately rejected the advice: "Learning, learning, and learning, and still he can not speak English. I don't learn and yet I speak quicker than you!"[12]

The need for English curbed the attraction of the multitude of small foreign-language papers—799 in 1880 and 1,032 in 1900—for people struggling to make a living in a new world despite emotional ties to an old.[13] In 1880, 92.9 percent of all American newspapers and periodicals were printed in English. In 1890, the proportion remained the same, although foreign-language publications increased; in 1900, English-language papers had grown to 94.3 percent of total circulation. Indeed, large metropolitan dailies answered the need for information. In 1880, four cities counted less than two residents to each copy of a daily paper. In 1890, there were fifteen cities with less than two people per copy, and two cities with less than one reader. In 1900, nineteen cities had less than two residents to one copy.[14]

These mass audiences had their beginnings in September 1833, when the initial number of the New York *Sun,* the first successful "penny paper" published in an American metropolis, promised its readers "all the news of the day."[15] The venture liberated American newspapers from their previous dependence upon subsidies from mercantile interests and political factions. The news appealed to readers eager to know, and the increased circulation attracted advertisers eager to sell. Both groups of customers provided increased revenue, although income from circulation outranked advertising for many decades. However, the need to attract and hold readers' attention created another form of dependency: it wedded the metropolitan press to sensationalism in order to capture the largest number of readers and thus command the highest advertising rates.

This sensationalism gave the new journalism a bad name because it formed a striking contrast to earlier practices. In the

1840's, after a visit to the United States, Charles Dickens conceived "The Daily Sewer" as an appropriate name for the typical American newspaper, which felt the constraint of libel laws less than the English press.[16] In their search for news, reporters dredged up subjects that had not been covered before, and the novelty of such topics as adultery, suicide, or rape, as well as the way they were treated, stirred readers.

Editors felt pressured to present stories in a form that would capture the interest of a passerby long enough to buy a copy. They realized that an appeal to imagination, rather than reason, influenced masses of readers. The roots of sensationalism lay not merely in the human craving for thrills, but in the nature of the modern city itself. The city's unbounded variety made it a great mystery. The routine of city government, with its police, courts, and prisons; the decorum of hotels and restaurants; the ritual of theaters and promenades; the action of auction houses and stock exchanges; and the etiquette of concert saloons and dance halls combined into an endless panorama of diverse scenes and fascinating individuals. The constantly changing city, one journalist discovered when he attempted to fathom urban life, grew "greater and more wonderful in its power and splendors" and "more mysterious and appalling in its romance and its crimes."[17] In 1891, a French journalist viewed American newspapers as "servants of the people," who wanted straight news as well as entertainment, and compared the metropolitan press to a large store, with its goods—stories—merchandised attractively so as to strike the shopper's attention as quickly as possible.[18]

Residents regarded the city as a mystery, stressed one writer who made it his business to satisfy their curiosity.[19] Some suspected that secrets were hidden among the throngs of pedestrians and vehicles crowding downtown. Others imagined them concealed behind the facades of row houses lining the sidewalks, or guarded by the fences set in the spacious lawns surrounding great mansions, or buried in the mazes of alleys, miles of streets, and blocks of houses. However, most lacked the time, training, and nerve to unravel the mysteries themselves. They turned instead to the metropolitan press, where they received coverage of the most newsworthy aspects of modern city life.

Given the capacity of most news reports to evoke the timeless appeal of dark crime, stark tragedy, and titillating sex, the metropolitan press actually told its stories with restraint. News of city life had to be up-to-date and reasonably accurate in order to give masses of readers the sense of sharing the action. The basic needs of communicating news to strangers produced subtle distortions, but these involved changes in emphasis and not outright lies.

At the end of the nineteenth century, however, the extreme sensationalism that characterized large newspapers facilitated the rise of the Yellow Press. That new form of journalism differed from the metropolitan press because it was willing to sacrifice credibility in its search for stories and forms of presentation that would thrill, startle, or shock readers. The Yellow Press, which seems to have received its name from an experiment with a colored comic strip called "The Yellow Kid" in 1895, crossed the dividing line between an exaggerated report of facts and a brazen display of lies.

In retrospect, it can be seen that the Yellow Press foreshadowed the demise of the metropolitan press in the opening decades of the twentieth century. The changing role of the United States in world affairs disrupted the symbiotic relationship between the metropolitan press and the modern city. It made city news just another topic, like events in Europe and Africa, Asia and Latin America. In addition, people had come to know big-city life. The modern city itself, as a form of urban settlement oriented around distinct foci of life, began disintegrating under the impact of the automobile. And finally, newspaper journalism developed new reporting styles with the advent of motion pictures, radio, and, ultimately, television.

The process of transforming events into news stories developed by the metropolitan press ended, for the most part, with a news-boy hawking his wares on a crowded sidewalk. Very likely he had never seen Daumier's lithograph of a woman vendor on a Paris boulevard who replied to a buyer unable to find today's news in her paper that it had been in yesterday's edition. However, the newsboy muffled any complaint about the quality of his newspaper with the intensity of his yells.[20] Calling out what he considered the leading stories of his paper, he produced the final distortion of the news before the reader's mind went to work. A visitor to the United States during the 1880's, who did not particularly like what he saw, observed that the lowly newsboys were the "controlling editors in American journalism," their "opinions in turn shaped by the prevailing interests of the public."[21] But the newsboys' approach merely completed the imaginative tampering with events that began when a reporter first encountered the facts.

Although the walls of the newspaper's city room daily admonished the reporter with slogans about accuracy and facts, he realized, as Theodore Dreiser learned before he quit news reporting in 1895, that his city editor wanted not merely accuracy, but a "flair for the ridiculous or the remarkable, even if it had to be invented," so that the paper, "and life itself, might not seem so dull."[22] The metropolitan press made certain that countless small reports reflected the magnitude of its subject. In the process, it coined new words that shaped urban patterns of speaking and thinking, gave old words new meanings, and wore others out.

The neologisms penetrated many areas of life. "Speakeasy" became well known during the crusade against liquor as the designation of an illegal saloon.[23] "Bohemian" exemplified the change in meaning of old words. It once had described any journalist; but reporters impressed by the significance of their work and eager to define themselves as a distinct group made sure no one confused a reporter any longer with a "bohemian," who became "a writer that wanders from one subject to another," a "ménager of trifles."[24] Excessive use inflated other words and stripped them of their meanings. The "first," the "most," and the "only" recurred in so many reports that they soon meant as little as "unique" or "best."[25]

The reduction of an event to a few phrases reached its ultimate in headlines that condensed communication to a minimum or emphasized one aspect of an event. "Both Bathed in Blood" was how the Philadelphia *Inquirer* reported an "Atrocious Crime Up Town That May End in Murder."[26] When facts refused to bend sufficiently to give the desired impact, the reporters molded language into a message system that invited readers to share secrets. "The plot thickens and the drama is fast deepening into tragedy," the chatty San Francisco *Call* began a description of a legal struggle between feuding newspapers.[27] The technique gave a news story the form of a personal exchange, laced with colloquialisms, fortifying the distortions of sensationalism with the flattering sensation of being addressed directly. A report in the San Francisco *Golden City* identified a politician as "a wily old fox. His latest exhibition of cunning was the entrapping of a young school teacher . . . into a discussion at Lincoln Hall before one of the largest audiences ever assembled in that building."[28]

The changes in the mode of journalistic expression stretched over many decades. Enlivening the prose of the metropolitan press, they slowly overcame antiquated usages. Old writing habits disguised as convention or cultivated as tradition weighed so heavily at times that it took until the 1890's before the news story lost its chronological straightjacket. Only then did reports assume an analytical structure and answer in the opening paragraph the impatient questions behind the five W's foremost on the reader's mind: who, what, when, where, why. That innovation facilitated the rapid extension of sensationalism into all areas of life, hastened the demise of the metropolitan press, and contributed to the spread of yellow journalism through the cities and towns of the United States in the 1890's.

Despite the movement toward casual language and sensational appeal, some sections of a metropolitan newspaper could rarely afford to color events so that they seemed bigger than life. Distorted accounts about legal decisions and money matters ran the risk of driving readers to more reliable sources as guides for their business ventures. The statistical language of the stock market report, the most technical of all pages, retained much of the mentality of the counting house that had characterized the mercantile newspapers before the rise of the metropolitan press.

In 1831, Alexis de Tocqueville foresaw that the "need felt by a great number of people to communicate with one another" would stimulate the rise of many newspapers.[29] Until then, the driving force behind a newspaper had been a job printer or book publisher, who issued a subscription list for a new journal and circulated it mostly among merchants and manufacturers. When the publisher thought he had sufficient subscribers for his venture, he would try to find a lawyer, physician, or teacher to supervise the publication, a man with enough political ambition, literary aspiration, or sense of civic responsibility to ignore the minimal salary.[30] In the heat of a political campaign, some of these men wrote partisan editorials that rivaled in eloquence the literary effusions of professional editors.

Mercantile papers kept the business community informed about current wholesale prices, imports and auctions, economic conditions in Europe, money conversion rates, ship arrivals and departures, and stock and bond quotations. They also reported activities from Washington and the state capitals. The politicians in power, the Democratic Republicans in most cases, claimed the loyalty of these mercantile sheets because they could dispense political patronage in the form of official contracts for printing government pronouncements. Federalist papers, originally established to maintain the political balance, quickly acquired the features of the mercantile sheets. The most successful journals filled about three-fourths of their space with advertisements and became "expensive bulletin boards for a small trading clientele."[31]

In 1820, the largest daily newspapers in New York City, the *Evening Post* and the *Commercial Advertiser*, had a circulation of two thousand copies. About half of that figure seems to have been sufficient for survival, supplemented by advertising and printing contracts. The cycle of presidential elections periodically stimulated the slow pulse of newspaperdom. In 1824, Philadelphia had

eleven dailies and New York City twelve, with a circulation ranging from one thousand to four thousand. By 1828, the press of the
United States counted 863 dailies and weeklies, with an annual
circulation of 68 million copies. Two years later, the number of
American newspapers had reached one thousand.[32]

The American journals of the 1820's, however, were newspapers
only in name. They published little news in the form of up-to-date
reports about events, and most of it appeared rather late. Except
for an occasional letter from a casual correspondent and the scanty
gleanings of a special correspondent in Washington or in a state
capital, an editor clipped the reports that suited his paper from
newspapers mailed to him from other cities. He continued pretty
much the journalistic practices of the printers of newspapers during the colonial period. Whenever a journal from abroad reached
his desk, he pasted together a summary of European affairs that
was at least several weeks old, if not several months. Apart from
editorials, little original writing found its way into his sheet. Reporters as such did not exist, but some local news got into the
paper through the editor's circle of acquaintances. English novels
were serialized freely before the existence of the International
Copyright Law. From the early 1830's, the political satire of the
popular "Major Jack Downing" provided a lighter touch.[33]

The demand for accounts of current events, a journalistic com-
modity of high market value in large cities, broke the dependence
of newspapers on party patronage and business enterprise. One
newsman who grew old with the new journalism observed that the
rise of the metropolitan press proved everyone wrong who had
been "educated for half a century in the belief that no journal of
any respectability could be established without the consent of politicians and the pecuniary aid of party."[34] Encouraged by the success of the London *Penny Magazine*, in September 1833 Benjamin
H. Day started the New York *Sun*. The rise of the *Sun* produced
other offshoots of the new journalism. In the span of six years, between 1834 and 1840, thirty-five penny dailies emerged in New

York City alone. Many of them lived only briefly, but the call for news lasted and during the 1830's influential penny papers acquired great names. In New York, the *Sun* and the *Herald* stood out. In Boston, several dailies opened in 1835 and the *Daily Times* in 1836. In Philadelphia, the first experiment, the *Cent*, was started in 1830, and the *Daily Transcript* began publication in 1835, followed the next year by the *Public Ledger*. And the first issue of the Baltimore *Sun* appeared in 1837.[35]

Much of that initial triumph of popular journalism was based on James Gordon Bennett's perception that the public would read almost anything as long as it was presented as news, as reports about events that had just happened. In 1835, encouraged by the response to penny papers, Bennett started the New York *Herald*, which he quickly turned into a leading metropolitan journal. His first editorial stressed his political independence and his endeavor "to record the facts . . . equally intended for the great masses of the community—the merchant, mechanic, working people—the private family as well as the public hotel—the journeyman and his employer—the clerk and his principal."[36] Along with straight news and suggestive gossip, plain accounts of actual happenings and imaginative tales of fancied ones, he served a steady diet of reports about murder, suicide, adultery, and rape that satisfied the readers' taste for the sensational. He fought city hall, boosted local enterprise, and, for good measure, fanned nationalistic sentiments.

In 1836, Bennett's telling of the story behind the Jewett murder and the Robinson trial demonstrated a new reportorial technique. The facts of the case added up to a mystery, remained one, and, consequently, made good copy. Someone had murdered Helen Jewett, a beautiful young prostitute, with a hatchet in a fashionable bordello and set fire to her body and bed. Circumstantial evidence led to the arrest of Richard P. Robinson, a handsome young bon vivant. Bennett went over the ground and the corpse in detail. "The perfect figure, the exquisite limbs, the fine face, the full arms, the beautiful bust, all, all surpassed in every respect the

Venus de Medici," he reported. Presumably he and his readers cherished reading the report, because he reprinted it twice, in successive issues.[37]

In his coverage of the case, Bennett left none of the proverbial stones unturned. He related his interview with the madam verbatim and began raising doubts about Robinson's guilt. His defense of the accused stirred up a violent controversy with the *Sun* and the *Transcript* that further boosted the circulation of the three penny papers. Speculations about the "real" murderer, the murdered woman, the wages of sin, and the morals of New York kept the case alive. Its grand finale, orchestrated in the *Herald* with daily transcripts of the trial, analyses of the testimony, and more moral lessons, culminated in the acquittal of Robinson by the jury.[38]

Bennett methodically invaded that sphere of life hitherto considered private and steadily broadened people's idea of what was news. In order to satisfy the desire for information about the intimate life of others, especially the rich, he violated contemporary canons of etiquette and propriety. He sensed the news value of the most diverse aspects of big-city life. He pioneered the emergence of a sports section by treating accounts of horse racing as news stories. He assessed the operation of the stock exchange and reviewed court trials, reported the ups and downs of Wall Street and covered church meetings.

Bennett's flexibility enabled him to adjust to the rate of change his audience tolerated. When he instinctively tried to make the front page his major news page, because his audience rejected the change, he suffered a setback and so, after a few months, he restored advertisements to their familiar place on page one; his readers did not seem quite ready to surrender wholeheartedly to the magic of printed news. When he was in need of copy, his sensational success and his rivals' failings constituted his favorite editorial topics. Inspired by his ingenuity, the *Herald* made news supreme in its columns and thus outdistanced the other popular newspapers, the mercantile press, and the political journals.[39]

Rising circulation figures made it easier for editors to endure protests against their journalistic excesses. Generally these figures lacked accuracy until advertisers insisted on more reliable counts. Yet, despite distortions, their steady increase attested to the popularity of the metropolitan press. This success baffled those who felt obliged to watch the cultural features of the cityscape. Philip Hone, patrician by instinct and, by accident, mayor of New York in 1825, pondered in 1837: "Everybody wonders how people can buy these receptacles of scandal, the penny papers, and yet everybody does encourage them; and the very man who blames his neighbors for setting so bad an example, occasionally puts one in his pocket to carry home to his family for their and his own edification." Hone may have done that, too, for he explained apologetically that one paper would not corrupt morals. "It is bad enough, to be sure," he added, "but the sale of one copy, more or less, will not make any difference in the circulation."[40]

The purchase of many single copies, however, did make a difference and produced the phenomenal expansion of the metropolitan press. By the beginning of the 1840's, Philip Hone had overcome his ambivalence and strongly ciriticized the "depraved and vitiated taste of newspaper readers," but as a true man about town he also recognized the intimate connection between the metropolitan press and the modern city. At the only moment in his many years as diarist when, as he thought, he lowered himself to quoting from the penny press, he cited a comment in a news report about a New York society ball which attempted to probe the larger meaning of urban life: " 'This is one of the most remarkable, curious, droll, incomprehensible cities, the capital of one of the greatest countries, that God ever tried to save from damnation, or the devil ever worked like a horse to get below!"[41]

Devils and demons had long tempted the curious with exposés of city life. In the first significant urban novel, published in Paris in 1707, one of them escorted a student through the air to watch the inhabitants of Madrid engaged in the frivolities and vices of the night.[42] In the opinion of Hone and other New Yorkers, penny

journalists played an analogous role. However, while the devil in
Le Sage's *Le Diable boiteux* titillated his companion with revela-
tions of places and people that did not actually exist in the real
Madrid, newspapermen reported the action and detailed the scene
of large American cities with precision. Readers could actually
identify segments of their daily life, stare at the scene of a tragic
event if they passed it, search for a face in the crowd, or recognize
one behind the window of a carriage.

At times, news reports drew readers physically to the scenes of
events, but the development of another form of reporting assured
that the hearts and minds of those who stayed away were there,
too. The human interest story set the basic elements of individual
human drama against the whirligig of life in the modern city. Journalists quickly realized that any news item contained the makings
of a great story, particularly if it involved a sequence of events that
took days, or weeks, to reach a conclusion.

These insights were put to good use, and in the process, elements of fiction entered into news reports and became facts, while
facts written as literature turned into fiction. Under the masterful
touch of Charles A. Dana, who after the Civil War acquired the
New York *Sun*, little chatty reports about the tragic or comic
events in people's lives gained dignity and importance as a new
genre of news writing. [43] News report and human interest story became major journalistic vehicles that brought information and
knowledge about urban life to the large audience created by the
modern city.

A San Francisco newspaperman who set out in disguise to experience what it meant to be homeless, without a job, and starving
demonstrated his mastery of the art in the fall of 1878. In relating
his adventures under the heading "Trying Tramping," he referred
to specific localities and made sure his readers could follow his excursion into the world of poverty-stricken men. His search for
shelter took them to the bales of hay piled like a gigantic wall along
the waterfront, teeming with men trying to find a place to sleep,
and to the lumber yards where others sought protection against fog

and wind behind the construction materials. His description of his nausea made his readers smell the stench of overcrowded rooms in windowless hovels. His despair on the city dump may have actually deepened their humanity for a fleeting moment as they read the lines that had them sifting the refuse with the fortunate poor, who found something to eat, some rags to wear, and earned two dollars a week for their work.[44]

The news report and human interest story tied the metropolitan press to another source of knowledge about the opportunities of city life. Previously, advertising had been done by means of voices, bells, banners, and signboards, as well as scribbled tackups, printed handbills, sandwich men, and inserts in the columns of newspapers. Now the increased circulation of the popular press gave merchants a new opportunity to address many potential customers; and because advertisements provided news as well as revenue, they gained importance for newspapermen.

In one form or another, advertisements had always been in newspapers. In the mercantile and political sheets of the 1820's, they filled the six or eight columns of one page in "squares" of ten lines, an inch or so in height. In a minute typeface, they called attention to the goods and services of the city's businesses, but spoke only to a small group of readers. These early advertisements appeared in papers aimed neither at a mass audience nor a mass market, but at highly select audiences instead. Space was frequently contracted for one year. The tempo of life was slow, custom assured continuity, and there was always something one businessman had to offer to another. Consequently, displays varied little, names hardly mattered, and, as if to make certain that things remained the same, the mechanics of printing limited typographical or illustrative innovations.

The new journalism stimulated new forms of advertising. Publishers and editors who saw the circulation value of local news recognized the business possibilities as well as the news values of want-ads. Benjamin H. Day promised in his prospectus for the New York *Sun* "all the news of the day" and an "advantageous me-

dium for advertising."[45] Help-wanted and situation-wanted ads of
two or three lines, instead of the familiar "squares" of ten lines, catered to readers looking for jobs or for servants. The social range of
the employer-employee groups broadened the appeal of the metropolitan press. Paid marriage and death notices provided an egalitarian counterpart to news reports of a society wedding or a state
funeral. The playbills of amusement centers, theaters, and museums attracted legions of pleasure-seekers to the newspapers. By
the end of the 1830's, seventeen columns of advertising appeared
in the twenty-four-column *Sun*, of which help-wanted and situation-wanted ads made up four.[46]

Given the news value and the financial significance of the advertisements, newspapers and advertising accommodated each other.
New journalistic practices mirrored new life-styles dictated by the
increased tempo of life in the modern city. Instead of restricted
space for a fixed sum per year, small units of space were now sold
by the day. The flat rate per insertion that had prevailed for more
than a century gave way to a line rate for most clients. When the
small advertisers realized that they needed more than one printing
of an ad to get a response, the papers began offering rebates for a
package of two or more insertions. The practice of restricting the
width of an advertisement to one column, because foundries produced column rules only in standard sizes, fell by the way in 1836,
when the New York *Herald* began using various sizes that made
possible the publication of a two-column advertisement and illustration showing an "Unparalleled Attraction" at Barnum's American Museum.[47]

In general, however, innovations came slowly; for decades advertisements struggled for recognition of their importance in the
metropolitan press. Insights about the mass market came more
slowly than insights about the mass audience; the desire to communicate about people seemed stronger than the desire to communicate about goods. Only gradually did the admonitions spelled
out in a pamphlet in 1869 take hold: "A man can't do business
without advertising; and the question is whether to call to his aid

the engine of the world—the printing press . . . or to go back to the days when newspapers, telegraphs, and railroads were unknown." But when the advice did gain a following, it stuck.[48]

For the new journalism, the production of certain forms of advertisements created some difficulty. Ambitious announcements required a much more sophisticated layout than the lines of type that went into a column of news stories, and their illustrations taxed the limited technology of the printing presses. The new demands of advertising also strained the obligation of journalists to do justice to all aspects of the vast social changes experienced in the modern city. Editors, who traditionally had done advertisements as part of their routine as printers, abandoned them when their attention became absorbed by their new function as newsmen. This preoccupation went so far that they sometimes treated advertisements as news. James Gordon Bennett announced in the *Herald* in 1848 that no advertising copy would run longer than two weeks, because he hoped to assure the news value of advertisements by preventing advertisers from using the same copy without change month in, month out.[49]

As businessmen, editors recognized the importance of advertisements for their papers, but they also discovered soon that more advertisements increased production costs by requiring larger issues. However, they kept taking orders for advertisements because they feared that advertisers would place their messages in the columns of competitors. In the 1870's, when the use of wood pulp was bringing down the price of paper, James Gordon Bennett, Jr., who had taken over the *Herald* from his father, still complained to Whitelaw Reid, publisher of the New York *Tribune*, that the growth of advertising troubled him: "Whole columns of it I print now at a loss, and I would gladly throw part of it out, if it were not that some of you fellows would pick it up."[50]

Advertisements could be trouble, but advertisers could become even more troublesome, or so the new journalists thought. Some editors granted favors to certain advertisers, provoking others to go to rival newspapers or to demand special treatment for themselves.

Most editors abandoned these problems gladly to business managers who, in an emerging business diplomacy, played small advertisers along but bargained intensely with advertising agents over the rates of large clients.

Large advertisers, merchants and manufacturers, almost automatically turned to advertising agencies to handle first the placing, then the planning and preparing of the advertising. Unlike editors, advertisers had had experience with all kinds of middlemen in the proliferation of their businesses. The advertising agent was another variety of intermediary in economic affairs, who worked out methods of accounting, developed categories of rates, arranged forms of payment, and produced acceptable ways to judge how well a newspaper performed for the advertiser's dollar. Advertisers recognized that it was pressure from the agents that persuaded the editors to develop an advertising policy and impressed them with the need for accurately reported circulation figures. The first compendium of such figures appeared in 1869.[51] Advertising agencies came into existence in an environment that put a premium on rationality and organization; they resolved friction between newspapermen and advertisers created by outdated practices, fluctuating rates, and strained feelings arising from uncertainty about the line between advertisements and news.

Increasingly, this ambiguous distinction troubled the newsmen. Complications arose when a newspaper staff, overburdened in its daily search for news, ran as a human interest story a sketch about a singer or author or actress that provided publicity for the artist and unpaid advertising for the impresario or publisher. Showman P. T. Barnum, dealing with highly praised Jenny Lind, and editor Robert Bonner, working with highly priced authors, built some of their successes on the astute manipulation of the dual nature of certain stories as both news and advertising.[52] The stories enthralled readers fascinated by the glamor of celebrated names or reports about huge royalties but yielded little advertising revenue. And the demand for them as news only intensified the problem until the concept "no ad no advance notice, no advance notice no ad" took hold.

Consumption of the growing quantities of news, in the form of reports, human interest stories, and advertisements, required time. Many people, tied for six days a week to offices, workshops, or factories, had leisure only on Sundays. Their desire for news overcame the opposition of moralists who considered the Sunday newspaper a violation of the Sabbath. "We shall be pleased," one of them had written in 1832 in response to rumors about a Sunday edition in New York City, "if the experiment were to end in showing . . . there is too much moral sense in our community to allow such a speculation proving profitable."[53] But his notion of community extended only to the limited number of residents who thought the way he did. Many newcomers to the modern city, particularly immigrants, greeted Sunday as a relief from the monotony of toil and regarded a newspaper on that day as a welcome diversion. Other residents became accustomed to special Sunday editions during the Civil War when extras related details about battles. Undoubtedly, the temper of the mass audience, which made up the following of the metropolitan press, favored the Sunday newspaper.

In general, newspapers accommodated to the work cycle of the city. Evening papers, bought on the way home from work, outnumbered morning papers about two to one in 1890, and about three to one in 1900.[54] In the case of the Sunday paper, the trend went from Sunday weeklies to Sunday editions of the large dailies. Although Chicago and other large cities also pioneered Sunday journalism, New York City set the pace. In 1842, one in twenty-six New Yorkers acquired one of four Sunday weeklies or a copy of Bennett's *Sunday Herald*. At roughly the same time, one in six residents purchased a daily. In 1850, one of every 2.2 inhabitants acquired one of the Sunday papers, which had a greater circulation than either morning or evening daily papers.[55] More readers on Sunday brought more advertisers. The interest of both groups required extra pages of features to maintain a balance between advertising copy and editorial material.

The sheer volume of news also taxed a reader's capacity to absorb the content of a newspaper and undermined his inclination to read an entire issue. The fact that such a monstrous subject as the city itself was the great news meant that news management became a necessity. This produced a departmentalization within the newspaper that readers grasped quickly because it corresponded to categories they understood better than the divisions by means of which municipal government struggled to adapt a rural democracy to the intricacies of urban life. In an age that also systematized retailing by way of the department store, people could relate to this rational presentation of life as news.

The new format divided the paper into sections and created subdivisions with the help of columns, corners, and pages. The sections of news reports, editorials, human interest stories, and advertisements imposed a rational order on a chaotic urban life. "The ancient practice of throwing all news items together into the columns of a paper without reference to either character or locality, is gradually but surely dying out," the *Journalist* stressed in 1887. "It is comparatively rare now-a-days to find a wedding following a murder, and a church dedication a raid on a disorderly house."[56] Instead, sections and subdivisions encouraged selective reading, a habit that appealed to people whose experience of modernity taught them to live life in segments and not as a totality.

These devices allowing selective reading perpetuated the mass audience by assuring the daily sale that provided the major source of income for newspapers during most of the nineteenth century, when revenue from advertisements was somewhat smaller. Before the advertising bonanza of the twentieth century, the urge to accommodate readers also stimulated a search for news that would attract specific groups of readers as well as large general audiences. Special audiences built up and sustained the total mass audience.

Many of the new editorial features of the Sunday newspaper spoke directly to women, who had been ignored by conventional journalism, with its masculine orientation, and were served only by a few magazines and specialized journals. The metropolitan press began systematically to court women, who represented an enormous group of uncommitted readers. Large advertisers followed suit when they realized that the changing life-style of nineteenth-century America was giving the woman of the household control over spending the family income. Attracting and holding women readers was an effective way to boost circulation and to satisfy large advertisers.

The task of attracting women involved more than the insertion of recipes. It required walking a tightrope between social progress and traditional attitudes, between old journalistic practices and necessary innovations. It took until the 1880's before the metropolitan press really found out how to serve women without arousing prejudices. Joseph Pulitzer managed to address women living in new social conditions without offending the sensibilities of his other readers, undoubtedly many women among them, who were reluctant to make concessions to the feminist movement by supporting the struggle for universal suffrage. Pulitzer's instinct for popular journalism, best expressed in his ability to respond successfully to the needs and opportunities of the moment, created a newspaper that spoke to women as well as men.

The casual way in which the metropolitan press came to address women was a product of big-city life. To attract and hold a female audience the *World* relied on interesting articles, mostly reports about fashion, discussions of etiquette, and advice on beauty that reflected the convention of the day, which considered home as woman's place and domestic life as her field. In November 1883, the *World* broadened its message with a column of "advice letters," supplemented by columns that expressed liberal ideas about women's concerns without committing the paper in any way. Although respecting the social conservatism of families in tenements and flats, these features, like shopping downtown, helped to undermine stereotypes and expanded the female domain. They struck a compromise between the new roles some women were carving for themselves and the old sex roles accepted by most of the immigrants and lower-income groups that made up the bulk of the readers.[57]

Most of the metropolitan press' appeal, however, was simply the result of the modern city's fascination for women as well as men, a fascination which newspapers such as Pulitzer's *World* were able to reflect. The policy of keeping away from controversial topics about women's rights pursued by Edward Bok after he became new editor of the *Ladies' Home Journal* in 1889 seemed the obvious one in the 1880's.[58] The managing editor of the *Independent* defended Bok's policy in 1909, saying that a publication "which wants a million readers, must adhere strictly to the conventions if it would keep up its reputation as a safe guide for the multitude. This may not be the ideal form of leadership, but it is common sense."[59]

Other metropolitan papers pursued a similar policy of not inciting controversy when speaking to women. Toward the end of the 1880's, when the Philadelphia *Inquirer* began devoting parts of its Sunday section to "women topics," the subjects ranged from beauty hints to child care and from "in-depth" features on city life to serialized novels. On January 5, 1890, "The Art of Dressing" illustrated a reporter's assumption that most people did not understand it. "Frolics for Children" made suggestions "to keep the lads and lasses in great good humor" after the holidays. Well-written accounts of general interest softened the impact of female news but attracted the interest of women readers. "M'Ginty Saws Wood" related a "tramp's" experience at a Wayfarers' Lodge, culminating in a bath without soap or towel and hard work for three hours "in return for a bed in an illy ventilated room and a wretched breakfast."

In the next Sunday edition of the *Inquirer,* the children's column gave way to one on "Capon and Mutton," spiced with the announcement that "Great Britain cannot equal us in Southdown saddles and caponized fowls," while the constant advice about the intricacies of fashion continued with "A Woman's Wardrobe." And so did the serial novel, *Imperial Millions: An American Monte*

*Cristo*, by the ever-popular Julian Hawthorne. Regularly the columns "In the Philadelphia Theatres" and "Brilliant Society Events" reviewed the plays of the week and announced in detail the coming receptions and fetes.

At about the same time, "Our Woman's Page," furnished by the Bok Syndicate, and a "Children's Page" constituted the major features of the Sunday edition of the St. Louis *Republican*, which averaged thirty-six pages. A full-page "Room and Boarders Directory" regularly linked one of the major occupations of women in the modern city to the advertising columns of the paper. "The Great Shadow," by A. Conan Doyle, was the serial story. On November 6, 1892, biographies of the author Elizabeth S. Phelps, Queen Olga of Greece, and Queen Margarita of Italy appeared along with illustrated hints of how "To Hang a Skirt" and how to arrange "Children's Teas." On January 8, 1893, "Work of the Women" discussed the progress of clubs and societies, "Hints on the Fashion" tackled midwinter hats and bonnets, and "Gravies and Sauces" had "their foundations elucidated by Miss Barrows of the B.Y.W.C.A. School of Domestic Science." On weekdays, "Our Women's Corner" filled the gap between Sunday editions.

The emergence of a woman's page furthered the compartmentalization of the metropolitan press and enriched its content. Other innovations in specific fields also strengthened the idea that a big paper printed not only news but also whatever people wanted to read, from sports to comics. Joseph Pulitzer staffed the first sports department of an American newspaper with experts to satisfy readers who took their diversions seriously.[60] He systematically expanded the sports reporting pioneered by other editors of the metropolitan press and by the *Spirit of the Times*, and *Clipper*, and the *Police Gazette*, the big three of American sports journalism in the nineteenth century.

In putting the sports page on the journalistic map, Pulitzer followed a trend of concentrating editorials on one page and financial news, stock market reports, book notices, and theater reviews on other pages. In the early 1880's, Pulitzer also took his first faltering steps towards the comic strip of the 1890's. His initiative helped add, within a decade, illustrations and cartoon strips to the metropolitan press, which ultimately came to be defined as a vehicle of news and entertainment.

The enthusiastic reception of illustrations and cartoons also underlined the importance of a newspaper's general appearance as a means of catching the attention of distracted or semi-literate readers. Along with its new content, the metropolitan press slowly gave American journalism a new format. Although some editors learned to make the title page their news page in the 1850's, it was not until 1883 that Joseph Pulitzer, over a period of several months, established the last (or right-hand) column, or columns, of the first page as the proper slot for the lead story. The development of multi-column headlines, which ultimately ran across an entire page, did not come until the 1890's.[61] It was primarily in content, however, and only secondarily in format, that the metropolitan press reflected the diversity of the modern city and made it comprehensible.

Like the city itself, newspaper growth depended on managerial and technological innovations. As readers and advertisers steadily increased, the newspaper became big business. The federal census report of 1840 was the first to recognize the press as a specific subject of investigation, in its volume on commercial and manufacturing enterprises.[62] Under the heading "Printing and Binding," the Sixth Census listed 138 daily and 1,141 weekly newspapers and 227 periodicals, with a $6 million investment and 12,000 employees. In 1880, the census enumerated 971 daily and 8,633 weekly newspapers. Although the number of daily newspapers had increased at each of the intervening censuses, the growth between 1870 and 1880 alone amounted to almost 100 percent.[63] Between 1880 and 1890, the figure for dailies almost doubled again, rising to 1,731, while weeklies grew about 50 percent to 12,721. And the amount of capital invested in newspapers and periodicals jumped from $15 million in 1870 to $126 million in 1890.[64]

As the nineteenth-century statisticians of the newspaper business emphasized, figures were difficult to obtain and comparisons difficult to make. In 1880, the Tenth Census report explained that the most casual examination of the tables of the Eighth or Ninth Census exposed the weakness of statistics. The report stressed specifically that "the well-known tendency of newspaper publishers to exaggerate circulation has revealed itself in several instances." The 1880 census avoided raising questions about capital investment in newspapers because the superintendent of the Ninth Census had found that "the census returns of capital invested in manufacturers are entirely untrustworthy and delusive."[65] Changes in categories of reporting between the Tenth Census and the Eleventh Census only increased the difficulty of securing a reliable overview.[66]

A discussion of the significance of the metropolitan press does not require sorting out all these unreliable figures. However, as a reflection of the rationality of what often seemed an irrational age, it is revealing that reliable figures did appear when advertisers inquired about the value of the publicity they were buying. Instead of waiting for publishers to furnish answers to questions mailed out by the Census Bureau, advertising agents themselves went after the information. In 1869 the first directory of the New York advertising agency of George P. Rowell & Co., intended "to increase our own business and best serve the interests of our customers," listed twelve daily newspapers in the United States with a circulation of over 20,000 copies and twenty-six with a circulation of 10,000–20,000 copies. It was the "first serious effort to ascertain and make known the circulation of newspapers," as Rowell liked to call his directory.[67]

Much sooner than the modern city itself, the metropolitan press demonstrated the limits of bigness in the form of strained finances. Staggering costs threatened a newspaper when a large circulation or changed format called for a new press, a bigger building, and more manpower. Publishers and editors occasionally suggested— perhaps to discourage newcomers from increasing the fierce com-

petition—that they made less money in the 1870's when the cost of
bigness began to show than they had in the 1850's when big business dawned for the newspapers.[68]

In 1879, Whitelaw Reid, successor to Horace Greeley at the
New York *Tribune* and son-in-law of the financier Darius O. Mills,
compared the costs of publishing the *Tribune* in 1859 and in 1879
in an attempt to justify the increased sales price. In 1859, the total
expenses had come to $130,198; in 1879, they were $377,510,
nearly three times as much. When Reid went into details, he used
figures from 1874 to compensate for the effect of the Panic of 1875
on prices.

Specifically, Reid pointed out the charge for the telegraph,
which had gone up from $11,679 to $51,729; the composing room
expenditures, which rose from $42,256 to $125,883, and the cost of
the editorial department, which grew from $43,125 to $188,829.
He emphasized that the *Tribune* had yielded a net profit of
$85,000 in 1859, as a two-cent paper, on a total revenue of half a
million dollars, and that in 1879 it earned $85,588 as a four-cent
paper. "We have made $85,000 as a 2-cent paper," he argued,
"have spent a half more and made only the same sum as a 4-cent
paper." Consequently, according to Reid, a return to the pre-Civil
War prices while maintaining "the present quality" would mean
"merely to plunge into bankruptcy at a gallop."[69] In the next decade, an English commentator on the American press supposed
that all successful publishers in the United States heartily en-
dorsed Reid's view.[70]

From the perspective of the publisher-editor, the metropolitan
press may not have been a truly great money-maker over the span
of years. But some publishers profited handsomely, and newspapers remained big business in the eyes of most of the residents of
the modern city, who had observed the rise of enterprises that
started in basement printshops and, without further capital, became large newspapers—such as the *Herald,* the *Sun,* and the
*Tribune* in New York, the Boston *Herald,* and the Philadelphia
*Ledger.* A large number of newspapers started without capital. In

New York City alone, 146 newspapers sprang into existence between 1833 and 1880, and 29 of them still flourished at the end of the period.[71]

The fortunes accumulated in journalistic ventures, as well as investment lost, exemplified the importance of money in the modern city. The success or failure of editors demonstrated to newspaper readers that wealth could be acquired by applying mind and energy to exploiting the economic potential of a democratic world that recognized few restraints on the pursuit of happiness. Evidence of journalistic achievement was present not merely in rising circulation figures and growing advertising pages but in bewildering machinery and magnificent buildings. In 1875, the granite and brick Tribune Tower rose 260 feet high, surpassed on the New York skyline only by the 286-foot spire of Trinity Church, and helped transform New York from a horizontal city into a vertical one. In 1890, the spectacular golden dome of the sixteen-story World Building overshadowed both, rising to a height of 310 feet.[72]

The success of the metropolitan press rested on effective organization of steadily expanding modes of operation. The practices pioneered by newspapers were models of the methods of new social institutions in the modern city. In order to assure a modicum of freedom for its heterogeneous inhabitants, the modern city depended on an orderly anarchy; but the social institutions it spawned—the metropolitan press, the department store, the baseball park, and the vaudeville house—themselves relied on efficient organization. Within its own context each furnished the order that curbed emotions and limited confusion. The pursuit of money led the new institutions to an intense kind of rational order unsuited for the modern city as a whole.

In the metropolitan press, the discovery, publication, and distribution of news ruled supreme, and the emerging system reflected that priority. As the newspaper grew in significance and size, specialists took over aspects of a job once handled by one man. Benjamin H. Day himself wrote and set in type the first four-page *Sun* he issued on September 3, 1833.[73] But the hunger of the mass audiences for information soon ended the one-man shop and stimulated a new technology in enterprises as yet barely recognized as an industry. The technological advances not only kept newspapers in business but also resulted in the development of organizational techniques to cope with bringing the story of complex cities and a chaotic world to the curious. In 1843, ten years after the appearance of the *Sun*, the multitude of new devices that the first U.S. Patent Commissioner faced convinced him that they presaged "the arrival of that period when human improvement must end."[74]

The metropolitan press developed rational management early in its operation, before American industry in general, which became really concerned only around 1880, when production began to outrun the capacity of the market to absorb goods at profitable prices. In a full-fledged metropolitan newspaper, experts ran editorial, business, production, and circulation departments under the supervision of an editor-in-chief or publisher. The department heads in turn surrounded themselves with specialists who covered all areas of gathering, producing, and distributing news as well as advertising.

In the 1870's, the efficient organization of Wilbur F. Storey's Chicago *Times* provided one apprentice journalist with a model for his later work as an executive manager of the Associated Press.[75] A managing editor, with a city editor at his elbow, took care of news and editorials, often delegating to sub-editors responsibilities for reports, features, and reviews to go on pages devoted to stock market and financial affairs, sports and entertainment, theater, art, literature, and women. A business manager, whose assistants oversaw the composing room and the press room, also handled advertising. Under the direction of a circulation manager, the finished product found its way into the hands of readers through street sales or subscriptions.

Two innovations facilitated the initial attempt of the metropolitan press to provide news for a mass audience—low prices and newsboys. Both made people who were not in the habit of reading a newspaper more willing to buy, and both remained weapons in the circulation wars of the nineteenth century. Prices did not stay as low as one penny for very long because, as a cynic observed, "it is safe to say that no one-cent paper was ever started . . . which did not contemplate, from the beginning, an increase to two cents as soon as it was firmly rooted."[76] With success came new standards of news coverage and feature writing, and the need for a higher price to pay for larger staffs and better equipment. But a paper as successful as the New York *Sun* continued to sell for one cent until the Civil War, when the hike in prices brought the paper up to two cents, where it remained for several decades.

Lowering prices was an effective competitive tactic during decades when, throughout the country, advertising furnished a little less than half of the revenue of a newspaper, and even less in the case of a big metropolitan newspaper with a large circulation.[77] Most editors depended on selling papers to growing masses of readers drawn steadily into the habits of daily reading, and a reduction or increase of the price by one or two cents weighed heavily in their success. It weighed even more heavily when the reduction came as a result of pressure from competitors and was taken by merchants as a sign that the paper was losing its significance as an advertising medium.

In the 1880's, Joseph Pulitzer, fresh from St. Louis, succeeded with the *World* in New York City through manipulating prices, an instrument of competition that had been sharpened by the *Sun* and the *Herald* in the 1830's. He reduced the *World's* price to two cents. That move pressured the *Times* to come down from four cents to two and the *Tribune* from four to three; their surrender forced the *Herald*, the *World's* great rival, to drop from three to two cents. An exuberant *World* saw the capitulation as evidence of its growing circulation and of the *Herald's* decline as an advertising medium.[78]

In the following decade, William Randolph Hearst arrived in New York City from San Francisco and beat the *World* at the old game. Pulitzer, in answer to the challenge of Hearst's *Journal*, lowered his morning edition to one cent and raised advertising rates. He promptly lost advertisers and then readers, too. Later, Pulitzer recalled how James Gordon Bennett, Jr., had reacted with his *Herald* after Pulitzer had appeared on the scene: "When Mr. Hearst came to New York, I did the same. I wonder why, in view of my experience."[79]

Like low prices, newsboys dated back to the beginning of the metropolitan press in the 1830's, when they began to roam the streets shouting their bits of news to attract customers. The practical Benjamin H. Day bypassed making the customary list of subscribers for his new penny paper and sold, cash in advance, one hundred copies of his *Sun* for sixty-seven cents to boys who pocketed thirty-three cents after they had cornered one hundred buyers. And more, if they were lucky: in 1836, when the *Herald, Sun,* and *Transcript* were stirring up New York with their reports about the Jewett murder, newsboys sold scarce issues for one shilling.[80]

The newsboys' running and yelling accentuated the heightened tempo and toughened tone of urban life and assaulted the public's eyes and ears—if not with news, at least with the name of the newspaper. "So entirely absorbed do these urchins become in their vocation," *Leslie's Weekly* explained in 1856, that they keep up their cries "along an entire block of buildings in which every house is closed and not a possible purchaser in sight."[81] Their ragged dash also shaped the aggressive salesmanship of street newspaper vendors who came to replace footloose newsboys at strategic downtown intersections.

The gradual development of small printing shops into publishing empires paralleled the more general application of an intensified technology to the task of living in the modern city. Printing innovation began in the 1830's and reached fruition in the 1880's. In 1847, the Philadelphia *Ledger* introduced Richard M. Hoe's tencylinder press, which the Lords of the Privy Council of Great Britain called in 1853 "one of the greatest steps ever made in printing"; but the needed development in type composition by machine did not come until 1886, when Ottmar Mergenthaler's Linotype machine solved the problem.[82]

Each step in the sequence of technological changes produced drastic advances. With "such mechanical facilities as even the best office could command thirty years ago a great newspaper of the present style would have been . . . inconceivable," one observer noted in 1878.[83] Benjamin H. Day began with men cranking his Napier double-cylinder presses until he turned to steam power in 1835.[84] The old presses which printed one hand-fed sheet at a time clearly failed to meet the demands of the metropolitan press for volume and speed, and inventors began trying to develop a press that would perform rapidly, print both sides of a sheet, and feed the paper mechanically.

In pace with the heightened speed of big-city life, rotating cylinders replaced the slow flat-bed movement of the old presses. Hoe's "lightning press" enabled newspapers with circulations of 20,000 copies to satisfy the call for news within two hours after going to press. In the 1860's, when the Civil War intensified the cry for news, curved stereotyped plates fitted to the printing cylinders made it possible to duplicate a page quickly and to run it off on more than one press at the same time. By the beginning of the 1870's, the web perfecting press introduced "the most noteworthy development of the past two or three decades," in the judgment of the census expert on newspaper technology in 1900.[85]

The new press printed, or "perfected," both sides of a continuing roll, or "web," of paper in the same run and cut the paper into sheets; attached machinery saved time and labor by collating and folding the papers. By the end of the decade, the St. Louis *Republican* operated the largest web perfecting press made, "with a capacity of 30,000 perfect papers per hour, printed, cut, folded and pasted, ready for delivery."[86] The introduction of the triangular form folder in 1881, in combination with the web press and the curved stereotype plate, laid the foundation of the modern newspaper printing process.

The successful use of variations of the web perfecting press depended on other technological advances. The development of fast-flowing inks kept step with the progress of printing machinery. Supplying cheap, tough newsprint was a problem in the 1850's because paper was made chiefly from expensive rag fiber. Then mills that made paper out of wood pulp began to deliver newsprint at lower prices. After the Civil War, a variety of processes perfected the production of paper out of wood pulp and superseded entirely the use of rags for newsprint. Consumption grew steadily over the next thirty years, and the price of paper dropped from nine to three cents per pound.[87]

Despite the advances in the technology of printing during the nineteenth century, however, type composition followed a process that went back to the invention of printing. While better machinery, cheaper newsprint, and faster ink facilitated the expansion of the metropolitan newspaper into extras and supplements as well as morning, evening, and Sunday editions, a typesetter still had to handle separately every single letter used to print a story or an advertisement. He composed letters into a line, fitted the lines into columns, and when the type had been used, he took the lines apart and put the letters back into their cases. In order to get out large volumes of reading matter quickly, newspapers had to increase their staffs of compositors.

Although patents for typesetting machinery dated back in Great Britain to 1822 and in the United States to 1840, Ottmar Mergenthaler's Linotype machine passed its practical test only in 1886. Operated by a keyboard, it released type matrices from a magazine, assembled them into a line or "slug," automatically justified them to the right length, cast them in a solid slug of lead, and then returned the matrices to the magazine for re-use. It vastly, though rather belatedly, increased the speed of composition.[88]

In the 1880's pictures found their way into the metropolitan press, not only ending typographical boredom but also appealing to semi-literate readers who relied on them as short cuts to the essence of a report. Up to that time, inferior reproduction methods had produced fuzzy pictures, and woodcuts and steel engravings were expensive because they had to be produced by hand by real artists. "If illustration was cheap, it was poor," the rule of thumb went; "if good, it was expensive."[89] New incentives to improve the process appeared in the 1870's when advertisements began displaying such objects as typewriters or sewing machines. The New York *Daily Graphic*, the first picture newspaper, used zinc etchings, photo-engraved line illustrations, and, in 1880, the half-tone process, which made cuts suitable for printing photographs and other continuous-tone artwork.[90]

In the mid-1880's, Joseph Pulitzer and his *World* staff made illustrations a major tool in the art of news reporting by using drawings as part of a news story instead of merely as fillers or curiosities. The paper had to battle not only custom but also technology, because high-speed presses complicated the printing of pictures. The experiments of the staff artists produced news illustrations, portrait drawings, political cartoons, street scenes, picture stories, and comic strips.[91] As their crude woodcuts gave way to sharp etchings, their innovation decisively shaped the appearance, content, and appeal of the metropolitan press. In 1893, *Harper's Weekly* judged that the question of pictures in newspapers "has been settled in favor of their use now by every considerable morning paper in New York," because "good pictorial work justifies itself wherever it can be achieved."[92]

News flowed faster as the demand for it increased, and competing editors resorted to ingenious devices to outdo their competitors. They relied on carrier pigeons, pony express, horse relays, and special trains for domestic news and utilized press schooners and steamboats to collect information from abroad as quickly as possible. New concepts of reporting and new uses of technology reinforced each other in the search for ways to get the news out ahead of rival papers. A New York *Times* reporter assigned to cover a speech by Daniel Webster in Boston wrote his copy on the return boat and passed the text to compositors who carried letters and cases with them to set the type; when the steamer docked in New York City, the speech was ready to go to press.[93]

The introduction of the telegraph in the 1840's enriched the diet of the young news-hungry industry by speeding transmission. In the early years, reporters attempted to defeat rivals by beating them to the telegraph office nearest a news source and preventing them from using the operator. A reporter for the New York *Herald* who covered the visit of the Prince of Wales to Niagara Falls in 1860 had to wait while the official party was delayed, but his editor instructed him to keep his hold on the only nearby telegraph operator by sending parts of the Old Testament to New York until his story had materialized and could be transmitted. Such schemes gave a newspaper momentary control over a telegraph line, but to have its own line was beyond the resources of any single paper.[94]

Economic necessity and the democratic nature of the telegraph resulted in press associations. Groups of newspapers recognized the wisdom of gathering news collectively, as New York papers had done in the 1820's when they joined forces and shared news collected from European packet ships. Such activities eventually extended to marine news, expresses from Washington, and dispatches on the Mexican War. Boston and New York papers shared news from England.[95] These and similar cooperative ventures lasted a few years without producing a common dispatch for all members, but paved the way for the formation of the New York Associated Press in the spring of 1848. This cooperative of six leading newspapers arranged with a Boston telegraph agent to receive, in one transmission, the latest news from steamships just approaching Nova Scotia.[96]

The enormous market value of news and the general economic trend of the age toward monopoly shaped the association. By the mid-1850's, the members had increased to seven and controlled wires through bargains, promises, and threats, selling their bulletins to other newspapers. New members had to terminate all relations with other news services and share wired material from their correspondents with all members of the association. From time to time newspapers rebelled and rival organiations arose, but the association retained its hold on the news during the nineteenth century.[97] Its operation speeded spectacularly the flow of information and lessened political distinctions because economy restricted reporting to one message for each story. This process fostered among newspapers a uniformity that defied the heterogeneity of the modern city and led to the emergence of a national press molded by news services.

The news association, with the telegraph as its instrument, tended to equalize American newspapers. It placed country papers on a par with the metropolitan press as far as access to news was concerned. The telephone, which appeared in the 1870's, quickened the tempo of news gathering in the following decade by helping reporters get last-minute details to the desks of their editors. But the idea of the "talking" or "speaking" telephone overcame the concept of news as only a printed message, epitomized by the metropolitan press.[98] Within a generation the telephone usurped the role of the metropolitan press as the provider of news about the modern city. Ultimately, with the addition of radio and television, electronic communications instruments undermined all newspaper journalism. But it was the telephone that first severed the intimate ties between the metropolitan press and the residents of the modern city, ties which had brought these newspapers into existence and sustained them.

The ingenuity of a group of journalistic pioneers had cemented this relationship between the newspaper and the modern city since the 1830's. As editors and publishers they saw the possibilities for an expansion of the journalistic sphere. They also perceived the potential of the metropolitan press for making a fortune, promoting reform, and, without becoming party papers, influencing politics by shaping public opinion. Historically, the fate of newspaper editors had depended upon their ability to satisfy the interest of the commercial community or to link groups of politicians into an ef-

fective party, but this new breed of journalists aspired to make politics independent of party or to capture, perhaps for themselves,
the nomination of a party.

The changing temper of American society supported the pioneers' drive for journalistic independence. With the broadening of
political democracy in the 1820's and 1830's, the common man
came to constitute a public not only with political aspirations but
also with opinions on the important matters that formerly had been
discussed only by the few who traditionally spoke for all.[99] Men
and women showed an insatiable curiosity to know things themselves and to think for themselves. They questioned conventional
answers and began looking for guidance to adapt the lofty ideas of
orators and ministers to their views. Before mechanization perfected the dependence of people on an industrial technology providing leisure and entertainment that came to characterize the
twentieth century, the experimentation with inventions and the
search to apply them produced a turmoil that stimulated many
people to know more than they had known before.

Their dominant concerns involved ordinary matters that
frequently lay outside the lofty realm surveyed by the sages of society. Philosophical abstractions, theological discourses, and
learned treatises failed to satisfy the need for quick answers to
questions about business, practical politics, and social life, so people turned for enlightenment to the newspapers. They welcomed
the publishers' help in struggling against political machines and
rampant vice. Frequently, the editor took over the role of spokesman or conscience of the community formerly filled by ministers
or statesmen.

The test of a minister's or statesman's worth might vary, but an
ordinary yardstick measured an editor's efficacy: his newspaper's
circulation figures. An increase meant more readers, greater influence, and higher income. Many journalists used the metropolitan
press to pursue all three, though quite a number of them had their
eyes only on the money. None of them, however, spoke about his
journalistic success as directly as James Gordon Bennett, who gave

it a social dimension that reflected his shrewd perception of popular attitudes bred by the modern city. In an age of extraordinary journalists, Bennett brought to the task special experience, born of failure, and intense confidence in his ability. "I am no novice in the business," he said in introducing himself to his readers in his first issue of the *Herald*, "and I cannot make a mistake in public feeling."[100]

Within a few weeks Bennett tied his drive for a mass audience to his readers' search for identity. He convinced the public that he and his *Herald* had a common self, and that their identification with the paper amounted to sharing his own identity as their spokesman. His success and the paper's growth were the readers' success and, in a world worshiping success, writing bout it came as naturally to Bennett as reading about it to his audience. In the context of that relationship, the stories covered milestone after milestone in mutual accomplishment. Through them, this Scottish immigrant, who had come to the United States in his twenties and was thirty-nine years old before the first issue of the *Herald* appeared, captured the readers' imagination and loyalty. Bennett did not start a "vast and important revolution" in newspapers, nor was he "the Napoleon of the American press," as he liked to claim, but he was the Napoleon of his readers, "one poor man in a cellar against the world" whose rise to wealth they shared vicariously.[101]

Bennett's rise to riches and that of other editors also enriched their readers' identity; but quite a number of journalists just got rich without any concern for their audiences. Wilbur F. Storey, who controlled the Chicago *Times* from 1861 to 1878, showed nothing but contempt for his readers. He printed everything that suited his personal interests, excusing his recklessness with the maxim that he considered it "a newspaper's duty to print the news, and raise Hell."[102] In his belief that people would buy what they found interesting, he pioneered a form of news coverage and typography that kept him one step ahead of his Midwestern rivals for almost a quarter of a century. Bigoted and bold, he secretly trained forty women typographers rather than accept the wage demands of a union in 1864; he also pioneered Sunday journalism with feature stories, leading to the appearance of the Chicago *Sunday Times* in 1866.

During that decade, Storey's mind cracked, depriving him of the limited sense of proportions he once might have had. Eight-column streamers and suggestive pictures were not yet part of American journalism because their technology had not yet been developed, but Storey pushed the potential of the metropolitan press for pernicious scandal-mongering and excessive detail to the breaking point. In 1875, tired of reports describing a murderer's last-minute repentance as the noose tightened, Storey made his headline scream: "JERKED TO JESUS."[103] His crudity and obscenity enriched no one but Storey himself, yet his brand of metropolitan press spoke to the loafers and toughs who liked their news raw, satisfied laborers and clerks who sought reprieve from the doldrums, and appealed to urbanites itching to flout convention.[104]

Despite the Storeys of the metropolitan press who saw newspaper journalism only as a way to riches, many editors and publishers strove to live up to its potential as a guide to a better society. In a setting where thousands searched daily for assistance in coping with the intensified problems of city life, editors found themselves in a unique position. In their editorials, they had an instrument for speaking directly to the burning issues of the day, compressing, so to speak, a minister's weekly sermon into daily print that addressed a specific subject in everyday language. They also discovered that they had in their news reports a much more subtle instrument for influencing their readers, one which recognized the shift of interest from sermons to news that people interpreted themselves.

Most editors responded resourcefully to the call for straight news. Their reports gave an illusion of neutrality that had more appeal than editorials which, although stripped of the theology of a sermon, still presented a distinct viewpoint. The novelty of objective news impressed readers, noted a journalist reviewing the development of the press at the beginning of the twentieth century.

In the face of the demand for straight news reports, he concluded, "the editorial never regained its old supremacy in American journalism," despite writers like Horace Greeley and E. L. Godkin in the East, Joseph Medill and Joseph B. McCullagh in the Midwest, and Henry Watterson and James C. Hemphill in the South, who had "great personal influence through their writings."[105] H. L. Mencken, recalling his start in journalism on the eve of the twentieth century, stated the case for news reporting equally bluntly: "If anyone in the city-room had ever spoken of an editorial in his own paper as cogent and illuminating he would have been set down as a jackass for admiring it and as a kind of traitor to honest journalism for reading it at all."[106]

Regardless of the overall trend, in exceptional cases the metropolitan press did produce a following for great editorial writers, particularly when their messages coincided with popular notions about the urban dilemma. Readers respected the editor Horace Greeley because he lighted tirelessly the path of progress, using a modern low-priced daily, the New York *Tribune*, as his pulpit. He had put out the initial 5,000 copies of his little paper, whose four pages contained less news and advertising than did a single sheet of the 1880's *Tribune*, in 1841, and "nearly succeeded in giving away all of them that would not sell."[107]

Undaunted, Greeley labored for three decades to make his newspaper "as sensitive to oppression" in "the next street" as in "Brazil or Japan."[108] Driven by his conviction and his ambition to help others, he ventured into the world of politics. Lacking the conciliatory manner that the modern city had begun to foster in others, he refused to compromise or to recognize another's virtues, while his outlandish dress and self-righteous idealism made him a target for ridicule. But while his excursions ended in frustrations and failure, his *Tribune* remained a forum of intellectual discussion and moral challenge unrivaled by any other metropolitan newspaper, with practical advice on urban life thrown in for good measure.

He who is "fit to come to a city," Greeley admonished the eager

young man, ought to understand "that he must begin at the foot of
the class, and work his way up." Such a newcomer "sees the advertisements of 'Wants' in the leading journals at an early hour each
morning, notes those which hold out some prospect for him, and
accepts the first place offered him which he can take honorably and
fill acceptably." Improving the quality of life was a constant goal.
In order to make job hunting easier, Greeley advocated on another
occasion "the creation of a spacious edifice at some central point in
our city to form a Laborers' Exchange, just as Commerce now has
its Exchange," where "any one wanting work may inscribe his
name, residence, capacities and terms, while anyone wishing to
hire may do likewise, as well as meet personally those seeking
employment."

Compassion for the poor of the large city filled other Greeley
editorials. Appalled by the "wretched, tumble-down rookeries now
largely inhabited by the poor," he urged a building reform leading
to decent "tenement houses" that would lodge "our whole laboring
population" far better "than they now are, at half the expense,
while room would be made on our Island for thrice the population
it can stow away under the present architectural anarchy." Again
and again one of his favorite themes emerged: "Dream not of getting suddenly rich" in the big city, because all avenues of advance
"are choked up by eager, struggling aspirants, and ten must be
trodden down in the press where one can vault upon his neighbor's shoulders to honor or wealth."[109]

Greeley's belief in his wisdom to discern the right, which allowed him to color news to suit his viewpoint, was challenged by
many residents of the modern city who considered themselves the
best interpreters of news. They preferred the ingenious leadership
of an editor like Joseph Pulitzer, who relied on news management
as well as on editorials to sway his readers. Although Pulitzer
upheld a concept of pure news reporting that stressed facts and accuracy, he emphasized subjects that supported the messages he intended to convey, walking the thin line that separated reform-
mindedness from radicalism. On the assumption that injustice

perished in the glare of publicity, he printed drastic and colorful news stories concentrating on miserable housing, impure milk, woman and child labor, strikes and lockouts, or fraudulent tax assessments, which implied that the *World* was on the side of its masses of readers. However, this impression did not alienate other groups, who often used the same material to prove the troublesome nature of the discontented poor.[110]

One of his chief editorial writers later dismissed Pulitzer's editorial policy in a rather abrupt fashion, arguing that "nobody wants to know what you think." People "want to know what they think," explained Arthur Brisbane, who ultimately employed his insight in the service of William Randolph Hearst.[111] Long after Pulitzer's death, one of the staff artists of the *World*, whose cartoons had castigated the greed of millionaires during Pulitzer's campaign to collect funds for a pedestal for the Statue of Liberty in 1885, suspected that the Pulitzer policy towards poverty and injustice was "nothing more than political or business expediencey" on the part of a "highly commercial gentleman who knew exactly . . . what sort of literature would most cheaply extract pennies from the lower classes."[112]

Pulitzer's respect for facts kept his *World* from becoming entirely an instrument of his ego that provided readers with newsy entertainment simply to satisfy its publisher's craze for power—as was the case with William Randolph Hearst, whose drive for self-aggrandizement did much to destroy the restraints most of the metropolitan press had observed for decades. In 1897 and 1898, he unleashed in his New York *Journal* the press campaign for United States intervention in Cuban affairs that culminated in the Spanish-American War. His manipulation of lies gave rise to the Yellow Press, marking the decline of the metropolitan press as an era in American journalism.[113] Yellow journalism reduced newspapers to a tool of power politics in the hands of news barons without concern for news reporting as an instrument of communication forged by the interaction of journalism, the modern city, and its residents.

News reporting in the metropolitan press was best done by journalists in direct contact with events and people. Reporters and cartoonists collected the news that editors presented and interpreted. Cartoonists depended on startling improvements in reproductive techniques and on audiences becoming receptive to images as well as printed words. Irrespective of the growing importance of pictures, the metropolitan press, by journalistic convention and because of the fact that gossip was word-oriented, relied for its essential success on reporters detecting news.

The call for news that brought the metropolitan press into existence in the 1830's also produced the reporter. As general assistant to the editor and publisher, he quickly became the newspaper's major provider of information. When the editor-publisher withdrew from the day-by-day running of the paper to supervise its management, the reporter came to occupy the limelight. He perpetuated the general public's identification of the newspaper with a person, assuming the role the printer had played in the seventeenth and eighteenth centuries. While his reportorial forerunners had specialized in parliamentary or marine reporting, the proliferation of activities in the modern city expanded the reporter's activities into most areas of life. His impudence and inquisitiveness became proverbial, and he discarded quickly most restraints that once had shielded topics from becoming the subjects of news reports. His constant exposure to disasters, conflicts, fires, floods, murders, riots, and wars perfected his ability to present news quickly to the reader.

A hierarchy of reporters emerged. Men who recorded the doings of police stations, courts, and city halls sought to surpass reporters who covered ballrooms, theaters, and sports arenas, and others assigned to the stockyard, the stock exchange, and the financial district. Assiduously they tried to get an exclusive "scoop" on a story or to secure a "beat" by publishing a report earlier than their competitors. Some followed armies and roamed battlefields as war correspondents; others were assigned, or stationed themselves, as correspondents at capitals, at home and abroad. All were out to get the news first and to report it in the most intriguing form to their editors and readers.

Women made their way into the metropolitan press as big-city reporters two decades before Elizabeth Cochrane established her reputation as "America's best reporter" in the late 1880's. Cochrane, as "Nellie Bly," exposed the chicanery of an insane asylum and raced Jules Verne's hero around the world. She and her colleagues followed the lead of Ann A. Stephens and Margaret Fuller who, in the 1830's and 1840's, wrote for large dailies about literature and social issues. The growing popularity of many female correspondents and columnists, among them "Jenny June," "Fanny Fern," and "Grace Greenwood," eased the movement of women into the ranks of distinguished news reporters. In 1889, *The Journalist* acknowledged their contributions in its first "woman's number," in the hope of becoming a paper not only for "all newspapermen but also for all newspaper-makers." [114]

Fascinated by the opportunity, women "plunged gaily into planning for a career in journalism," as Ida Tarbell recalled about her own venture. [115] As news-gatherers, they themselves were news, celebrated by the most modern artistic expressions of the day. A "picture play" of 1895, "a triangular partnership between the art of fiction, the art of the tableau vivant and the science of photography," imagined the heroine as a reporter interviewing Chauncey M. Depew, picturing both in the authentic New York Central office of the railroad magnate. [116] General recognition strengthened the credibility and influence of female journalists. It produced by-lines, the ultimate indicators of a reporter's success, and, in the first decade of the twentieth century, started William Randolph Hearst's "sob sisters" on their specialty—reporting murder to boost circulation. [117]

Although their styles varied, many reporters, at one time or another and in one form or another, made use of a reportorial device developed and perfected by the pioneers among them. The interview, quickly incorporated into the new journalism, touched one of the basic impulses on which the metropolitan press was based—people's urge to gossip. Since the interview was also a major technique for obtaining information, its actual dialogue had often vanished by the time the published story appeared on crowded pages. But when presented in its pure form, it gave readers the illusion that they were part of a conversation, directing through a reporter questions at someone they hoped to talk to at least once, but probably never would.

James Gordon Bennett, who first published an interview in dialogue form in the metropolitan press, retained both questions and answers specifically to give *Herald* readers the feeling that they were actually present. After all, he was there as their reporter, "on public duty," as one police officer explained to an irritated crowd when he admitted only Bennett to the scene of a crime.[118] The treatment of verbatim court testimony, again in question-and-answer form and modeled after both John Wight's amusing London Bow Street police reports of the 1820's and the metropolitan press' own human interest stories from "real life," further widened the appeal of the interview as a technique of bringing readers to the scene of the action.[119] "It is the duty of a great newspaper to furnish the fullest possible account of the great events of the day," as a reporter covering one of the spectacular parades of the 1890's eloquently put it, "so that those who cannot read, can see it; those who cannot see, can hear it, and those who can read and see can doubly enjoy it, and everybody be made happy."[120]

Newspapermen relied primarily on printed words to re-create events until the mid-1880's. In 1884, Walt McDougal's first cartoon in the *World*, "The Royal Feast of Belshazzar Blaine and the Money Kings," put thirty thousand uninvited guests at the sumptuous table of the Republican presidential candidate and his millionaire friends, in a caricature of James Blaine's ill-advised New York dinner with some of the richest Americans. Spread across the entire top of the front page, the cartoon added images to words as food for the readers' thoughts and stirred demands for more drawings in the newspaper. "Such events as the opening of the Brooklyn Bridge," McDougal recalled, "Grant's funeral, . . . the electrocution of Gibbs, . . . the first tryout by Edison of his gramophone, . . . all had to be sketched, because . . . all photographs had to be converted into . . . line drawings before being engraved."[121] The other papers quickly imitated the *World* and speeded the incorporation of the drawing into the metropolitan press to illustrate news reports and human interest stories and in the form of the comic strip.

Comic strips further curtailed the role of the printed word in newspapers. This long development had begun with the reduction of gossip to succinctly written reports or human interest stories with a specific point. The next stage shortened an article to the concentrated language of a headline that offered a report's significance at a glance. Then advertisements reduced a commercial message to the bold promises of sales slogans or the pleasant surprise of entertaining jingles. In the final stage of the process, words almost seemed superfluous and at times were superfluous, as audiences became increasingly wearied by logically arranged words as a vehicle of opinion.

Although the physical size of newspapers grew over the years, as news, feature stories, and advertisements steadily increased the number of pages, the significance of the printed word diminished as the foundation for a coherent argument, an enlightened speculation, or a logical exposition of facts. People who did not speak English found it more convenient to respond to pictures. The precise meanings of words gave way to mental associations with images that placed no priority on the literacy of one particular culture. In its final stages, the metropolitan press reflected the changing patterns of thinking in the modern city. New ways of receiving messages linked people less to printed words, which because they were specific to one culture could create ambivalence and stimulate divisions, and more to messages conveyed by images. Pictures spoke indiscriminately to heterogeneous groups of residents through their elementary appeal and linked people to each other as democratically as did their common pursuit of money.

Its importance as a social force, its role as a political tool, and its

success as a business venture often obscured the cultural importance of the metropolitan press in the lives of city people. By identifying and explaining the role of diversity as the way of life in the
American modern city, the metropolitan press helped to make
diversity comprehensible and acceptable. Its news and stories covered, in flagrant violation of former newspaper practices and social
convention, everything that happened in the modern city. The
mass audiences craved this new journalistic fare. Their experience
of living with capricious chance and constant change conditioned
them to embrace the assumption that anything could happen in
their lives. That attitude made the newspaper reports plausible,
justified them, and gave them significance as object lessons on how
to cope with the vicissitudes of modern life.

Human interest stories related the complexities of urban actions
from the perspective of village life. Their intimate scale made it
possible to identify people "lost" in the shuffle of daily life or
bypassed in the pursuit of riches, their misery ignored by neighbors as well as officialdom. "Who Kate Sweeny was or where she
came from it is almost impossible to tell," the New York World
explained about a young woman who suffocated in her sleep when
the sewer overflowed her basement room in a tenement.[122] But
the report gave Kate Sweeny in death a bond with her fellow citizens that life had begrudged her. The readers in the slums could
not help but recognize her as a neighbor because they saw the circumstances of her death closely tied to the conditions of their own
lives. That day, glancing at the World, thousands of strangers recognized that they had lost someone they knew.

Such stories identifying "lost" people fostered the recognition of
divergent life-styles as a distinct element of the modern city.
These reports presaged the short stories of O. Henry collected in
The Four Million and The Voice of the City (some having first appeared in the World)—stories that deftly expanded the concept of
the elite "Four Hundred" as the only people worth noticing. Theodore Dreiser's exposure as a reporter to the sufferings of rootless
people haunted him, as shown in "The Rivers of the Nameless

Dead," the concluding story of his stark pictures of New York life in *The Color of a Great City*.

The portrayal of life's complexities in ways that stimulated their acceptance was assured by the attention the metropolitan press gave to myriads of events that happened hourly and demanded to be registered daily. The news value of the unknown overcame ignorance perpetuated by convention and encouraged tolerance born of knowledge. Frequently, explanations of various customs informed readers of the rationale behind other approaches to the task they all shared, handling city life. News stories furnished the pieces for an Aristotelian mosaic of modern city life, composed of an infinite variety of paths to the good life taken by seemingly infinite numbers of individuals according to their inclinations or wealth.

The experience of living day in and day out alongside the lifestyles of other people eroded preconceptions and ultimately left its mark on people in the form of a growing cosmopolitanism. This was sometimes happily demonstrated as a willingness to masquerade at a party as someone else, one of the strangers from the next block. Urbanites may have done so even more enthusiastically when newspapers specifically recorded the extraordinary nature of their borrowed identity. In February 1874, the report of the annual Bal Masqué of a San Francisco social club concentrated on these seemingly incongruous combinations of names and disguises: Fannie Levy as a Spanish girl, Amelia Rothschild as Pocahontas, Esther Goldstein as a Scottish lass, Sarah Henry as l'Africaine, Annie Abrahams as a Polish princess, G. P. Kaspel as an old Yankee, Louis Tobias as a Negro, and Richard and Otto Alexander as Siamese Twins.[123]

Recognizing the multitude of life-styles composing the modern city, the metropolitan press identified the democratic base of the urban world. It held out a measure of political and social freedom that appealed to migrants running away from the restraints of the countryside as well as immigrants escaping from the bondage of their homelands. Messages about behavior implied in news reports

and spelled out in editorials guided masses of people to an urban
identity. Underlining the democratic foundation of society they
guided immigrants to an American identity. Human interest
stories related how some immigrants had succeeded and explained
why others had failed. Such stories seemed neither to sermonize
nor to lecture, but just to give facts, as newspaper readers understood them, thus presenting lessons of attitude and behavior that
demonstrated the American promise of success and failure.

The promise of an American identity held out to a mass audience made the metropolitan press itself a distinctly American phenomenon. In the second half of the nineteenth century, newspapers in Great Britain, France, and Central Europe shared some of
the characteristics of the metropolitan press or, like the weekly
London *Penny Magazine*, even antedated the first successful
American penny paper. However, these European newspapers differed in one decisive way from the American metropolitan press:
they emphasized primarily news and editorials and slighted the
human interest story.

The difference between the American metropolitan press and
European newspapers mirrored the distinction between American
and European cities. The character of European newspapers can
be accounted for by the relative homogeneity of the residents
there. The city masses of Europe shared a distinct social status as
urban proletariat and consequently possessed a class-consciousness
and identity that their American counterparts lacked. The more
limited amount of democracy in European societies led these
masses to struggle for political freedom and to look to their newspapers for news and comments guiding their attempts to increase
political democracy and their own personal freedom. Addressing
the urban proletariat directly, the European newspapers speaking
to the crowds in big cities were instruments of ideology and constituted a political press.[124]

While the political ideology of some central European newspapers at times pointed toward totalitarianism, the American metropolitan press reinforced the basic democratic tenets of American

society by recognizing differences among people. By identifying and describing the human reality of each resident, it protected the complex freedom and tenuous individuality of urban life that had previously been endangered by the routine and anonymity of the modern city. By extolling common features of behavior, based on new customs and ideas about life, the metropolitan press contributed to the Americanization of immigrants as well as the modernization of Americans. Fostering respect for differences among people as the essence of life in the modern city also paved the way for the emergence of more uniform behavior.

Another contribution to uniformity by the metropolitan press was its fostering of a distinct urban mentality. It facilitated communication among strangers in large cities through the development of markedly urban patterns of thinking and speaking. Reports and advertisements began to change conventional modes of thought and speech. "Swindled Clergy, Widow Confesses," a headline stated bluntly under the eight-column streamer that announced the signing of the Treaty of Paris and the end of the first World War in the New York *Times*.[125] Headlines, slogans, and cartoons presaged the trend toward reducing communication to a brief message.

In its symbiotic relationship with the American modern city, the metropolitan press recognized people as individuals, apart from their existence as part of the masses. Beyond that, it identified them as persons who formed special groups. In beginning to address women directly, large newspapers singled out a potentially powerful segment of the urban population. Through their control of the family purse and as downtown shoppers, women stimulated the coming of a new form of retailing and became the vital concern of the emerging department store.

# IV
# DEPARTMENT STORE

"Hanging on the skirts, very literally, of indecision," a small boy wearily trailed his aunt through the splendor of the "ladies' great shop" in New York City in the early 1850's. Five stories high, A. T. Stewart's magnificent Marble Palace "bravely waylaid custom" on the Chambers Street corner of Broadway. It regularly interrupted aunt and nephew on their way home from a dentist's office on Wall Street, confronting them with displays of fashionable life familiar to the boy from reading *Godey's Lady's Book*, the first American women's magazine, while waiting his turn in the dentist's chair. Shopping gave his aunt "the familiar Stewart headache from the prolonged strain of selection" and exposed him to "the enjoyment of our city as down-towny as possible," Henry James recalled in his old age.[1] Their experience reflected some of the impact of a new urban institution, the department store, on the residents of the modern city.[2]

The modern city, providing the economic incentive and the physical setting for new enterprise, produced the department store. The city stimulated the expansion of the retail market, improved communications systems, and generated a new building technology. Swept along by the tide of progress, residents steadily expanded the range of their consumption beyond food and material for clothing; the ambience of the large city encouraged many people of modest affluence to aspire to an air of solid comfort, if not luxury. Changing life-styles engendered a new pattern of urban life. Making money absorbed men, while women sought to realize their growing expectations through the purchase of household furnishings, ready-made clothes, children's toys, and other fashionable goods. These new desires took all sorts of women into the heart of the city, hastening the emergence of a new kind of store, one that displayed conveniently a large variety of goods under one roof and served shoppers obligingly.

The department store was the focal point for a novel form of downtown life. Its imposing appearance lent dignity to other, smaller shops that had gained a foothold among wholesale establishments and warehouses, hotels and churches, banks and offices. Its alluring presentation of merchandise attracted legions of women. Horsecars, trolleys, and cable cars facilitated the invasion of what had been—with the exception of a trip to church on Sundays, an occasional visit to a dentist, or a carriage ride to the theater—predominantly the austere world of draymen, clerks, merchants, lawyers, and bankers.

The palace of merchandise towered over the parade of pedestrians and the lines of streetcars that discharged women on the sidewalks skirting it. Coachmen and cab drivers quickly recognized that the curb in front of the main entrance had a special significance for their passengers. It was the starting point for a successful shopping spree and the best place to pick up returning customers carrying bags and bundles. These activities projected some of the order and safety of the store interior onto the sidewalk, reassuring those women who felt ill at ease in the hustle of porters and messengers or under the stare of loafers and workmen. The extravagant size of the plate-glass display windows also bestowed an aura of security and splendor upon the downtown streets, making the clean, smooth sidewalks into a woman's world—even though the glass might be "easily shivered by a boy's marble or a snowball," as Philip Hone feared when he first saw Stewart's Marble Palace in 1846.[3]

"There is nothing in Paris or London to compare with this dry goods palace," the former mayor of New York noted with satisfaction in discussing the significance of the first department store in his city.[4] However, he was wrong. Similar stores did exist elsewhere. General economic and social trends produced analogous institutions of retailing in most industrially advanced countries by the middle of the nineteenth century. Internal policies and external operations were roughly the same wherever such stores emerged as a big-city feature, though some variations from country to country, reflecting the weight of custom and tradition, added distinctive touches to the emergence of the new mode of retailing between the 1840's and the 1890's.

In each case both the rate and nature of economic growth and the conditions and expectations of urban life influenced the transformation of dry-goods stores selling fabrics into stores offering ready-to-wear clothes and a large variety of other goods conveniently arranged in various departments. The visions of entrepreneurs and the aspirations of women were also factors: needs barely recognized one day were fulfilled the next by novel services that department stores were well suited to provide for awakened consumers. This interplay between buyer and seller accounted for both the similarities and the variations in the development of the full-fledged department store.

The lack of agreement on the definition of a true department store limits any search for the so-called first department store, as it does, for instance, the identification of the first skyscraper.[5] However, the conflicting ideas of historians reflect subtle differences in the social conditions that gave rise to the variations among the emerging stores in France and England, and illuminate the unique features of the department store in the United States. Although in 1827 the German architect Karl Friedrich Schinkel, in his search for utility and beauty in domestic architecture, sketched a department store that achieved "the highest degree of both novelty and quality" in design, it was not until the end of the century that Berlin had enterprises that as buildings, businesses, and social institutions measured up to department stores in other countries.[6]

In France the phenomenal growth of industry in the 1840's and

1850's stimulated changes in retailing that led to the appearance of the *magasin de nouveautés*, as Parisians called dry goods.[7] This new kind of store carried textiles, hosiery, and gloves, which established storekeepers had considered and sold as exclusive lines of their specialty shops. Other features of these new emporiums were equally startling. Organized into departments, they brought order to the jumble of the general store, relied on marked and fixed prices, allowed customers to look around freely, and reimbursed them or exchanged their purchases if they were not satisfied. Their proprietors learned to buy in bulk from manufacturers on discount and to rely on high turnover, special sales, and constant advertising to compensate for their low prices. Their business flourished. In 1844, the largest of the *magasins de nouveautés*, the Ville de Paris, had 150 employees and a volume of annual sales of about eleven million francs.

Economic and social changes guided the expansion of the *magasins de nouveautés* into department stores. Textile manufacturers entered large-scale production and demanded dependable retail outlets. A national railroad network linking textile mills to city stores strengthened the big business of production and distribution and provided an organizational model for devising and operating large enterprises. In addition, simplified manufacturing processes and semi-skilled workers debased the crafts of traditional tailors and shoemakers with ready-to-wear that came to be bought increasingly in place of hand-tailored clothing, second-hand clothes, and handmade shoes. Although ready-to-wear touched only the fringes of women's fashion, its appeal, assured by low prices and immediate satisfaction of the desire for a new possession, hastened the flowering of new retail stores based on rapid turnover of merchandise. In turn, the increasing sales encouraged more production, and the concentration of the expanding consumer market in large cities led to new sales techniques that appealed to growing numbers of urban residents.

The surface prosperity of the Second Empire also contributed to the rise of the department store. Its social whirl provoked a clamor

for luxury goods, but social reform was also fashionable, giving cur-
rency to the idea of providing underprivileged groups with access
to some features of the comfortable life. Additionally, any concern
for a measure of social justice made sound economic sense because
it increased consumption. Although the demand for consumer
goods taxed the resources of retail merchants, enterprising bankers
extended credit to expand businesses, and ingenious storeowners
went to work with low prices and special sales to assure a rapid
turnover of their stock and to attract new customers *en masse*.

The general migration to the cities contributed heavily to the
success of department stores. In the case of Paris, which had been
transformed into the dazzling showcase of Europe by Louis Napoleon and George Haussmann, the population doubled during the
first half of the nineteenth century to more than a million inhabitants. During the following decades it increased by another
600,000. As a by-product of the renovation of the cityscape, newly
opened tree-lined boulevards facilitated cross-city traffic, providing
splendid opportunities for leisurely promenades that encouraged
window-shopping. By 1860, public transit moved about 70 million
passengers annually.[8] Railroad trains brought customers from the
countryside into the city and took back to the provinces goods ordered by mail from the catalogues of large stores.

In a typical process, this movement of people would inspire the
proprietor of a successful *magasin de nouveautés* to buy a valuable
commercial site at a strategic crossroad, acquired fortuitously when
the property became available as a result of city planning on an imperial scale. He then experimented with new marketing techniques based on steady advertising and constantly changing displays. The success of this merchandising concept would ultimately
lead the merchant to acquire an entire building for the operation of
his store, in contrast to traditional shops that were restricted to
one dark, ground-floor unit of a residential building. The extension
of a store into adjacent buildings or the move into a magnificent
new structure transformed the *magasin de nouveautés* into the
*grand magasin,* the department store.

While most *magasins de nouveautés* failed to make that transition, the success of the Bon Marché in Paris reflected the organizational talent and the imaginative leadership of Aristide Boucicaut. It underlined his genius for combining daring and caution in the pursuit of innovations. He had learned retailing in a *magasin de nouveautés* in the 1830's. After becoming department head, he managed in 1852 to acquire 50,000 francs, which enabled him to become joint owner of the Bon Marché, another *magasin de nouveautés*, with twelve clerks in four departments and an annual sales volume of about 450,000 francs.

Eleven years later, Boucicaut bought out his partner with the help of one of his countrymen who had made a fortune as a confectioner in New York City. In 1869 he laid the cornerstone for what came to be regarded as the first French department store. When he died in 1877, Boucicaut had created what Émile Zola in the early 1880's called "la poème de l'activité moderne."[9] Zola had researched the Bon Marché for the setting of *Au bonheur des dames (Ladies' Delight)*, his novel about Parisian society staged against the background of a rising department store.

Boucicaut had built a store that surpassed the *magasins de nouveautés* of the 1850's and 1860's. In the fourteen years he controlled it, the sales volume rose more than tenfold to 73 million francs annually and the number of employees to 1,788. However, if diversification of merchandise was a mark of the true department store, then the Bon Marché experienced a rather limited development during his reign. Boucicaut expanded his stock cautiously, because he had risen with *nouveautés* when he first entered retailing and always considered them his special merchandise, separate from household items, toys, tables, chairs, upholstery, stationery, and books. In his *grand magasin de nouveautés* he consequently encouraged an ever-greater variety of dry goods by dividing rapidly growing departments into new units. Furthermore the Bon Marché emphasized respectability and shunned a mass clientele, the corollary to the "democratization of luxury" for which department stores began taking credit in the 1880's. The Bon Marché remained basically a store for affluent women until the 1890's.

The *grand magasin* that Boucicaut established evolved into a full-fledged department store only in the 1880's, after his death. However, Boucicaut created the modern department store as a specific building type on the European continent when he commissioned a new structure for his Bon Marché in 1867.[10] His vision of it was enriched by the fusion of architecture and engineering that grew in the artistic soil of Paris, creating what Zola called "la cathédrale du commerce moderne."[11] When finally completed around 1880, its facades, elaborate as well as monumental, radiated the luxury and solidity that befitted a store selling distinction and respectability. Its corner rotunda drew people in toward the magic of the large windows grouped between the entrance portals leading into lavishly decorated grand halls that trumpeted the greatness of the store through the dramatic use of space.

A flood of daylight illuminated the interior, adding dimensions to Zola's felicitous metaphor. Through the sacrifice of the central floor space in the upper stories, light fell from glass domes into the central court, past two tiers of iron galleries and their *passerelles*— small iron bridges that allowed customers on the upper galleries to cross the great hall directly. In the center of the building, the graceful grills and spectacular double revolution of a majestic iron stairway radiated modern elegance. The extravagant steps enticed women, long accustomed to climbing the stairs of tall apartment houses, to the upper floors.[12] The whole structure inspired the passerby to gaze, to shop, or to buy as the three ways to share its splendor. To use a contemporary phrase that linked the department store to a museum or a world's fair, this "musée de marchandise" transcribed into modern idiom the *richesse, goût de la couleur, luxe*, and *volupté* of Parisian life. It was this same quality that contemporaries admired in Charles Garnier's new Opéra.[13] This accomplishment set the Bon Marché as much apart from its counterparts in London as did the special development of retailing in England.

Although England set the pace for commercial and industrial growth at the middle of the nineteenth century, no rising mercantile palace accompanied the beginnings of the department store in

London. There, the modern age had found its symbol in the Crystal Palace of the Great Exhibition of 1851, which displayed the raw materials and the manufactured goods of the world. Like a gigantic emporium, the enormous hall with its countless exhibits bespoke organizational drive and ability. The sense of purpose and dedication to order caught the attention of about 400,000 sightseers daily, women and children, laborers and clerks. The visitors admired in particular the section of manufactured items, such as cottons, woolens, silks, velvets, leather goods, clothing and finery, furniture, mirrors, and decorations. This merchandise not only demonstrated the productive capacity of the most industrially advanced nation in the world, but also held out the promise of a better life.

Several kinds of stores made some of these riches accessible to the average person. Although they had few departments in the strict sense, their arrangement pointed toward a clear division of merchandise as the way to cope with the growing complexities of retailing. "Heavy" and "fancy" goods were the basic categories of wares in a draper's shop (dry goods store). Fabric with woven or printed designs made up the bulk of the business because women bought it for sewing their own dresses or to supply to their dressmakers. Gloves, hosiery, ribbons, lace, and handkerchiefs constituted "fancy" goods. Finally, there was a section of small wares—mostly threads, buttons, and needles—and a section of ready-to-wear, primarily long, drab woolen cloaks for women.

Great bazaars came closest to creating the atmosphere of a department store. They occupied large halls, with or without a gallery, where small traders rented a counter or a stall. In addition to dry goods, they carried an enormous variety of merchandise—jewelry, cutlery, children's dresses, toys, sheet music, and ornaments—as well as refreshments. Exploring the pretentious Pantheon Bazaar, George Augustus Sala, one of the most fashionable recorders of London life during the 1850's, found himself in a "labyrinth of avenues between triple-laden stalls, all crowded with ladies and children." Some of the traders operated shops in long colonnades or covered arcades, where they sold everything, Sala felt, that he could do well without.[14] However, all these forms of retailing—dry goods stores, bazaars, colonnades, and arcades—still lacked the efficient organization or the diversified merchandise of a department store.

William Whiteley's single-minded pursuit of the great emporium of goods conjured up by the Crystal Palace contributed to English retailing.[15] He had learned his trade in a country drapery store and developed an expertise in imported ribbons after he came to London, but he lacked the means to break into the fashionable establishments in the center of the city. The physical expansion of London in the early 1860's provided him with an opportunity to launch the kind of business he envisioned, on Westbourne Grove in suburban Bayswater. He speculated that the metropolitan railway would bring customers to his door. When one of the termini of the London Underground Railway linked the West End with the City and connected with a nearby station of the Great Western Railway in January 1863, he felt able to challenge the assumption that a new, large store in a suburb would be doomed. Two months later, he started a shop with two female clerks and an errand boy.

His store flourished immediately because he allowed customers to browse freely and view his merchandise in attractive window displays or on well-arranged tables. His wares were reasonably priced and clearly marked, and he let them speak for him, shunning sensational sales or extravagant advertising. To lace, trimmings, ribbons, and other fancy goods he added silks, linens, mantles, dresses, jewelry, furs, umbrellas, and artificial flowers. All of these departments soon thrived, with dresses and silks leading in sales.

Diversification and expansion went hand in hand. Within a year, the number of his clerks rivaled the size of the staffs of the leading neighborhood stores. In 1867, Whiteley leased his second shop, near the first one, and embarked on a system of expansion made feasible because property changed hands frequently in the suburbs. In the course of the next few years he occupied an entire row

of shops, and ultimately he possessed several clusters of shops on
Westbourne Grove and adjacent streets that made up Whiteley's.
In 1876, he had fifteen shops and two thousand employees. At the
time of his death in 1907, he owned twenty-one shops, most of
them remodeled from old structures.

During the years in which the Bon Marché structure was being
built in Paris, William Whiteley also gave his shops the dimensions
of a department store. However, he concerned himself exclusively
with the extension of merchandise lines and service, rather than
with architectural considerations. Consistent with his ambition and
in response to the solicitations of his customers, his store became,
as its name indicated, the Universal Provider. Whiteley ingeniously buttressed his expanding dry goods departments with customer services. A real estate agency and a restaurant became parts
of his complex in 1872, and a cleaning and dyeing establishment
was included in 1874. During these years he also introduced stationery and foreign departments. Carpets, trunks, and china and
glass, as well as the sale and repair of furniture, followed in 1875.
Adding provisions to his line of merchandise represented the most
momentous step of that year, when the Universal Provider began
selling meat, poultry, eggs, vegetables, butter, cheese, biscuits,
and chocolates. In the next year, Whiteley's shops added a hardware department with house and building decorations as a special
feature.

In 1876, the amenities included, besides rest rooms a reading
room with reference books, a hairdresser's salon, a restaurant, a
telegraph bureau, a post office, and a funeral parlor. "Mr. Whiteley will take charge of you from the cradle to the grave," the London correspondent of the New York *Daily Graphic* quipped, "and
give you your meals as you go along—if you can pay for it."[16]
Before Whiteley's propaganda began compensating for the intense
dislike that local merchants and businessmen expressed for his emporium on Westbourne Grove, the Bayswater newspaper reported
that some of his activities produced "the most hideous eyesore that
an English visitor can look upon" and added emphatically: "We do

not want to Americanize the Grove."[17] And yet, it was Whiteley's
adherence to customary English ways that, in the 1870's and
1880's, kept him from creating what became a sign of modern
life—of Americanization, as some of his critics called it—a full-
fledged department store.

Steeped in the tradition of English retailing as commercial trans-
actions conducted in individual shops, Whiteley thought of himself
as London's shopkeeper. He regarded his emporium as "the first
great instance of a large general goods store in London, held under
one man's control," in the words of the 1911 edition of the *Encyclopaedia Britannica*.[18] He followed the operations of large
stores in Paris and New York, but his innovations in retailing did
not break with English usages, and when he tried to record his enterprise for posterity he chose ways fitting the conventions of English society. He attempted to commission W. P. Frith, one of the
favorite painters of his day, to do a canvas to be called *Whiteley's
at Four O'clock in the Afternoon* and only stipulated that "the
whole length of the shops should be shown, care being taken that
the different windows should display the specialities." But even in
this he seems to have stepped out of bounds because Frith, distinguished by royal patronage, politely declined the commission, although "greatly interested" in Whiteley, "that extraordinary
man."[19]

Whiteley, as a merchant prince, retained a shopkeeper's deference to nobility, hoping to see in his painting "aristocracy making
their purchases" and "nobility and gentry stepping into their carriages."[20] He catered to the ladies in a sequence of shops and
through an efficient delivery system that gave a sense of exclusiveness. In the summer of 1879, when the peripatetic George
Augustus Sala found his way to "Wonderful Whiteley," he noted
that the customers belonged "exclusively to the well-to-do
classes." The store's setting in "the centre of a new, prosperous
and refined district" and the general tone of English life also kept
Whiteley's from contributing to that Americanization of life that
the Bayswater *Chronicle* dreaded—the excessive mingling of all

classes of people determinedly pursuing the advantages of urban innovations.[21] This mentality was expressed by the novelist Anthony Trollope: "I wish we had nothing approaching" the department store, he commented, "for I confess to a liking for the old-fashioned private shops."[22] The Universal Provider obliged, remaining, in Sala's words, "Whiteley's Shops—a chain threatening to stretch to the crack of doom."[23]

The social dynamics of the modern city in the United States generated the momentum that brought the full-fledged department store into existence. This store not only sold great varieties of goods, constantly advertised in newspapers and conveniently displayed in an impressive building, but also served large numbers of women from all segments of society and made the presence of women a distinct attribute of the downtown section of the modern city. In contrast, throughout the second half of the nineteenth century, the absence of women in the center of London, Paris, Berlin, or Vienna struck American travelers in Europe. At the beginning of the twentieth century, an Italian visitor to Boston, "fighting his way along Washington Street" through "a solid immovable congestion of femininity," concluded that "the Public is here a common noun of the feminine gender," since the "whole world of women in the city, and from its suburbs, apparently, betakes itself to the shops every day."[24]

The department store made the new phenomenon of a feminine public possible. Its rise accompanied that of the modern city. In New York, which, with one million inhabitants, offered the largest department store market, in the 1860's and 1870's, the department stores that emerged during these two decades still accounted for almost half of the city's leading department stores a century later.[25] The department store thrived on the concentrated urban markets that clamored for goods and on the industrial sector of the American economy, which eagerly sought new outlets for its products. It brought about the decline of many small retail shops that could not keep up with the systematic marketing of goods on a large scale. Railroad lines and urban transit speeded the flow of merchandise as well as the movement of people from their homes to stores that sold inexpensive products. The advance in building technology provided practical as well as lofty structures that permitted spacious displays and attracted attention as expressions of that boundless energy generated by the modern city. Slowly the metropolitan press became the primary medium for the advertisements of the department store.

In 1846, an anonymous pamphlet directed attention to the new mode of doing business in New York. Its author considered the kind of organizational genius and executive ability which A. T. Stewart represented indicative of "the paramount tendency of the age . . . to systematize." A commercial house, with "several heads properly organized, may divide its labor into various departments of buying, selling, and management," the author explained, and "become perfect in its adaptedness." In his view, Stewart carried out "what must be apparent to every reflecting mind the proper plan of business—to render a Dry Goods store a grand magazine."[26] In the following year, *Hunt's Merchants' Magazine* expressed admiration for the departmental organization of a Philadelphia dry goods store which had perfected the new form of business organization.[27] The management of any firm along departmental lines created "a beautiful thoroughness" that "is becoming more and more part of our national character," *Putnam's Monthly* stated in 1853.[28]

The American national character, only vaguely defined in the first place and now being modified by the impact of large waves of immigrants, encouraged and accommodated new methods of selling and buying. "We are so busy in improving what the Past has bequeathed to us, that we forget we owe it anything," *Harper's* "Easy Chair" explained in 1854.[29] The expansion of merchandise beyond the conventional limits of a dry goods store was accepted readily by New Yorkers who, accustomed to thinking of their city as a great clothing emporium fed by ready-to-wear factories, put everything "used for covering the human body" into the category of dry goods.[30]

Although the sale of dry goods provided the start for most department stores, in some instances other products made up the core of the merchandise. A few major department stores developed from jewelry, crockery, and hardware shops, such as E. J. Lehmann's Fair in Chicago in 1875. At times a department store emerged because retailing on a big scale in a magnificent building seemed the most profitable way to use a downtown lot or a large structure. The Emporium in San Francisco grew out of a real estate speculation when first developed in 1896.[31]

The extension of the circle of customers to include women from all walks of life occurred as a matter of course. The practice of calling any woman who might buy something from a merchant a "lady" coincided with the rise of new businessmen in the modern city. In 1825, A. T. Stewart, fresh from Belfast, offered his goods "for sale to the Ladies of New York" in the *Daily Advertiser*.[32] With this extension of the term went the egalitarian assumptions that began to shape the relationships among customers in a store. "Testify no impatience if a servant-girl, making a six penny purchase, is served before you," Miss Leslie's *Behaviour Book* counseled in the 1850's. "In all American stores, the rule of 'first come, first served,' is rigidly observed."[33]

In the late 1840's and early 1850's, women "squeezing toward the counter of the last new emporium" represented a familiar sight in the changing downtown scene.[34] In his editorial accompanying the opening of Stewart's Marble Palace in 1846, *Herald* editor James Gordon Bennet stressed that "as long as the ladies continue to constitute an important feature of the community, the dry goods business must be in a flourishing condition."[35] The Panic of 1857 convinced other segments of the public that the woman shopper had definitely arrived because the recession, in the language of *Hunt's Merchants' Magazine*, "brought us the lady buyer."[36]

The financial crisis of 1857 drastically tightened the supply of money in the United States. The shortage drove shopkeepers to desperate measures in their attempts to raise enough cash to meet obligations. It sanctioned certain business practices that hitherto had been used only by reckless men to drum up business quickly. Cost sales, fire sales, shipwreck sales, distress sales, and panic sales succeeded each other, and the tumbling prices heightened the delight of shopping for women who used their time to look around extensively to find the best buy. At auctions, the stock of bankrupt tradesmen fell cheaply into the hands of more fortunate merchants who indiscriminately added the merchandise as new attractions to their repertories of goods. During the late 1850's, the "inevitable dry goods stores," which before the Panic had already been notorious in New York for crowding churches out of the downtown district, fostered a "rage for building superb business palaces" that filled "acres of brick with gorgeous marble and stone fronts and converted New York into a city of palaces." [37]

Among these calico palaces, occupied by such firms as Lord & Taylor—whose name is still a household word—A. T. Stewart's new uptown store stood out as the epitome of a true department store. Erected between 1859 and 1862, the breathtaking building covered the entire block between Broadway and Fourth Avenue, Ninth and Tenth streets, and was separated by Astor Place from the Cooper Union, another New York landmark exhibiting and distributing through shows and lectures the practical accomplishments of the age. Various designations, such as "Stewart's Tenth Street Store" or "Astor Place Store," referred to the store by its location. However, no name did justice to the significance of the building as did "Stewart's New Store," which distinguished it from the Marble Palace, now clearly "old" after sixteen years of renovations and additions. That name also suggested, albeit unintentionally, the novel achievement embodied in one enormous building devoted to the sale of a great variety of goods to a large clientele of women.

Many features of the building bespoke the special nature of the store. A. T. Stewart, "an enthusiastic advocate of cast-iron fronts for commercial structures," often used to compare the iron front dressed in white paint "to puffs of white clouds." The cast-iron facade, with plain columns and molded arches in the Venetian manner of the Italian Renaissance, rose five stories in height, "arch upon arch," eighty-five feet above the sidewalk.[38] The artistic economy of John Kellum, a New York architect with expertise in iron fronts, immediately touched the practical sense of the masses of people who daily thronged the store, "as they do an exposition," A. T. Stewart thought.[39] Kellum's plain design shunned the hideous filigree work and elaborate pattern of fluted columns that had discredited the first iron fronts when they appeared in the 1840's. Instead, he reduced the four enormous walls of the store facing the surrounding city to rows and rows of windows that brought "ample light" into every corner of the building.[40]

The merchant's conviction that "everybody will know it is A. T. Stewart's" kept the facade free from signs and advertisements and increased the distinction of the magnificent building.[41] The purity of the cast-iron design also added a definite American note to the city's eclectic architecture, one contemporary commentator stressed. He felt that such "a chaste and airy edifice of iron" formed a happy contrast to the pretentious marble palaces and bulky brick offices that crowded the densely built-up business quarter. An observer standing "on any of the four corners of Stewart's immense dry-goods store," he argued, could not mistake its "lightness and grace for anything but iron," and iron he considered "emphatically an *American* building material."[42]

Stewart's intimate knowledge of the urban scene inspired his choice of building styles. The "graceful dome" that rose ninety feet above the main hall of his old Marble Palace owed much to the splendid rotundas of two New York landmarks, City Hall and the Merchants Exchange. His use of a rotunda in department store construction in 1846 shaped commercial architecture for some time. Stewart himself may have been influenced by the wide publicity given fifteen years earlier to Frances Trollope's Graeco-Roman-Turkish Bazaar in Cincinnati, the only commercial building to use dome, rotunda, and stairway before the Marble Palace, as part of her concept of combining the dissemination of culture with the sale of merchandise.[43]

Formally sanctioned in the 1870's by Boucicaut's use of the dome in his Bon Marché, the rotunda's charm kept it a feature of department store architecture long after electricity and fire hazards had made it obsolete, as many buildings constructed in the 1880's and 1890's indicated. In 1896, the first San Francisco department store, the Emporium, opened with a central dome and kept the rotunda until 1957, through its reconstruction after the earthquake and fire of 1906. The most stunning example appeared in 1902, when Marshall Field & Co. in Chicago opened a new store, built by the firm of D. H. Burnham, with a gigantic Tiffany glass dome.[44]

Stewart shaped the development of the department store in various ways. In building the New Store, he boldly defied conventions and flew in the face of the praise his contemporaries had heaped on the Marble Palace, which added distinction to a generally drab cityscape. Calling it a "white marble cliff" when marble was considered a singular "ornament to the city," New Yorkers regarded it as a "model" giving character to the city's architecture.[45] Their enthusiastic approval launched the *palazzo* mode barely two years after the *North American Review* had proclaimed its greater virtue for American architecture over that of the Greek Revival.[46]

With the design of his New Store, Stewart turned against the tide his Marble Palace had helped to create. The choice of iron, the hallmark of industrialization, over marble in the midst of the Civil War gained approval as a result of the general preoccupation with military technology, from cannons to trains and from ironclads to bridges. But behind his daring also stood sound economic sense, because the iron structure permitted wide windows that opened to all floors the daylight that cumbrous walls faced with marble had kept out of Stewart's downtown store.[47]

Almost immediately Stewart's New Store fulfilled the promise its visual impression made. The efficient arrangement of the uniform interior highlighted the sense of purpose and expressed dedication to service. An enormous skylight admitted sunshine directly into the vast main floor. Its simple harmony of lines, formed by the individual panels of glass, did not obstruct the flow of light, correcting a shortcoming of the Marble Palace, where daylight had to struggle past the ornamentation of the rotunda and "the elegant lantern in the dome."[48] The carefully arranged space, with counters and aisles symmetrically disposed, gave the ground floor and the open circle of upper stories the appearance of a utopian order that was a relief after the orderly anarchy of modern city life that engulfed the building.[49]

In Stewart's New Store, a minor feature of Edward Bellamy's utopian vision seemed to have come true, a quarter of a century before *Looking Backward* appeared in 1888. There it was, a warehouse for an entire city, "where the buyer, without waste of time and labor, found under one roof the world's assortment in whatever line he desired."[50] The novelty of the displays heightened the impression of boundlessness conjured up by the great variety of goods. Prefabricated household furnishings, ready-made clothes, mass-produced toys, fashionable stationery, and inexpensive books helped make Stewart's the largest retail store in the world. Its departmental organization ordered countless displays with "military precision," *Harper's Monthly* noted, the whole machinery working, "as it were, by electric touches."[51]

Alexander Turney Stewart, to give at least once the full name that seems to have been used sparingly during his lifetime, kept strict discipline among his 2,000 employees. His absolute authority resulted from an intimate familiarity with all aspects of the business. An immigrant, a well-reared Ulster Scot holding a Dublin Trinity College degree, he had built up his organization methodically since the 1820's, when he began in a dry goods shop measuring twelve by thirty feet on lower Broadway. Although he seemed almost inaccessible, maintaining the granite-like reserve that often goes with a Scottish ancestry, he constantly managed to impress his clerks on the floor with his standards of service. His customers liked the bland friendliness he showed them. His honesty gained him their loyalty, which compensated for his shortcomings: he advertised extensively but poorly, and banned displays from his store's show windows and interior. His salesmanship stressing service was what attracted a steady stream of customers.

A shrewd trader, who sold on credit but always paid cash for his purchases, Stewart ran several eastern mills that manufactured woolen goods, cotton and silk, ribbons, threads, blankets, and carpets. He operated offices and warehouses in Great Britain, Ireland, France, Germany, and Switzerland to control his imports. His European buying organization, the outgrowth of annual trips he began in 1839, served as a model for other American retailers. The range of his business corresponded with his success, and in three years before his death in 1876, the combined wholesale and retail sales amounted to $203 million.[52]

Stewart's careful business calculations undoubtedly contributed much to his accomplishment. However, his determination to keep abreast of general trends of urban and industrial growth made him also a brilliant entrepreneur. A sequence of daring moves revealed him as a good judge of human nature and urban expansion. Against the wisdom of the 1840's, he built his Marble Palace on a corner lot of the penny or shilling side of Broadway, where he could acquire real estate cheaply because most merchants preferred the other side of the street where pretentious stores attracted well-to-do customers. The spectacular store immediately drew the dollar trade across the street, with "the beautiful carriages of the millionaires stopping on the shilling side of Broadway to purchase dry-goods."[53] When he located his New Store further uptown in the early 1860's, in another act of seeming folly, he had assessed the population movement of the surging metropolis correctly and found his customers already uptown.

The image of his business, the variety of his merchandise, and the organization of his enterprise provided the foundation for a full-fledged department store. In addition, the orientation of his services toward large numbers of women gave his store its cultural significance as the focus of a new community. The grief expressed in the faces of women listening to the announcement of Stewart's death in front of his New Store, captured by one of the best nine-teenth-century American illustrators in *Harper's Weekly*, sug-gested the bond that linked them to the store.[54] About forty years later, Gordon Selfridge, who had come to London from Chicago's Marshall Field in 1906 and started a department store, coined the phrase that explained the constant stream of women shoppers in such a store: "You know why they come here?" he asked. "It's so much brighter than their homes. This is not a shop—it's a commu-nity centre."[55]

The social functions of the department store turned around the needs of women shoppers who emerged as directors of family con-sumption in the middle of the nineteenth century. These services, at first piecemeal accommodations rather than systematic pro-grams, assured the popularity of the department store among women who regarded the new activity of shopping as a relief from the boredom of familial confinement or the drudgery of domestic routine. In a long-range perspective it can be seen that shopping actually provided the framework of a gilded cage keeping women from their share of freedom. However, in the 1860's and 1870's the ability to shop in the center of large cities seemed to the large number of women crowding the department store a form of real emancipation. It was a small but tangible token, like the indepen-dence Elizabeth Cady Stanton had urged on the wife of her Con-gressman in 1854, when she induced her to buy a much-needed stove without her husband's approval or company.[56]

The attention the department store devoted to its female cus-tomers changed the urban environment and made downtown streets attractive to women. Clean and orderly sidewalks became an extension of the store. The displays in the large plate-glass win-dows added the diversion of window-shopping to the pleasures of the promenade. Women came downtown purposely to see and to be seen, to chance meeting a friend in the store's hospitable atmo-sphere, or to enjoy shopping in company. They arrived in numbers that continuously called for more services. In 1883, a cartoon face-tiously labeled a group of window-shoppers a neglected class be-

cause the storekeeper had failed to make provisions for their comfort and they were forced to inspect the exhibits of a clothing store
sitting on piano stools.[57] Under these circumstances the department store and the upgraded downtown also furnished a setting
that placed on an equal footing with each other women who might
have suffered from a sense of inequality if they had visited one
another at home.

Dreiser's Sister Carrie, who cringed when she compared her
small flat with rich Mrs. Vance's apartment, managed to recover
some of her equanimity during mutual shopping sprees, seeking
"the delight of parading here as an equal."[58] The department store
also permitted fleeting identification with ladies from the upper
crust of society who visited it as part of their carefully timed pursuit of pleasure. Women aspiring to the air of solid middle-class
comfort could find it, at least temporarily, in the atmosphere and
appearance of the new downtown center of their life.

The appearance of the department store heightened the illusion
of shared luxury among the shoppers. In the form of a marble palace, a cast-iron showplace, a sprawling grand depot, or a masonry
castle, it emphasized dedication to the ideal of shopping as an endless delight. The fact that no offices or other tenants crowded the
building's upper stories signaled its commitment to a sole purpose.
Rows and rows of large windows filled it with daylight and relieved
the shopper's dependence on gas lighting for the many purchases
that involved a decision about the colors of fabrics. Elevators accommodated customers who felt reluctant to climb more than one
flight of stairs. These features symbolized prosperity and prestige.
Above all, they emphasized convenience.

The arrangement and display of the merchandise reinforced the
leisurely atmosphere the store sought to create. The division into
departments assured easy access to goods, contrasting with the orderly confusion of the general store and the exclusive air of the
specialty shop where gloves or shawls waited in boxes for the right
customer to call. Clearly marked prices on wares attractively displayed on tables and counters made social equality an element of

the convenience of a store catering to a cross section of the population; for pre-established prices eliminated the possibility of any embarrassment that might have arisen had the sudden disclosure of a price taxed the shopper's means excessively.

Haggling over prices had gradually disappeared from the retail scene in large cities during the first half of the nineteenth century, although the practice continued in smaller cities as a "regular and accepted part of retail buying," with formal discounts given to so many groups that "the occasional person who did not ask for a cheaper price paid too much for his goods."[59] In large stores, however, where many sales were made by many clerks, bargaining was quite understandably passé—proprietors saw no way to entrust setting prices to the numerous and often inexperienced sales people on the floor. Furthermore, a department store management recognized that feature of human nature that aspires to get something for nothing—or, at least, for less than it seems to be worth. Thus came the introduction of the bargain table and the bargain basement, as stores catered to the economic as well as the psychological needs of some of their customers. In 1888, John Wanamaker created in his Philadelphia store a Bargain Room "into which our other rooms will empty all those goods that block their way to serving customers quickly with style and size sought." Edward Filene's Automatic Bargain Basement, a distinct innovation introduced in Boston in 1909, featured unsold goods at reduced prices in order to generate high turnover and to clear the other floors of distress merchandise.[60]

Most stores backed extensively the claims they made to attract customers. They buttressed the policy of accurately advertised merchandise with money-back guarantees, if a customer was not satisfied. John Wanamaker summed up his attitude with a "trinity of square-dealing":

> All goods to be sold openly,
> All traders to be treated alike,
> All fraud and deception to be eliminated.[61]

Some stores, like Marshall Field in Chicago, gave short-term credits and billed monthly, occasionally offering discounts for cash. Others, like Macy's in New York, had no charge accounts at all for many years. All avoided excessive markups and instead sought profits on volume, selling at low prices and low margins. The key to a high stock turnover was extensive local advertising, coupled with price reductions on slow-moving items and extensive customer service.[62] Rapid turnover provided the cash needed to buy in quantity the latest lines and thus to be responsive to ever-changing consumer demands.

The orientation of the department store toward service and mass merchandising was reflected initially in the spectacular selection and convenient arrangement of its merchandise. But new facilities became essential when large numbers of customers spent several hours in the building. Rest rooms and lounges led the way to restaurants and reading rooms. At the end of the nineteenth century, nurseries for customers' children, mail-order services, complaint and credit counters, check-cashing windows, post offices, and ticket agencies quite naturally joined the features of the department store because women wanted these services.[63]

Customer service became the credo of department store personnel. "Public service is the sole basic condition of retail business growth," John Wanamaker emphasized in 1900, while in 1916 the designer of a model store called it a "Service Store," because "every detail has been laid out with the customer's convenience in view."[64] As different as their approaches to retailing and management may have been, most of the legendary builders of great stores—Aristide Boucicaut, William Whiteley, A. T. Stewart, Rowland H. Macy, Isidor and Nathan Straus, Potter Palmer, Marshall Field, Gordon Selfridge, John Wanamaker, Jordan Marsh, and Edward Filene, to name the better known among them—made service a tenet that they upheld meticulously during their regular walks through the aisles of their stores. Through example and exhortation, with fines and dismissals, they impressed the staff with their determination to carry out the policy of service. Their routine rounds and sudden appearances drove the point home to clerks and customers alike.

At such moments, shoppers saw their yearnings to be served answered by a patrician merchant who personified the store's written policies. Clerks saw the owner's art of salesmanship giving dignity to their own skills in a society that considered waiting on people a menial task, somewhat below the dignity of free men and women. A millionaire who greeted his customers and responded to the grievances of a shopper on the crowded floor of his store elevated an obsequious act to the level of a public service, well respected and highly regarded in a professedly democratic society. The Chicago novelist Ernest Poole recalled that as a boy shopping with his mother, he would stare at a "cold-souled courtly merchant" with "a low voice and charming manners," as "he moved about the store with bright observing smiling eyes": Marshall Field, "the richest man in Chicago and ace merchant of the West."[65]

In the 1870's and 1880's, Marshall Field stood out among Chicago merchants who sought to make their department stores servants of the public. He followed approaches to the "carriage trade" and the "shawl trade" that had been laid out by Potter Palmer, his one-time business partner. Field used equality of service to create a social no-woman's-land that allowed upper- and lower-class women to shop together. He made both groups essential actresses in the drama of shopping and spending. A poor woman's self-esteem was elevated by her ability to share a display counter with a rich woman, who in turn achieved her satisfaction from the admiration of clerks and customers. Field's salesmanship made easier the use of the "pecuniary canons of taste," Thorstein Veblen's term for the basis of a new gentility that considered all people equal who had the money to acquire certain goods, indicating they knew which possessions mattered.[66] Although Field at times handled customer-store relationships on the floor of his emporium and actually saw to it that the lady got what she wanted, his skillful

displays of merchandise and well-timed promotional campaigns ensured that his customers "wanted things and services that money
alone could buy."[67] These things and services he sold.

Field's success depended to a great degree on making his store
"irresistibly attractive" to customers.[68] He, and the other great retail merchants, incorporated personality into their cult of public
service. Before marketing research made retailing a science, they
knew instinctively that not only the quality and price of the merchandise, but also the image and identity of the enterprise, attracted people to shop a particular store. Each was the personification of his store, and because they could not wait on every
customer personally, they relied on the store image they created
to convey the impression that they were indeed serving their public.

If this magic failed, floorwalkers stood ready to reinforce the
elusive sense of the owner's presence with a touch of managerial
involvement. They substituted diligence for those features of the
owner's style they were unable to copy. They also extended the
doorman's measured greetings cheerfully into the more remote
departments where they served as "a politely convenient living
directory."[69] The notion of public service they maintained pervaded the entire house and also extended to the store detectives,
who discreetly dealt with thievery as an accident best kept out of
earshot because the sight of one apprehended thief could conjure
up the fear of pickpockets everywhere and undermine the harmonious ritual of buying and selling.

The great number of well-categorized employees made that harmony possible, but most remained hidden from view. The sales
clerks, the group most directly in contact with the customers,
served the public in the most literal way. Although they waited on
individual customers for ten hours a day and for roughly six dollars
a week in the 1890's, they considered themselves not as servants,
but as friendly counselors who provided information about materials, comments about quality, and advice about style to untutored
women shoppers.

Increasingly, women assumed the role of sales clerk as the opportunities of the city lured men elsewhere. By 1900, due to the wide range of better-paid jobs open to men, women became the dominant sex behind the counters.[70] Most managerial jobs were closed to them, although Margaret Getchell rose from cashier to superintendent in Macy's during the 1860's and became one of the first women to attain an executive position in American business.[71] On the other hand, management and customers welcomed women clerks as especially competent sales people. Unlike men, who only tolerated the changes in retailing, young women adjusted quickly to the new ways of selling because the department store represented an economic start for them. They cherished being in urban surroundings that removed them further from domestic chores than did waiting on tables in a restaurant or sewing clothes in a sweatshop. Here, they did not rely on tips, but earned wages. They were able to experience something of the glamor of the big city and meet interesting people. The seasonal help even endured wholesale dismissals preceding the slack months and came back willingly when needed.

Furthermore, the female sales force fit better than men into this new kind of store that replaced the hard sell with an emphasis on service. They easily accepted the novel requirement of attention to the orders of all superiors, essential to the operation of a store no longer run by a single proprietor. They adapted smoothly because they did not bring to the job the burden of outdated practices. To them, strict regulations and disciplined operating procedures were not impersonal or degrading but primarily new, because they had no memories of "the good old days" in the life of a "real clerk."[72] To be sure, they resented some rules, particularly the store's demand that they stand continuously during their long working hours, and they managed to bypass other edicts they found unreasonable. Massie, "a deep-tinted blonde, with the calm poise of a lady who cooks buttercakes in a window," one of the 3,000 clerks in O. Henry's "Biggest Store," chewed tutti frutti "when the floorwalker was not looking" and "smiled wistfully" when he did.[73]

Quite naturally, female clerks also meshed smoothly with the department store's female clientele. They knew what these shoppers wanted because they themselves desired similar possession. The customers, for their part, found it easier to share their intimate desires with them than with men. Fitting new garments was also simplified with the help of sales people of the same sex. Constantly exposed to fashionable goods and demanding customers, the clerks themselves became models of stylish elegance, smartly dressed like O. Henry's Miss Claribel Colby, who personified the "thousand girls from the great department store." When they needed a new gown, like Maida in "The Purple Dress," they skipped meals or starved on skimpy diets and, with the encouragement of management and employee discounts, they spent an inordinate amount of their meager salaries on their wardrobes.[74]

Shopping as a new social art and the department store as a new social institution rose simultaneously, complementing one another. The personnel's commitment to service, the atmosphere of ease and luxury, and the magnificence of the building awed many customers unfamiliar with the idea that they, too, were entitled to service. Under these novel circumstances, they felt relieved, as well as flattered, by the attention and assistance they received. But many people who were pretending to be as affluent as they craved to be lacked experience in shopping for the luxury goods of the new manufacturers, particularly dress goods and household furnishings that came ready-made from the factories. While the specialty shops carried these lines too, the department store strove to take the lead with the newest items. Its lavish displays, conveniently arranged and clearly priced, also provided a wide range of choices in one location, allowing customers unfamiliar with such objects to absorb information about goods just by wandering through the store, without revealing their ignorance as could have happened in an exclusive shop where a haughty sales clerk might have taken any inquiry as an admission of social inferiority. Women shoppers who went into the department store with one purchase in mind invariably left it with many new ideas. Thus clerks and customers learned that shopping as a social art involved acquiring a share of the better life in the future by dreaming of it in the present, both savoring the moment when the purchase actually took place.[75]

Indeed, the buying stage of shopping appeared as the most widely visible sign of female emancipation in the modern city. A Chicago *Herald* political cartoon, reprinted in other newspapers of the Midwest, portrayed that concept in a comment on the presidential campaign of 1892. A young woman representing *the* American shopper briefly interrupts her window-shopping at a dry goods store in order to straight-arm William McKinley into what in that year seemed political oblivion, with an imperious gesture that clearly indicates she is not buying.[76]

In their daily lives, women also responded alertly to the dictates of necessity and the lure of opportunity, and some may even have followed consciously Elizabeth Cady Stanton's advice to "Buy, Buy" as a welcome expansion of their domestic routine. For the most part, they spent the salaries of white-collar workers, professional men, and small entrepreneurs, who had begun earning just enough money to keep the cash tubes of the department store humming with pouches of coins and to keep the women busy making change in the basement cashroom. Buying on credit was not a common practice among these people who were just learning to buy things they did not need, but had not yet discovered that they could do so with money they did not have.

There were of course ladies among the ranks of customers who could afford the purchases they made in the new department stores. Their presence and style set standards of behavior that raised the expectations of women from less affluent homes and led them to buy some new item as the most direct way to prolong the association with the rich which the store induced. Much of the store's success depended on the intensification of desire through the shopping process that helped create this identification. The consideration with which A. T. Stewart and Marshall Field wel-

comed enormously wealthy ladies to their stores indicates that
they appreciated the fact that the visits of these influential people
induced vast numbers of other customers to patronize their stores.

Window displays and store decorations also played a major role
in stimulating demand. The department store, growing with the
new technology of construction, new forms of management, and
new systems of communication, quickly utilized these innovations
to influence people. The activities of pioneer owners soon swept
aside A. T. Stewart's restraints. Potter Palmer, originally an upstate New York merchant who once had bought his goods wholesale from A. T. Stewart, opened his Chicago store with fanfare. His
window of gloves and hosiery, black silk and white cotton, skillfully
arranged against a background of crepe shawls, stirred the city in
the fall of 1852. Novel phosgene lamps illuminated the display at
night and radiated their brilliant light onto the murkey street. In
1878, in his Philadelphia "Grand Depot," a rambling old freight
depot of the Pennsylvania Railroad converted into a huge dry
goods and men's clothing emporium, John Wanamaker first used
electricity to light an entire store "as in daytime." At the time of
the Chicago World's Fair in 1893, Marshall Field & Co. had
blended displays and exhibits into such an artistic achievement
that advertisements could declare the entire store "an exposition in
itself."[77]

Advertising had previously been drawn into the service of
the department store, but it took John Wanamaker's genius for
promotion to make it a major force. His messages telling consumers to buy the latest item appeared on every fence, construction site, and empty building in Philadelphia; even the
curbstones advertised his offerings. Before he opened his store
in 1861, he littered the city with a series of handbills that built up
curiosity. He took in $20.67 on his first day of business, and
promptly spent $20 on advertisements in the Philadelphia *Public
Ledger* announcing a sale of complete men's suits for $3—since he
had suddenly acquired the stock of a bankrupt ready-to-wear
maker of men's suits. Within ten years he ran the largest men's re-

tail clothing operation in the United States, an accomplishment announced in 100-foot-long signs along the train tracks leading into the city. He marshaled parades, gave a suit to everyone who returned one of the large balloons he released, and sent costumed employees through the streets blowing hunting horns from tallyho coaches that were pulled, not by four horses as was customary, but six.[78]

John Wanamaker went all the way with his promotional campaigns, and he did the same with newspaper advertising. Most early department stores advertised modestly, but regularly, in newspapers. In New York, after the Civil War, Lord & Taylor and Macy's moved into double-column-width advertisements, a long step away from the tiny display ads used extensively by A. T. Stewart and Arnold Constable & Co.; but Wanamaker outdid them by advertising daily, using more space on a newspaper page than his competitors, and enlivening the descriptions of goods with hints about their usefulness.[79] His first full-page advertisement appeared in 1879. By 1890 other stores were copying his methods so liberally that they furnished Wanamaker with additional publicity, enabling him to accompany his messages with announcements such as the following: "17 quotations found in the East and the whole advertisement copied bodily in the West."[80]

Wanamaker understood that truncated messages about new merchandise in the advertising sections of a newspaper could not systematically make casual readers regular shoppers in his store because women also liked to hear the story behind the new dress coats or kitchen utensils. He therefore sponsored advice columns about style, etiquette, and fashion trends that subtly prepared readers for the next novelties to appear in his exhibits. His store talks in newspapers informed his customers about the latest innovations in the store to make shopping easier, detailing the functions of service centers or providing instruction on how conveniently a novel safety catch could be installed on an apartment door. Soon these messages began spilling over into regular advertisements and helped to make advertising more literate as well as more honest. In 1896 Wanamaker acquired Stewart's New Store. Its magnificent building had for years been defaced by hideous slogans and gaudy banners that the executors of Stewart's estate had used in a vain attempt to save their declining business. The modest tablet Wanamaker placed at the main entrance reflected his intelligence as well as his integrity as advertiser. It read:

> JOHN WANAMAKER
> FORMERLY
> A. T. STEWART AND CO.[81]

The work of John Wanamaker reflected yet another aspect of the sophistication of retailing, one which shaped the department store as well as the shopper. His use of display advertising and paid newspaper columns helped educate the consumer and thus contributed to the rise of the knowledgeable downtown shopper who ultimately freed the department store from its dependence on the wholesale side of the business, which had filled the orders traveling salesmen drummed up in country stores and provided some of the support for the lavish extension of the retail operation.[82] Creating large groups of customers, new concepts of shopping and selling expedited the expansion of a store like Macy's in New York, which in the 1860's, without the support of a wholesale operation, grew from a small clothing and fancy dry goods store into a department store by adding different lines and acquiring adjacent shops.[83]

Advertising messages and advice columns awakened large numbers of women to the art of calculated shopping based on deliberation and selection. Women who supplied their families' needs by buying in the department store came to rely on these forms of publicity for keeping in touch with the latest styles and offerings. Department store newspaper advertising also introduced women shoppers to a concept of obsolescence that merchants considered quite acceptable. The fashion cycle kept alive the demand for merchandise without violating the ethics of the business vis-à-vis the quality of goods. Changes in taste shortened the life span of a garment or a lamp much more effectively than the use of cheap material or shoddy craftsmanship could have done, without stirring suspicion of creating resentment among customers, who greeted "something new" with delight.

The fashion cycle, which sustained the rising department store by making shopping a perpetual social drama, received its impetus from the freedom of modern city life, which abrogated the political, social, and economic restaints that in the pre-modern age had curbed extensive social use of fashion. It did away with innumerable ordinances and conventions that had once governed life from cradle to grave. In the 1670's, new laws of the Free Imperial City of Frankfort in Germany not only determined the dress of its citizens but also regulated the kind of meals and the number of guests permitted at baptisms, weddings, and funerals.[84] Although such extreme sumptuary laws did not work in the English colonies in North America because the temper of the people and the nature of the setting eroded the instruments of coercion, some dress regulations existed. In 1676, the Suffolk County Court severely admonished a former Boston servant girl for excess in her apparel.[85]

The economic opportunities of the modern city vastly expanded the range of participants in the fashion cycle, and the tempo of life accelerated the speed with which one style succeeded another. More and more people strove to outdo one another in their attire, and as soon as one style became established, new ones emerged. The less impressive people's position or family background was, the more they relied on fashionable appearance as a credential. Jane Addams explained the sound economic sense behind a working woman's spending most of her income on appearance: "Her clothes are her background and from them she is largely judged."[86]

Men and women on the make swelled the ranks of stylishly dressed people, and their numbers increased the chance that the vogue of any particular fashion would have an abrupt end. In the free air of the modern city, anyone with money could aspire to become a social aristocrat by staying just ahead of the next turn of the fashion wheel, while anyone not rich but intent on getting ahead in life could draw closer to the leaders by acquiring a ready-made version of the made-to-order dress or suit of a style-setter. "There is a tide in the affairs of (wo)men that, taken at the flood, leads on to Fashion," an advertisement for a St. Louis department store explained in the 1890's, tying the fashion cycle directly to a department store—"That Kind of Flood is Always at Barr's." In Philadelphia, Wanamaker's emphasized: "What the public *desires,* we must *do.*" [87]

The democratization of the fashion cycle through the department store depended also on new, practical components that gained significance as the number of participants continually expanded. The days of owning one working dress and one Sunday suit became numbered as modern city life created more and more social pressures. The promenade required different attire from the parlor; shopping called for one dress, a social call another. The office and the theater each made different demands on one's wardrobe. People who wanted to belong needed to know what was appropriate for a specific occasion, so that at least their dress, their furniture, or their food would indicate that they had arrived or showed promise of being part of the charmed circle of insiders. The department store selling these status-conferring accouterments provided guidance by means of displays, advertisements, and advice columns that, in turn, increased the demand for the goods.

Dress requirements were correlated with the seasons, particularly in the field of ready-made clothes, and thus added new complexity to the female shopping expedition. Spring, fall, summer, and winter emerged as divisions of the fashion year promulgated by the department store. Each signaled the automatic beginning of a new fashion cycle. Christmas and Easter became high points of fashion, as did the summer vacation and the opening of school in the fall. Colors, cuts, and trimmings changed with them. Wool gave way to silk, and silk again to wool. Full-page advertisements in the Sunday papers of the metropolitan press eliminated any possible confusion for people tied to the wheel of fashion. "It wasn't a cyclone! Nor a 'landslide' that took St. Louis by storm last week and set all the Ladies to talking," the announcement of "Barr's Grand Value-Reducing Sale" clamored. "OH, NO! It was an Avalanche of New Spring Goods," which produced "the greatest sacrifice" of "strictly first-class fine wool dress goods."[88]

The time-honored device of the sale quickened the tempo of style changes. By the 1890's new features had been added to the repertoire of inducements used in the 1840's. "Miss January" and "Mr. Merchandise" came out in costumes at Wanamaker's in January 1888, and launched their sale as "The White Occasion." The sensational language of the advertisements and that of the news columns of the metropolitan press reinforced each other. Nouns like "bomb" and "crash" and adjectives like "desperate" and "solid" spoke not only of the social conditions of the 1890's but also of the department store sales of the period, which fluctuated between "slaughter" of prices and "sacrifice" of goods. Shipwreck sales diminished when big stores moved inland, but trainload sales increased, and grand anniversary sales and white sales were institutionalized. An emphasis on great selections of goods and on low prices, and a lack of restraint, characterized most promotions. In 1893, a St. Louis department store proclaimed itself, on the occasion of a spectacular sale, "by popular vote the headquarters of the North American Continent, both as regards to variety and low prices."[89]

Sales and seasons produced a constant succession of changes. Highlighted through new displays in store windows and on bargain tables, and introduced with advertising campaigns in the newspapers, the frequent turns of the fashion cycle camouflaged in a superficial way social and cultural divisions among the residents of the modern city. The cycle encouraged the egalitarian activity of department store shopping, and thus steadily increased membership in the society of consumers and stimulated identification across social classes. The process also established a distinct urban identity, because access to downtown shopping facilities was essential for participation in the latest fashion trends.

The department store made shopping itself fashionable. It gave status to what had been drudgery and added an element of diversion to the lives of women who could afford to play the game. "Fashionable Shopping in New York" was the caption of a large woodcut illustration of Stewart's Marble Palace in a *Herald* advertisement in September 1846, on the occasion of the store's opening.[90] The department store captured an audience of women shoppers who found a female enclave amid splendid settings and constantly changed scenes which matched well the ever-changing modern city.

By its very nature, shopping in a department store became a public act that educated people for living in the city. Successful participation demanded that the shopper possess not only money but also the poise to assess shrewdly the offered goods. It involved familiarity with the ways of the world and knowledge of the value of things. Buying, the culmination of shopping, constituted yet another measure of success. Though the goods people bought reflected well-established divisions among them, the egalitarian features of shopping diminished these inequalities and linked shoppers as an interest group. Through their shopping and buying activities women acquired not only a knowledge of what to buy but also the power to determine what was sold. Women's consumer's leagues began using that power in the 1890's, when the spread of the department store enabled them to touch all the major retail outlets with one boycott.

Most women welcomed the adventure of downtown shopping, which for many was not only a fashionable activity but also a truly urban one. They went window-shopping, strolled through the stores, gazed at the displays and each other, chatted with friends, listened to clerks' explanations, assessed the articles and other shoppers, bought something they considered a bargain, and under fortunate circumstances went home with the feeling that they had not only done something women were supposed to do, but had actually enjoyed doing it. This, experience, repeated almost daily, intensified their identity as modern urban women.

This new identity also engendered stress. At the beginning of the twentieth century one observer, sketching her impressions of "typical American women on a typical shopping tour," discovered "the anomaly that the longer they take to shop, the less they actually buy." She saw women "poorly clad, pale and irritable from fatigue," moving from counter to counter, "fingering, pricing, commenting, passing on, hour after hour," with "an ice-cream soda in the basement" as their "only lunch." This was followed by a "complete rearrangement of hair in the 'Ladies Parlor,'" and "a slow stroll through the Art Department," in a routine common to "tens of thousands of our women in every city in the Union."[91]

The identity of the modern urban woman acquired its distinct character through her relationship with the department store. In response to the lure of shopping, women became a presence in the downtown section of the modern city. As shoppers they exercised daily control over the household budget; this not only gave them a growing measure of independence but also earned them the special attention of merchants, who recognized their purchasing power as the sine qua non of large-scale retailing. Moreover, though the women who worked as sales clerks may have earned low salaries and worked long hours, this form of employment opened up a major female avenue into the male-dominated urban job market. The total effect was to introduce women as a new social force in city life.

A broad cultural perspective suggests a simile from the *Communist Manifesto* of 1848. Summarizing the history of industrialization in the Western world, Marx and Engels argue that the bourgeoisie liberated countless peasants from the "idiocy" of rural life and chained them to the factory. Analogously, the department store freed large numbers of women from the isolation of domesticity and chained them to a novel form of servitude—shopping as a social obligation.[92] With the feminization of shopping, the department store turned a chore into an elaborate process that oriented most residents of the modern city toward money as the common denominator of urban life.

Shopping also reinforced the separation between two spheres of life, leaving the acquisition of the funds for shopping to man while making the task itself a woman's affair. Ultimately, shopping and increased consumption may also have shaped the subtle relations between some men and women in an age that reinforced the ideal of middle-class marriage with layers of convention. In Dreiser's *Sister Carrie*, Mr. G. W. Hurstwood enjoyed himself thoroughly in Philadelphia during a brief escape he had engineered from the demands of his Chicago home life. On his return the whole incident was glossed over, "but Mrs. Hurstwood gave the subject considerable thought. She drove out more, dressed better and attended theaters freely to make up for it."[93]

Both men and women felt the social impact of the department store in other realms as well. They witnessed the transformation of the center of the city, which, during working hours at least, had been almost exclusively a male domain, into a downtown area where clean sidewalks enticed women to linger in front of store windows without fear of being harassed by draymen and crowded by office boys. The department store brought into the bustle of downtown the civility that most men had reserved for those aspects of city life they considered properly the social sphere. Thus the store added a new charm to the modern city by opening the city center to the civilizing influences of women and visitors from out of town, making urban life, in the words of Henry James, "so much more down-towny."[94]

Much of that new urban charm stemmed from the substitution of a shopping district for a wholesale or business district as the core of the city. Magnificent buildings and attractive sidewalks introduced into the downtown section the same sense of spatial order that the department store had brought to large-scale retailing. In a world barely touched by concepts of city planning, this innovation expressed the promise of an ordered urban life. In addition, as the destination of large numbers of women shoppers the department store furnished a focal point for expanding urban transit systems. This validated the downtown district as the center for the flow of people as well as of goods. As the heart of the modern city this district sought to create and attempted to satisfy in the most concentrated form the population's infinitely expanding demands for goods and services.[95]

With its far-ranging utility, the department store reflected the culture of the modern city. It constantly assessed people's hopes for a better life and responded to their dreams. As a creative social force, the department store sustained the shared experience of shopping, produced a new form of communal life, and provided links among heterogeneous people. Ultimately, the department store gave urban life a downtown focus, not only bestowing charm and civility but also evoking democratic qualities that enriched the urbanity of the modern city and reaffirmed its egalitarian nature.

# V

# BALL PARK

Old men, young men, and small boys, usually "confined in offices, shops, and factories," packed the Polo Grounds on May 30, 1888, for a baseball game between New York and Pittsburgh, "and saw the popular sport to their hearts' content." The early-comers had crowded the grandstands, forcing the latecomers onto the green field, where "they formed a horseshoe around the playing lines and took a sunbath." The spectators yelled, "jumped like colts, clapped their hands, threw their hats into the air, slapped their companions on the back, winked knowingly at each other, and . . . enjoyed themselves hugely." On that afternoon, according to the account of a New York *Times* reporter, 13,333 "anxious sightseers" experienced in the ball park the quintessence of urban leisure: watching others do things.[1]

The scene, barely a few years old, seemed timeless to the spectators. Engulfed by the surging city, an urban tide flooding the land with a sea of houses, the baseball field exposed within its boundaries the remnants of a ravaged countryside in the form of scarred ravines protected by their ugliness from building construction. Here, with weathered wooden grandstands and solid clapboard fences as dikes, a lake of grass contrasted with the surrounding shades of brown. Its green faded away around the bases, where the intense play had turned the grass to dirt, a baseball diamond without a diamond's glitter. Oblivious of this, however, thousands of spectators looked only for the sparkle of perfection in the play on the field. To them going to the ball park meant surrender to the spell of baseball and to the motions of the players—now frozen into a stance, now sprinting with a will, throwing, batting, catching, or chasing the ball—while enjoying the suspense of America's favorite game.[2]

In addition to the excitement, a visit to the ball park provided men with a new perspective on life in the modern city. Watching a professional baseball game, as well as knowing its ins and outs, turned them into true spectators who not only saw the events on the field but also could sense their significance for everyday life. The experience made crowds of people conscious that rules regulated the happenings of their world, too, and that beyond the fences of the ball park, restraints tempered the competition to get ahead in the world.

Thousands and thousands of men, frequently mystified by the operation of the economic sphere or the actions of their fellowmen in public office, saw in the ball park how rules affected one sector of modern city life, the athletic contest. In ways they could perceive, the spectacle demonstrated the regulation of one of their elementary drives—competition. When their knowledge of the rules of baseball put them in a position to detect how at times some players tried to win by getting away with infractions, city people came to an understanding of how regulations operated in the free-for-all of the modern world. A quick assessment of the swift action on the diamond revealed that restraints curbed the struggle for success, ordinarily pursued obtrusively by reckless men or obscured by the hustle of daily life. This insight reassured the spectators that elements of order permeated the turmoil of the modern city.

The freedom to share the intense competition and the slight leisure that the modern city granted most inhabitants distinguished some of the social functions of baseball and ball park in nineteenth-century America from the roles of games and arenas in earlier societies. From its beginning, the city had fostered spectator sports, but frequently depending on a ruler's will or a priest's ritual to grant throngs of people the leisure to enjoy them. Quite early, political ambitions and religious needs nourished a popular desire for more and better diversions that only professional athletes could satisfy. Although the large numbers of spectators already suggested in antiquity the commercial potential of games, it was only the individual freedom and the economic incentive provided by the modern city that turned sports into an industry.

The practice of conducting an entire game according to established rules signaled the arrival of spectator sports as big business in the nineteenth century. Apart from their basic function of distinguishing one sport from another, rules made a game a socially acceptable outlet for emotions. By regularizing procedures, they fostered interest, shaped the sport to the liking of spectators, and provided the framework for a sequence of related events leading to a championship. The use of rules set the big-city spectacle apart from impromptu play, which is attractive because it is freely improvised, utilizes make-believe instead of rules, and provides the pleasure of assuming roles.[3] Rules also heightened enormously the popularity of a contest because they facilitated betting on the results.

The impact of rules on the outcome of a game remained doubtful until promoters dependent on paying spectators and people eager to get their money's worth ensured impartial and constant enforcement. The modern sports entrepreneur pursued a course analogous to that of a Roman emperor who in principle was supposed to decide a duel between gladiators himself according to well-defined standards but who in practice may frequently have accepted the verdict of the crowd because he had allowed the entire circus to be staged in the first place to please them.[4] The promoter altered and shaped the rules of a game until the action suited the greatest number of people and then worked to give them the impression that all went according to the regulations.

Although the fans paid admission to sports spectacles and thus influenced their development, general social and cultural trends also affected the diversions of nineteenth-century urbanites. The

A policeman gives directions to a girl who ventured downtown, into the confusing center of the modern city that once had been the domain of men. Courtesy of The Bancroft Library, University of California, Berkeley.

A Jewish immigrant from Eastern Europe awaits the Sabbath eve in a coal cellar, at the end of the nineteenth century. The sign leaning against the wall at left advertises a bootmaker's custom-made products in Yinglish, a pre-fusion stage of Yiddish and English. Photograph by Jacob A. Riis, Jacob A. Riis Collection, Museum of the City of New York.

Long lines of stalled streetcars struggle to find a gap in the cross-town traffic in downtown Chicago during the first decade of the twentieth century. Chicago Historical Society.

Mount Auburn Cemetery, opened in 1831 near Boston, anticipated the rediscovery of nature in the urban environment through the municipal park. From *Meyer's Universum* (Hildburghausen, Germany, 1853), 220–21.

The narrow fronts of brownstones on New York's Forty-sixth Street document the vanishing dream of the single-family home in the modern city, shattered by steadily rising real estate prices. Museum of the City of New York.

The two tiers of Callowhill Street Bridge, at the waterworks in Philadelphia's Fairmount Park, linked the concern for practical solutions of urban problems with attempts to incorporate rural scenes into city life. From *Philadelphia and Its Environs*, 3rd ed. rev. and enl. (Philadelphia, 1875), 66.

Many city people found shelter in crowded tenements. An artist exposed to public scrutiny their conditions, which contrasted favorably with the secret misery of the surrounding hovels. His concept of tenement life reflected reformers' hopes of creating decent living conditions, shattered almost immediately in the face of waves and waves of newcomers to the modern city clamoring for shelter. From James D. McCabe, *New York by Sunlight and Gaslight* (Philadelphia, 1881), 560–61.

Early apartment houses in the modern city were known as "French Flats." Parisian models lent respectability to New York's Stuyvesant Apartments of 1869, apparently the first structure built as an apartment house for several families. Museum of the City of New York.

The illustration for the lead article about "Parisian 'Flats'" in *Appleton's Journal* for November 1871 accentuated the mansard roof of slate, iron, and tin of the Stevens House, an early New York apartment building. From *Appleton's Journal*, VI (November 18, 1871), 561.

A newsboy selling *Harper's Weekly* startled the window shoppers on Boston's Washington Street in the 1850's. Newsboys became a regular feature of the big-city scene with the rise of the metropolitan press in the 1830's. From John A. Kouwenhoven (comp.), *Adventures of America, 1857–1900: A Pictorial Record from Harper's Weekly* (New York, 1938), plate no. 6.

In the 1840's and 1850's R. Hoe & Co. in New York produced several new printing presses to keep in step with the growing demand for up-to-date newspapers with large circulations. At this ten-cylinder press men fed the sheets of newsprint into the type-revolving press, while automatic grippers, or fingers, took the printed paper from the feed board. From Harold E. Sterne, *Catalogue of Nineteenth Century Printing Presses* (Cincinnati, 1978), plate no. 338.

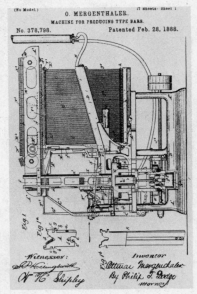

A page from Ottmar Mergenthaler's patent application shows the linotype machine that in the 1880's overcame a recalcitrant technology hampering the mechanization of typesetting. From Fritz Schroeder, *Ottmar Mergenthaler* (Berlin, 1941), [98].

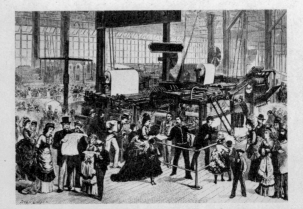

In 1876, the speed and efficiency with which a web perfecting press printed and folded 15,000 copies of a newspaper in one hour fascinated visitors to the Centennial Exposition in Philadelphia. From Kouwenhoven, *Harper's Weekly*, plate no. 171.

Whether or not they could read English, the message of the first full-page cartoon, spread across the front page of the New York *World* on October 30, 1884, reached all city people. It informed them about a dinner millionaires gave for James G. Blaine, the Republican presidential candidate. Newspaper Collection, The New York Public Library, Astor, Lenox and Tilden Foundations.

The ambience of metropolitan life encouraged people of modest means to aspire to an air of luxury, and ready-made clothes enabled some of them to realize part of this dream. Touching first the fringes of women's fashion, as in this skirt factory in New York City in the 1850's, ready-to-wear hastened the flowering of the department store based on the rapid turnover of goods. From *Harper's Weekly*, III (February 19, 1859), 125.

A. T. Stewart's "New Store," seen from the corner of Broadway and Tenth Street in New York, opened in 1862. The plain columns and arches of the cast-iron facade appealed to the practical sense as well as to the merchant's imagination that saw the front, painted white, as a huge cloud against the blue sky. From *Architectural Record*, I (October–December, 1891), 246.

The artist who sketched the former Stewart store in the 1880's (when it was under new management) succumbed to the spectacle of the department store in adding a sixth floor to the building. Courtesy of The New-York Historical Society, New York City.

Charles Stanley Reinhart's drawing "Announcing the Death of Mr. Stewart—Scene in Front of the Tenth Street Store" captures the impact of the news on A. T. Stewart's customers, the women of the modern city, for whom the department store had become a cultural institution. From *Harper's Weekly*, XX (April 29, 1876), 345.

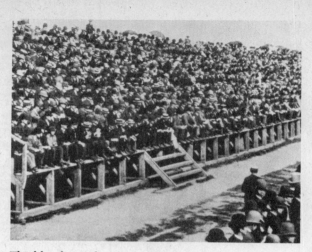

The bleachers, the uncovered stands for spectators in a
ball park, were once known as the "Bleaching Boards,"
as indicated on Joseph Hall's photograph accompanying
an article on "Our National Game" in the 1880's. From
*Cosmopolitan*, V (October, 1888), 445.

The wooden grandstands of a Boston ball park of the 1890's could not hold the many
spectators, who spilled over onto the bleachers and the field. Courtesy of National
Baseball Hall of Fame, Cooperstown, N.Y.

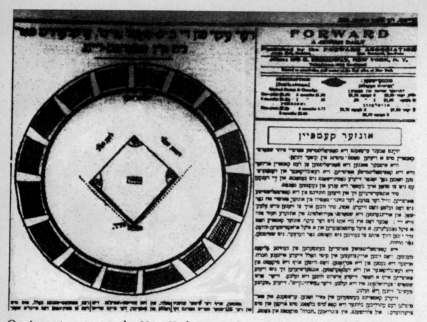

On August 27, 1909, the New York *Forward*, a Jewish daily published in Yiddish, exposed its readers to *the* American game as they would experience it "uptown" at the Polo Grounds. The article, "Der iker fun di base-ball game, erklert far nit keyn sports layt" ("the essentials of baseball explained to people unfamiliar with sports"), and the three-column-wide diagram of a ball park reflect the power of baseball over people and languages. Newspaper Collection, The New York Public Library, Astor, Lenox and Tilden Foundations.

In the 1890's the vignette of the regular vaudeville column in a major theatrical journal extolled the essence of the popular entertainment in the modern city: variety. From *Dramatic Mirror*, XLI (December 24, 1898), 90.

Vaudeville houses aspired to leave their mark on the cityscape. The Twenty-eighth Street front of the Fifth Avenue Theatre in New York managed to rival other urban palaces. From William H. Birkmire, *The Planning and Construction of American Theatres* (New York, 1901), 16–17.

The switchboard of the "Marble Engine-room" in Keith's New Boston Theatre was an essential part of the show. Spectators passed it on their way into the dynamo room before attending the performance. From Birkmire, *American Theatres*, 56–57.

"The Nawns' " routine about life in an Irish household provides a glimpse at an 1890's vaudeville act that brings out the realism of the entertainment, often obscured by nostalgia. From *Dramatic Mirror*, XLI (December 24, 1898), 90.

The poise of Lulu Glaser (*above left*) and Lillian Russell (*above right*) made a star's appearance on the vaudeville stage memorable. Gertrude Vanderbilt (*below left*) conveyed vaudeville's free spirit through her dances, Harry Houdini (*below right*) through countless escapes. Marius de Zayas sketched these performers for Caroline Caffin, *Vaudeville* (New York, 1914), 30–31, 66–67, 80–81, 192–93.

Eva Tanguay, ruling queen of the musical comedy stage, moved into vaudeville in 1906. Her singing and dancing made her *the* star for many vaudeville audiences. Harvard Theatre Collection.

disintegration of traditional society that accompanied the rise of the modern city undermined forms of popular recreation that were rooted in a predominantly agrarian social system. The newly emerging leisure culture was molded according to the requirements of capitalist society and industrial production. Unlike their ancestors in pre-industrial societies, relieved from incessant labor by climatic vicissitudes and rewarded for prolonged toil by seasonal feast days, in general the residents of the modern city learned to be satisfied with brief but more frequent opportunities to enjoy themselves.[5]

This formula suited their working hours, which could stretch through day and night, with some workers idle while others toiled if factory shifts required several sets of men. In consequence, the sporting events which attracted the most attention came to be reduced in length. However, the number of contests and of competitors increased and provided a steady stream of excitement that fitted most people's schedules and directed the use of leisure time toward relaxation rather than rest. In this way the spectator sports, which rose as business enterprises with the modern city, conformed to the needs of its residents.[6]

Men anxious to be distracted from their arduous daily routines provided a natural market for the product of the new industry. As soon as they had learned to live for the moment that temporarily freed them from work, they felt the urge to extend the diversion provided by spectator sports into their working hours. Presumably they had always talked on the job about athletic feats they had witnessed, but now, if they missed an event, they began looking at the columns of the metropolitan press to keep up with their pastime. They also relied on special forms of communication to bring distant contests closer.

Founded in Baltimore in 1829, the *American Turf Register*, the first sports magazine in the United States, paved the way. The New York *Spirit of the Times*, initially devoted only to racing, started covering other sports in 1831. In 1853, the New York *Clipper*, which became the major American sporting journal in the sec-

ond half of the nineteenth century, began sailing the journalistic
seas loaded with news about sports and the theater, underlining
the bond between varieties of diversions and spectacles. These
journals and newspapers and magazines steadily increased the
number of sports covered, as well as the size of their audiences.

This new focus of popular attention proved irresistible to journalists. "We would rather chronicle a great boat race . . . or a
cricket match . . . than all the prize poems or the orations on
Lafayette that are produced in half a century," *Harper's Weekly* reported in 1857.[7] Stories about walking and running races, boxing
matches, sailing regattas, and baseball games not only circulated
information about athletic accomplishments but also established
national standards of excellence. Reports of records established
one day and broken the next diffused a historical consciousness in
the modern city, among a people without a common history. They
steadily expanded the vocabulary of sports writers and stimulated
patterns of speaking that made sports jargon part of everyday
speech.

The apostles of play expressed their insights into sports practices
with a new terminology that frequently originated in London journals. Some of these phrases became so genuinely American that
their English origin faded away. "A Chinaman's chance" did not
originate in the California of the 1850's, as one might have suspected, but rather in the London *Weekly Dispatch* of the 1820's,
which called a light-hitting boxer a "china man" because he
seemed as likely to break with rough handling as porcelain. Other
British terms supplanted American ones. "Fan," short for "fancy,"
an English expression for a devotee of dog fights and boxing
matches, replaced the American term "crank" for a sports enthusi-
ast, although in the 1890's James Cardinal Gibbons of Baltimore
still explained rather apologetically to an audience that he was not
a "baseball crank."[8]

Spectator sports spread almost as quickly as the sports lingo.
They thrived on a network of cities connected by railroad and telegraph. The emerging sports industry soon was distributing its

products to a national market. Cities furnished facilities and human resources in the form of tracks and arenas, professional athletes, and paying spectators. They provided the settings for sports activities in which both individual sportsmen and teams flourished, creating the framework for staging the selection of national champions. Above all, the intensified urbanization of the nineteenth century led to the acceptance of games and races as urban extravaganzas, because the cities attracted people with leisure in search of entertainment and sheltered others seeking escape from the doldrums of daily toil.

Most conventions rooted in the morals of seventeenth-century puritanism and the vigor of eighteenth-century industrialism, which regarded popular recreation as frivolous and unproductive and blocked the growth of spectator sports, fell by the wayside in the modern city. In the middle of the nineteenth century, ministers and physicians spearheaded a campaign against excessive labor, extolling recreation and play as remedies for the seemingly overwhelming American urge to work. Later, leaders of the Social Gospel Movement promoted industrial man's right to his recreational leisure and helped remove repressive laws that interfered with an individual's use of his free time. Baseball itself, which as *the* American sport observed Sunday laws where they were enforced until 1933, became a primary force in lifting the restrictions on play. Finally, the modern city produced self-made men who set their own leisure hours, as well as laborers who benefited from flexible working hours. Both groups turned up in sufficient numbers at the racetrack and in the ball park on weekdays, if Sunday laws prohibited sports activity, to make spectator sports profitable enterprises for entrepreneurs.[9]

The new sports spectaculars also drew into their orbits the legions of spectators urban life seemed to produce quite naturally. The modern city's ever-changing sights, the intensity of activities, and the contrast of life-styles created by the unequal distribution of wealth turned many residents into observers. The splendor of the cityscape also bred *flâneurs*, who turned observation into an art and easily became habitués of grandstand boxes and ringside seats. The flux of the modern city daily created new forms of life that encouraged the heady defiance of convention. This heightened the attraction of outlawed boxing contests and, for that matter, of all spectator sports. These novelties commanded so much attention and so disrupted what was left of the established order of things that one of the arbiters of the age disdained them as "a public nuisance." [10]

Alarmed by the impact of the crowds that spectator sports attracted, another self-appointed judge of his generation reached a similar verdict. In 1842, after a visit to a racetrack, Philip Hone felt that the "crowd and the dust and the danger and the difficulty of getting on and off the course with a carriage are scarcely compensated by any pleasure to be derived from the amusement." An accident reinforced his idea that the masses were no proper spectators. "The tens of thousands of the sovereign people who wished to see this race" had planned to take a commuter train, he related, "but the numbers were so great" that the locomotive stalled. "The mob who had provided themselves with tickets . . . became riotous, upset the cars, placed obstructions on the rails, and indulged in all sort of violence." [11]

Horse racing was the most popular spectator sport in the United States until the rise of professional baseball. Boxing was a close second. The traditional, age-old appeal of the two exerted a strong influence on the residents of the modern city. The racehorses and pugilists demonstrated feats of elementary strength, disciplined in man's favorite animal and unleashed in two fellowmen who seemed to revert, at least in the eyes of some commentators, to the level of animals. The speed of horses and the stamina of boxers increased people's fascination with sports; and exposure to track and ring prepared Americans for baseball as the great spectator sport in the closing decades of the nineteenth century.

The popular sports of mid-nineteenth-century America taught city people what to look for in a contest. In a manner of speaking, they prepared spectators for the task of watching a baseball game, expanding their horizons beyond the immediate concern with winners to discovering how victory was achieved. A swift horse sharpened their powers of observation, an agile boxer opened their eyes to finesse, and both demonstrated the efficacy of discipline and perfection, which loomed large in urban existence. The comments of sport journalists expanded these lessons, tempering impulsive enthusiasm with a shrewd reservation that grew out of knowing the ins and outs of a sport as well as the wheeling and dealing behind the scenes. The writers increased skepticism about as well as appreciation of any accomplishment and provided the rising generation of sports spectators with a frame of mind that allowed them to be both involved and detached, watching a spectacle and learning from what they saw.

Horse racing fascinated city people. They craved rural scenes, and the racetrack recaptured some of the gaiety and turmoil of a horse fair in the country. In addition the elegant side of these sights reinforced the reputation of racing as the Sport of Kings and the pastime of millionaires, and with these allusions the horse's special position in human society.

In myth, legend, and fable, the horse occupied a distinguished place because of its faithfulness and generosity, valor and speed. However, the fact that only the horse among the big domesticated animals had accompanied man into the modern city, pulling hacks, streetcars, or beer wagons and carrying policemen, may have meant more to the racetrack crowd than any memory of Pegasus speeded along by his wings or Achilles mourned by his chariot horses.

The racetrack also developed city people's fascination with swift motion and sudden action, which the ball park was to cultivate to the utmost. This growing preoccupation with speed pervaded many areas of life that were unrelated except by an infatuation with fast horses. It generated Leland Stanford's support of photographer Eadweard Muybridge's scientific study *The Horse in Motion*, published in 1878, and established the popularity of artist Frederic Remington's horses in action. It also changed the character of horse races, revealing how people's notions of what was worth watching shaped the nature of emerging spectator sports.

After the Civil War, the standard four-mile race, which involved winning two out of three heats, disappeared, and even three-mile tests, once considered a concession to younger horses, fell by the wayside. Watching heats came to bore people chafing at the monotony of daily routines. The heats vanished entirely as a new trend developed favoring more contests per day, shorter races, and the use of younger horses. Increasingly dash racing fans became more deeply involved in the results of a race than in the event itself, because betting made the thoroughbreds a potential source of money for everyone.

Gambling on sports was widespread in the modern city just as gambling in one form or another had always permeated the life of the nation, from lotteries in England that financed the colony of the Virginia Company to lotteries during the American Revolution that provided funds to pay soldiers fighting for independence. Betting provided a way of responding to a world of change and chance. Poor men became rich overnight, and rich men poor; and between these extremes of good luck and bad lay a wide range of chances that cried out to be exploited by betting on a race or fight. Gambling appealed to some city people as a mark of gentility, or struck others as an exciting diversion from everyday problems. For some, it also affirmed a deep-seated suspicion about the inclination of heterogeneous people to transgress the morality of the lawmakers.

Betting deepened almost everyone's fascination with horse racing, beyond the rather small number of people concerned with improving the breed—one of the favorite justifications for staging races in the first place. The owners of horses had always considered wagering a part of the proceedings. Before the Civil War, auction pools in which the entries in a race were sold to the highest bidder gave spectators a chance to share what many considered the best part of racing. In the second half of the nineteenth century the spread of bookmakers further accommodated organized betting and tightened its grip on the sport. Good odds could make a betting coup more profitable than the modest purse given to the owner who had saddled a winner. Fans learned the track records and pedigrees of the horses, and this knowledge contributed to a state of mind which made them ready to question the results of any race.

The atmosphere of jockey clubs, stables, and paddocks provided grounds for speculations about imagined or real manipulations of horses by owners, grooms, and trainers to influence the outcome of races. Public indignation over actual frauds resulted in outlawing races in several states. If the desire for betting action in the poolrooms contributed to the new character of horse racing, as some people suspected, the changing atmosphere of the racetrack hardened the feeling that races were run more for betting and less for horsemanship and improving the breeds. Until the pari-mutuel system of betting, in which the winners share the total stakes less a percentage for the track management, gained acceptance in the first decade of the twentieth century, horse racing barely covered "its hideous reality" with "the mantle of social respectability" and remained under a cloud of suspicion.[12]

Boxing, the other popular spectator sport, shared the charge tainting racing—that insiders fixed the outcomes of races in order to influence the betting on horses. It was held in special disrepute because prize fighting rarely seemed to control its brutality. In 1853, the editor of the New York *Times* found it inexplicable and humiliating that boxing bouts could take place at all, with "public sentiment opposed to animal brutality in any shape," but at the same time he made sure that his paper cashed in on the news value of the contests.[13] Although frequently outlawed, boxing held its own in the back rooms of waterfront dives and tenderloin saloons where men like "Chimmie Fadden," a hero of popular fiction at the turn of the century, took any well-to-do "student of human nature" to observe the proceedings of "de Rose Leaf Social Outin' and Life Savin' Club."[14]

Aversion to the repulsive features of prize fighting remained

strong throughout the nineteenth century, but it diminished somewhat when a systematic refinement of boxing techniques led to
new rules that did away with bare fists; wrestling and holding in
chancery; and continuing each round until one boxer went down
and the entire fight until one man, or his supporters, gave up. The
1880's, when John L. Sullivan methodically began using a right
blow to his opponent's jaw to end a match quickly with a knockout,
marked a new era. He demonstrated his innovation in four-round
boxing exhibitions with gloves; however, in his last championship
bout he still fought seventy-five rounds with bare knuckles under
the old London Prize Ring rules. On that occasion, as on many
others, the elementary test of strength, conducted in a narrow ring
in plain view, fascinated spectators. It also commanded the attention of fans in distant cities, who crowded hotel lobbies, saloons,
barbershops, and poolrooms waiting for messages from telegraph
operators about the details of the endurance test.[15]

Although other spectator sports also entranced the residents of
the modern city, they neither drew the number of people the racetrack attracted nor produced the excitement the boxing ring generated. With growing regularity, rowing and yachting matches followed one another year after year. Billiard exhibitions and walking
races were popular attractions, while cricket and football occasionally drew large crowds. All these sports developed urban fol-
lowings, but none was as distinctly urban or reflective of the life-
style of the modern city as trotting races.

Big cities made fashionable the driving rigs used in trotting.
People rode fewer and fewer horses for transportation or pleasure,
but a businessman or lawyer might step from his home or office
into a buggy and speed down the avenue and through the park for
fresh air, exercise, and a friendly brush with other drivers. These
outings regularly attracted onlookers fascinated by the speed and
elegance a trotting horse could achieve if kept to the gait. However, the rapidly growing cities limited any direct role in the action to a wealthy few, so that when the straightaway turnpike re-
ceded into the country and deprived spectators of their share in

the show, clubs began building tracks where they raced trotters regularly before appreciative crowds.

Trotting and other popular diversions in the second half of the nineteenth century foreshadowed the role of baseball as the big urban spectator sport. The display of the harnessed and efficient movement of a crack trotting horse or of the systematic, refined technique of a new-style boxing champion introduced into people's enjoyment of leisure an appreciation for standards of performance. The attempt to perfect these qualities in professional baseball players during a season evoked analogies to the industrial discipline of the work force in the modern city.

The fascination with controlled energy, symbolized by the central position of the Corliss steam engine in the major hall of the Philadelphia Exposition of 1876, at times reached extremes. It stimulated the enormous popularity of such seemingly inhuman endeavors as heel- and toe-walking races. The unnatural technique employed in this sport led some who tried it to conclude that they "were straining every nerve and muscle to get ahead, but had entered into an insane compact not to employ the natural and obvious means of doing so." [16]

Popular sports, connecting the urban population with a rising sports industry, shared a potential for educating as well as entertaining crowds of spectators. Among these spectacles, baseball occupied a special position as the most popular and most organized of all spectator sports in the last decades of the nineteenth century. It was the most convenient way for city people to enjoy themselves and also to demonstrate a commitment to standards of excellence in a leisure-time activity. Within a generation the game had made the transition from a pastime for gentlemen to a social institution illuminating the inner workings of new patterns of urban life.

Baseball conquered the United States in the decades between 1840 and 1870, which saw the standardization of the diamonds, the organization of teams, the refinement of rules, the establishment of game schedules, and the first grand tour by a professional baseball team. The game descended remotely from English ball games, one of them called baseball as early as 1700, and directly from the English game of rounders. In America it spread as a base-running game under various names, such as Town Ball, Round Ball, Goal Ball, or One o' Cat, according to the locality or the number of players, until the name "baseball" won out. Suffering from an attack of chauvinism at the opening of the twentieth century, baseball moguls decreed that the game had been invented by Abner Doubleday in Cooperstown, New York, in 1839, and, in their own words, "forever set at rest the question as to the Origin of Base Ball."[17] From that time on, baseball acquired an official beginning and a distinctly rural American origin, reinforced by the sandlot motif of its supposed centennial in 1939, which included a barn, house, church, and school as the appropriate background.[18]

Historical evidence links baseball, as we know it, with the modern city. In the early 1840's a group of New York gentlemen who on sunny days enjoyed playing ball games in a lot at the corner of Madison Avenue and Twenty-Seventh Street formed the first association and in 1845 adopted the first set of modern rules. These merchants, brokers, and physicians enjoyed dining and playing together. In 1846 their Knickerbocker Baseball Club played its first match against another team of gentlemen, the New York Nine, in a popular summer resort across the Hudson River. The New York *Clipper* considered that contest the beginning of baseball "as now played" in its preview of the Centennial Year season of 1876.[19] Social as well as athletic exclusiveness distinguished these early gatherings. More often than not, formal challenges initiated the contests and social events concluded them. Soon uniforms—white shirts, blue trousers, and straw hats in the case of the Knickerbockers—added another stylish note.[20]

Despite several efforts to create a uniform game, there were no generally accepted rules regulating strikes and balls until the Civil War. The time the play consumed was still of little consequence, and games often dragged on, endlessly it appeared, because the man at bat, the "striker," waited for the pitch that suited him or hoped to tire out the pitcher. Often, local circumstances dictated the number of players as well as the layout of the field, the distance between bases, the size of the diamond, and the position of the umpire.[21]

The aristocratic setting of the game vanished during the 1850's when new clubs sprang up in New York, Brooklyn, Philadelphia, Baltimore, and Boston. Fascinated with baseball, laborers, mechanics, and clerks put onto diamonds teams that rejected the assumption that the Knickerbockers arbitrated the game simply because they had organized it first. The Knickerbockers themselves never really took their obligation as arbiters seriously because they feared that an improved system of play would produce more clubs and undermine their dominant position. The competition demonstrated the mounting need for a useful structure for the sport. In 1857, many people may have agreed with the editor of the leading sports paper, the New York *Spirit of the Times,* who considered the successful organization of the German Turnverein Association and of other immigrant sports organizations a challenge to develop "some game peculiar to the citizens of the United States."[22]

The agitation for uniform baseball regulations led to the formation of scores of committees to draft guidelines and to ask the mayor of New York to allow baseball games in Central Park, a bastion of cricket. In 1858, the search for more order brought together delegates from twenty-two clubs who established the National Association of Base Ball Players. Although a far cry from a national unit, the Association placed all clubs on an equal basis by forming a rules committee, establishing procedures for new clubs to join the group, and regulating players, umpires, and scorers. Following the time-honored American practice demonstrated by churches, political parties, labor unions, and charity groups, it grew from the local level to a state, regional, and ultimately a national organization.[23]

The informality of play contributed to the rapid spread of baseball through the country before the Civil War because it allowed men to conduct the game in many ways, according to the number of available players or the condition of the field. In 1859, the game reached New Orleans, where seven teams played intraclub games abetted by strong support from the volunteer firemen. In the same year newspapers reported the operation of a baseball organization in St. Paul, which followed the lead of another Minnesota club founded two years earlier. The Eagles baseball club was organized in San Francisco in 1859.[24]

Contrary to these facts, the Civil War frequently has been credited with breaking down the geographic concentration of the game on the East Coast.[25] The military conflict, so the story goes, curtailed the games staged in the North, but players and spectators as Union soldiers or Confederate prisoners brought baseball into the South. There they knocked the ball around in bivouac during a campaign, behind the lines of a siege, in a training camp, or in a stockade to relieve the monotony of the war.

Undoubtedly, the soldiers provided a captive audience, but one spectator figure from a baseball game during the Civil War borders on the incredible. On Christmas Day, 1862, a team representing a regiment of New York volunteers and a hand-picked nine from other regiments met at Hilton Head, South Carolina, before "about 40,000 soldiers."[26] That could be considered an attendance record for a sports event in nineteenth-century America; however, the report seems to have come from a player, Abraham G. Mills, who in 1907 as president of the National League also chaired the committee that created the Abner Doubleday myth.

In reality the Civil War did hasten the emergence of baseball as a game that was played everywhere in the same way. The young men liked to throw, hit, and catch, and when they met on a field as strangers they needed a standard game so that they could enjoy a contest without prolonged arguments. Whether bored by army life, ordered by officers to attend games, or fascinated by baseball, soldier spectators contributed to the emergence of a standard game because they needed to know not only what went on but also what to anticipate in order to enjoy themselves. Far from home, they watched strangers, and their interest centered more on the play as a whole than on an individual player in the field. When these captive audiences vanished with the end of the war, the systematic baseball reports in the sports press and the metropolitan newspapers sealed the uniform character of the game and contributed to the emergence of professional baseball as the great urban spectator sport.

The reports, tables, and statistics that the leading American sports journalists compiled in the 1860's and 1870's enabled thousands of spectators who flocked into the ball parks of the big cities after the Civil War to follow both teams and games methodically. An English immigrant, Henry Chadwick, saw himself in his old age as the "head gardener" who had raised the "now giant oak of the American game of baseball."[27] His didactic discourses in the New York *Clipper* expressed the fundamental rationality of the age, so often obscured by sentimentality. He considered it "important and necessary" to give "the full record of each season," and his readers' responses reinforced his view.[28] The accuracy of his scientifically oriented approach underpinned the emotional support given the game during the 1850's by William Trotter Porter in the New York *Spirit of the Times*. This editor, also credited with publishing the first box scores, had put emphasis on "inside" human interest stories and called baseball "our National Game."[29]

Chadwick's statistics became an integral part of baseball reporting, occasionally enlivened by the journalists of the metropolitan press with human interest features. In the 1870's, game statistics and baseball gossip were the mainstay of the Philadelphia *Sporting Life* and of the St. Louis *Sporting News*. However, from 1877 on, the proverbial man on the street received much of his information about the game from the New York *National Police Gazette*. This periodical, with its sweeping coverage of sensations of many varieties, reached masses of readers on a national scale. It enhanced its circulation enormously by offering reduced subscription rates to hotels, barbershops, and saloons.[30]

The writings of Henry Chadwick and his colleagues ball an identity and helped popularize game and p'

upheld faith in baseball as a noble and clean game when the fans'
enthusiasm lagged in the face of reports about fixed games, gambling scandals, warring leagues, and protracted infighting between
owners and players for shares in the new sports bonanza.[31] The
sports writers' work also helped sell the idea of a sports page to the
editors of the metropolitan press. "Regardless of what the present
generation of baseball reporters is doing to promote the welfare or
add to the box office receipts of the club owners," a well-known
baseball writer argued in the 1920's, "the sport owes its popularity
and probably its continued existence to earlier generations of
scribes."[32] Their stories prepared the ground for the flowering of
baseball journalism in Chicago in the 1880's which produced a new
style of sports reporting by weaving wit and satire into the stories.

Before the emergence of the Chicago style of baseball reporting,
accounts of games frequently read like market reports, with little
of the game's excitement emerging from the sober lines. Much of
the success of the first baseball writers rested on the novelty of the
ball park experience, still fresh in the spectators' minds when they
saw the box scores. However, after this appeal wore off, only true
fans found that journalistic fare palatable. Ordinary newspaper
readers not especially interested in the game initially looked for
something more readable and entertaining. This apathy vanished
when the language of the popular Chicago papers, unconventional
and vibrant, appeared in inspired baseball stories that intrigued
and informed.

In the 1880's, Chicago reporters expressing the raw energies of
the wildly growing city added slang and frivolity, metaphor and
simile to baseball reports and turned them into news that at times
qualified as lead stories. In 1913, the Charleston *News and Courier*
called the resulting style "a distinctive and peculiar tongue, . . .
not English, . . . not precisely slang, . . . full of idiomatic eccen-
tricities, rich in catch-phrases and technical terms, wonderfully
expressive and in the highest degree flexible."[33] This novel approach gave such a remarkable importance to baseball that in the
same year the *Nation* slyly wondered why the baseball language

"should so far outdo the feats of the players whom it glorifies."[34] It also affected general reporting.

In 1896 a Chicago newspaper editor sent one of his baseball reporters to help cover the Democratic National Convention and to write a follow-up on the reception of William Jennings Bryan's "Cross of Gold" speech. The language of the sportswriter's story on the front page of the Chicago *Daily News* on July 9, 1896, documents one aspect of the impact of baseball on modern city culture. It enlivened what had been the rather staid and dull form of political reporting in an attempt to describe the "almost indescribable":

## HOW BRYAN SWAYED THE CROWD.

### SCENE AFTER HIS REMARKABLE ORATION WAS ALMOST INDESCRIBABLE.

When Bryan's words: "You shall not crucify mankind upon the cross of gold" rang out over the throng there was a pause, a break of the smallest fraction of a second. The orator turned and made ready to leave the stand.

Then from the rearmost wall to the speaker's stand, from end to end of the gigantic hall, came like one great burst of artillery the answer of the convention: "You shall not crucify mankind upon the cross of gold." Roar upon roar, crash upon crash of fierce, delirious applause.

The people, men and women, were upon their chairs, their hats were in the air, their handkerchiefs tossing like whitecaps on the winter sea. Flags were flying, waving, streaming; the broad stripes of old glory were intermixed with the banners of states and territories and the pennons of the candidates.

Far down in the rear of the hall a woman was on her chair waving her cloak, blue with red lining, and the alternate flashes of red and blue blazed more conspicuous than any other banner in the hall.

People sprung upon Bryan as he struggled toward his chair. They leaped at him like hungry wolves and hugged him and crushed him in their strong arms. Old men, white with age and with the frenzy of the hour, tottered to him to grasp his hand.

Young men stood on the seats and strove to strike approving hands upon his shoulders as he passed by. His progress to his seat was such as never any Roman coming home to triumph had—the orator was literally whirled off his feat and borne on by the struggling masses of frantic friends.

Then some one in a western delegation uprooted the blue guidon that marked the place of his colleagues. In a second twenty other guidons were twisted from their sockets, and the men who tore them free were crowding toward the spot, where Bryan, bewildered, half frightened, panting, yet proud and satisfied, was fighting off the caresses, the adoration of his myriad friends. Over the head of the Nebraska man the blue guidons were clustered. More and more the group grew in numbers every second.

As each blue guide post was added to the throng the crowd simply joined delirium to its previous frenzy. Round the hall, waving the guidons on high, marched the men of Florida, of Illinois, of Idaho.

Twenty other states followed and there would have been but one man before the public eye could a vote have been taken then. Presently, exhausted, the banner-bearers sought their places—Bryan sunk utterly wearied into his seat—the mightiest demonstration of many a convention year was over.

Most of the names of the journalists who forged the new style and formed the new order of baseball reporters are forgotten, but Peter Finley Dunne achieved an eminent place in American journalism as the creator of Mr. Dooley, the fount of big-city wisdom. By the time one writer compared the sound of a hard-hit grounder ripping toward the shortstop through the unmowed grass of the infield to "the hired man eating celery," the new trend had spread to other Midwest cities that quickly followed Chicago's lead.[35] By way of Cincinnati and St. Louis, Louisville and Pittsburgh, the Chicago style reached Boston, New York, Philadelphia, and Baltimore, where it came to be amalgamated with other journalistic innovations. Joseph Pulitzer's *World* had produced the first sports page in the 1880's, and William Randolph Hearst's interest "in stories of the great American game" led to the development of the modern sports section in his New York *Journal* in the 1890's.[36] Other journalists updated the publication time of baseball reports and made the afternoon instead of the morning paper the chief carrier of baseball news.

In general, improved reporting helped transform baseball from pastime to spectacle by making watching a spectacular victory more significant than actually playing a mediocre game. Gentlemen of leisure who had once played baseball now sought exercise and conviviality in other games. Growing numbers of spectators more than made up for the loss of this support and brought more teams that played to win onto the fields. Local rivalries intensified. When the best team from one city met its opposite from another, the match laid the groundwork for intersectional rivalries that culminated in the struggle for the national championship. They attracted a following deeply involved in the intensified drama of luck and skill, eager to see how the victor capitalized on both.

This increased exposure to spectators and to other teams raised the level of the game. As the contests produced exciting scenes and drew large crowds more regularly, the clubs caught on to the changing atmosphere of the game. They began charging admission and paying good players to devote their lives exclusively to baseball as the best way to maintain a winning team. In 1862, in Brooklyn, William H. Cammeyer built the first enclosed baseball field in the country, graded the diamond, erected a clubhouse, and charged admission. He viewed baseball as another business venture made possible by the modern city, but his dream of getting a monopoly on the game fizzled when teams built their own ball parks. It vanished totally in 1871 when New York shook off political boss William M. Tweed, whose patronage control over baseball-playing firemen had tied a New York club to Cammeyer's Brooklyn park. Cammeyer left his mark on the atmosphere of the ball park by playing at the beginning of a game a popular song, "The Star Spangled Banner," which in 1916 by presidential order became the official anthem of the United States. His practice of charging admission had been previewed four years earlier at a Long Island race course, where 1,500 spectators paid fifty cents each to see the first game of the 1858 championship series for the national baseball title.[37]

Commercialization and professionalization went hand in hand.

Young men quickly spotted baseball as a new road to fortune and fame. The growing demand for good baseball put a premium on good players and induced more and more clubs to offer gifts or money to attract them. The practice violated the Association rule against paying players, so that at times clubs used unrelated salaried jobs to attract athletes who were in effect being paid for playing baseball, thus evading the regulation. Rumors about a player getting money under the table circulated as early as 1860. Albert J. Reach, soon to star as infielder for the Philadelphia Athletics, is said to have played for a straight salary in 1863. In the following year, leading New York and Brooklyn clubs began playing for shares of the gate money of a Brooklyn field that usually charged ten cents admission. With amateurism on the way out, so-called rounders or revolvers among the players deserted their teams at the first sign of better conditions elsewhere.[38]

Baseball's changing scenario led to new roles and produced new standards. The president of a club, by sheer necessity, became its business manager and the playing captain became the manager of the team. With a man's athletic abilities now clearly of greater concern than his social position in 1868, the National Association of Base Ball Players terminated its futile struggle against the monetary practices that produced professional players. The group accepted a recommendation of its rules committee to recognize two distinct classes of players, amateurs and professionals, in an attempt to straighten out the confusing variety of players.[39]

Similar considerations motivated Henry Chadwick to champion an all-professional team. The New York *Clipper* writer realized that the game could survive as a big spectator sport only if played by professionals. In his preview of the 1868 season he stressed the professional status that distinguished the Cincinnati Red Stockings from the other good teams he discussed: the New York Mutuals, the Brooklyn Athletics, the Troy Haymakers, the Chicago White Stockings, the Philadelphia Athletics, and the Baltimore Marylands. He strongly supported the Cincinnati arrangement, which had each player under contract for the entire season at a negotiated rate of pay ranging from $800 to $1,400. In the ensuing campaign for professional teams, journalist and team complemented each other well. Chadwick's articles emphasized that playing baseball was a genuine profession, which served the public with entertainment. The Red Stockings, during a spectacular tour through the centers of American baseball in 1869, demonstrated that professionals played the best baseball by completing an undefeated season. The followers of more than a thousand active baseball clubs recognized the significance of this achievement.[40]

The fabulous success of the Red Stockings quickly determined the future of the game as a spectator sport in the modern city, but it took several years to find an appropriate structure to implement the change. A score of clubs, following the new hiring practices, put together strong teams and attracted audiences without devising a stable organization appropriate for big business. Ten teams founded a professional league in 1871 but kept most of the old arrangements, changing only what mattered most to them. They added "Professional" to the title of the disintegrating amateur organization and paid their players openly. However, they restored honesty to baseball in name only, because the game became an excuse for betting among players and spectators, and crooked play followed, as in every sport where betting took hold. "Old-time baseball men are chary, even to this day," a journalist explained in 1909, "of talking about the crooked deals which they witnessed in that time" because of "the wholesale slaughter of tainted players which occurred later."[41]

The new industry experienced dismal years, but open and definite professionalism also made the conduct of the game into something approaching a system. The momentum of money squelched the hopes of small-scale speculators who had dreamed of exploiting the new bonanza by luring players and spectators to their own teams. The big clubs built or took over ball parks and clubhouses and organized a game schedule that glorified inter-urban competition on a national basis. Carefully timed and rigorously enforced, a progression of home games against visiting teams and of road games on the home field of the opposition provided a sequence of contests between rivals strongly identified with particular cities. Methodically, all events led to determining a league champion.

General business trends indicated that gentlemen sportsmen sacrificing profits in return for public esteem were on the way out and underlined the significance of strict organization assuring a monopoly for the new economic venture. Although breach of contract and bribery, drinking and gambling tarnished the image of baseball, in Boston Harry Wright and other members of the disbanded Cincinnati super-team maintained discipline and won the Association championship for four consecutive years. In 1875, when the original clubs had shrunk to seven, the first major professional baseball league folded, but the presence of the professional players it had developed and the economic potential of professional baseball brought the National League into existence in the following year.[42]

The modern business structure of big-time American baseball grew around the organizational framework conceived in the 1870's. Attempts to break the monopoly of the National League gave rise to the American Association in 1882. Within two years the rivals were able to agree to end competition over cities and for players. The Association failed in 1890; however, ten years later, another major league formed—the American League. From 1900 on, big-time baseball operated within the context of two league championships, figuratively called the Pennants, and soon added a play-off series between the champions called the World Series.

From its start in 1876, the National League of Professional Baseball Clubs, to give it its full title, meant business. Its owners established themselves as masters of the game. William A. Hulbert, the first League president, engineered the developments. In contrast to some of the gentlemen players, political bosses, or gambling operators who had previously dabbled in managing baseball, he was a member of the Chicago Board of Trade who used his managerial experience to lay the foundation for another flourishing business. Hulbert was "a typical Chicago man" in the eyes of Albert G. Spalding, who pitched for him before becoming a successful manufacturer of sporting goods. As booster of his city, Hulbert "never spoke of what *he* would do, or what *his* club would do, but it was always what *Chicago* would do."[43] He set up an oligarchy of club owners who ran the game efficiently. With draconic measures he restored the surface honesty of the sport and the public confidence in its operation that seemed so essential for good business.[44]

The governmental and economic structure of baseball became autocratic, but the atmosphere of the ball park preserved the appearance of freedom. The public, fed up with corrupt practices, largely ignored the undemocratic features of the new regime, which, in turn, struggled to square the owners' business monopoly with democracy and even make baseball its symbol. "Possibly there is no corporate body . . . with which the public comes into closer . . . contact than this association," a lawyer pointed out in 1910, "and it possibly knows less of its inner nature and working machinery than of other bodies which . . . have their being away from the limelight."[45]

The establishment of the National League offered new economic opportunities for poor men who could play baseball well; but the clubs held the power, not the players, whose contracts tied them to the organization. Strict control of city franchises, which the old Association had given away for a song, guaranteed not only the clubs' monopoly over professional baseball but also their hold on professional players, who now came to depend on the League for their livelihood. "The idea was as old as the hills," Albert G. Spalding explained in his later years, but it had never been applied to baseball before. "Like every other form of business enterprise," he argued, "Base Ball depends for results on two interdependent divisions, the one to have absolute control and direction of the system, and the other to engage—always under the executive branch—in the actual work of production."[46]

In order to assure the success of the new industry in terms of attracting paying spectators, the first systematic organization of an

American spectator sport set out to refine the rules of baseball in such a way that the competition in the ball park would be of a nature to absorb the interest of large crowds. Skillful manipulation of the rules paid off. The "game has long since become an art," a Russian man of affairs living in the United States observed in 1895, "and committees meet constantly, now in one place, now in another, to adjust the details of the rules."[47]

Before these technical refinements—indeed, two decades before the last major rules changes of the 1890's—modern baseball was already drawing crowds of city dwellers because it spoke to them as a game that reflected aspects of their own lives. Thus the introduction of regulations into most phases of the contest affected not only the conduct of the game but also the atmosphere surrounding it. More and more spectators became convinced that the game fitted uniquely into their modern world. "Anything goes" was the message they eagerly distilled from the behavior on the baseball diamond because their familiarity with the rules of the game indicated to them that certain plays reflected actions they experienced daily in the modern city. The rules of the game seemed strict, but the etiquette governing the players' behavior seemed lax. The game's enormous success as the most popular spectator sport in the closing decades of the nineteenth century was based on this relationship between baseball and the larger society.

Any notion that gentlemen may once have had about the proper conduct of a ball player or the correct form of making a play vanished with the emergence of professionalism. The idea governing the related game of cricket—that some behavior on the field was "not cricket"—never took hold in professional baseball. Its players, Bruce Catton concluded in his reflections on the game, "have borrowed nothing from the 'sportsmanship' of more sedate countries; they believe that when you get into a fight you had better win, and the method by which you win does not matter very much."[48] As soon as the skills of the professionals turned the drama of sport into an exhibition, Lewis Mumford stressed in his assessment of mass sport, the rule became "Success at Any Price" instead of "Fair

Play."[49] The disappearance of a tacit understanding about the conduct of the game, as well as the necessity of basing a judgment call on an observation made in a fraction of a second, increased the interaction between player and umpire on the field.

The intense rivalry encouraged the player constantly to seek advantages by bending a rule or trying to get away with an infraction. "Boys, you've heard the new rules read," the captain of the New York Giants would say in beginning his annual talk at the opening of the season during the 1880's; "now the question is: what can we do to beat them?"[50] A generation seasoned by the Civil War began to assume that any behavior, however outrageous, was acceptable in baseball, too, and this feeling may have generated the metaphor that spoke of baseball as war. "Infractions are expected by the crowd, and hence by players, umpires and managers," explained Walter Camp, who almost singlehandedly shaped the rules of American football, in 1910. "In the long run, the people make the law," he added, unwittingly identifying the spectators' influence over the enforcement of the rules with the workings of rules committees eager to attract the largest crowds.[51]

For the people in the ball park, the umpire represented the voice of authority. To the spectators he was a convenient target for their frequent irritations and deep-seated frustrations both within and outside the ball park. The umpire became a personification of the rulers of their lives, who in the workaday world remained hidden behind the whirl of urban life, the faceless corporate structures, the anonymity of technocracy, and the mystery of public affairs. During the strife-ridden 1880's and 1890's, in their urge to identify and challenge a villain in the drama they lived, the crowds ignored any distinction between the rules committee of the league that had made the regulations and the umpire on the field calling a play.[52]

Thus the grandstand crowds had a field day in exploiting to their hearts' content the pressure put on the umpire. Over decades of changing styles of play he was called on to decide the legality of the tricky delivery (a new overhand pitching style), unusual batting tactics, fielding aberrations, and base-running maneuvers. What mattered was that all decisions allowed the spectators to challenge vehemently and vociferously the ruler, clearly identified from the 1880's on by his dark blue coat and cap.

On the surface the umpire appeared to exercise an authority like that of some other powers that regulated life. Like constables and clerks, he also lost his standing as a gentleman. Though he had once been specifically honored because refereeing evidenced his intimate knowledge of the game, the rise of baseball as a spectator sport had made him just another member of the cast of characters in the show—at times a villainous buffoon. Before the introduction of the double umpire system at the beginning of the twentieth century, the single man working behind either the pitcher or the catcher frequently cut a pathetic figure.

Definitely not omnipotent and hardly omnipresent, the umpire was abused or even mobbed on the field by spectators and players, and ridiculed or slandered in the sports papers as "the mortal enemy" of everyone, if "he does not especially favor the local club."[53] Among the many fatuous comments on umpire-baiting, few rivaled the explanation that rowdy fans were merely exercising their democratic right to protest tyranny. Any protection the league might have extended to the umpire, and he received none, would have interfered with his actual role. Shaping the game to maximize attendance was of utmost significance to the club owners, so that they tolerated the rowdy behavior of players, managers, and spectators as long as it enhanced the excitement of the game.[54]

This desire for an exciting spectacle eventually led to new rules speeding up the moments of spectacular action in the game and also to the introduction of protective equipment, because gloves and face masks allowed men to make without injury the rough, fast, and exciting plays of the game, in bursts of speed, that most people waited for. Speed occupied the spectators, who were constantly under pressure to match the hectic tempo of the modern city. The action in the ball park demonstrated to them that it was possible, after all, to keep up with the fleeting moment. The experience related to their world Shakespeare's line "The Spirit of the Time Shall Teach Me Speed," which the *Clipper* displayed under its title.[55]

If there had ever been a choice between cricket and baseball, the hustle and bustle of the American modern city turned the scales decisively in favor of the latter. One reminiscence about the 1850's commented, "Young America looked askance at a game that required a day and sometimes two days to play to a finish," because "such a waste of time" seemed "beyond all reason."[56] In 1854, a Scottish publisher encountered the tempo of life in the United States and concluded that "American minutes would seem almost to be worth an English day.[57] Christy Mathewson, an outstanding pitcher of the first decade of the twentieth century, expressed the logic of coupling baseball with speed when he said, "The American public wants its excitement rolled up in a package and handed out quickly."[58]

Although the players' concern for protection introduced gloves and catcher's masks into baseball, these innovations escaped being ridiculed as unmanly because the age worshipped the result they produced—memorable moments packed with action. Baseball had been played with bare hands until the glove began appearing in the early 1880's, supposedly after a shortstop had used a crude version to protect his hand. Other players followed his example when they noticed that he did not have to ease off catching the ball, could meet it solidly, and got his throw away faster than the other infielders. The spectators, who liked what they saw, supported the change, and sporting goods firms soon began furnishing gloves to professionals. A few years earlier, the first body shields had permitted the umpire to stand behind the catcher and enforce the strike and ball rules in a way that heightened the game's drama. The introduction of the mask and the fingerless glove with light padding on the palm in 1877 allowed the catcher to become the director of team action on the field, an effective way to coordinate the play.[59]

In addition to the protective devices, the change from the large six-ounce elastic ball to the hard regulation ball hastened the transformation of a pastime into a spectacle. An ironic twist of circumstances accompanied these developments. While the new equipment opened up baseball to everyone it also made the professional game the exclusive domain of specialists. Hundreds of agile, hard-throwing men who had not qualified for old-time baseball because they were not born with hands and arms for barehanded fielding replaced the so-called natural players. They did not have to worry about protecting their hands while catching the ball, and their swift plays quickened the pace of the game. New waves of players, each raising the standards of performance, quickly drove each other out of big-league baseball. They constantly advanced the quality of the game, heightened the level of competition, and increased the expectations of spectators until only a handful of big-league-caliber experts could participate.

Less became more early in professional baseball, but the enthusiastic spectators caught on quickly and watched more carefully. Gloves and masks contributed to the decline of the high scores that characterized mid-nineteenth century baseball by allowing steady improvement in pitching and fielding. This intensified a trend marked by revoking the old straight-arm delivery restriction which had forced pitchers to obtain speed only by an underhand throw or a wristy jerk of the ball. In 1900, Adrian C. ("Cap") Anson, after his retirement as manager and captain of the Chicago club, called the high scores of old-time baseball "performances impossible in these days of great speed and curve pitching."[60] In 1859, in the first inter-collegiate baseball game on record, Amherst beat Williams 73 to 32. When the celebrated Cincinnati Red Stockings ruled in 1869, they trounced an opponent 103 to 8, and that was only about half the largest number of runs ever scored in an old-style game. However, at the turn of the twentieth century big-league teams rarely scored more than 10 runs per game.[61]

By that time only sandlot baseball, with the help of the mitt and, from 1896 on, such literary embellishment of baseball virtues as the feats recorded in *Frank Merriwell* by Gilbert Patten, had acquired some of the free and open features that many people identified with the sport.[62] Boys and men tried to emulate the professionals on empty streets and vacant lots, in parks and on playgrounds. In big cities amateur clubs sometimes attracted more fans than the professionals. Eighty thousand people saw the game between the Telling Strollers and the Hanna Street Cleaners for the Cleveland championship of 1914. One year later, in the same natural amphitheater, more than 100,000 cheered the victory of the Cleveland Indians over the Omaha Luxus for the world amateur championship.[63] In 1917 Frederic L. Paxson saw the rise of sports in the United States as another "safety valve" replacing Frederick Jackson Turner's frontier. Baseball "succeeded as an organized spectator sport," he observed, but it contributed something neither racing nor boxing could "in turning the city lot into a playground and the small boy into an enthusiastic player."[64]

Street baseball, which could be played in a limited space and required no expensive equipment, advanced immensely the cause of play in an urban world.[65] In 1868, *Leslie's Illustrated Newspaper* reported on "playing Baseball Under Difficulties in the Streets of New York" and emphasized that boys "will play . . . in spite of all travel and obstruction."[66] A need for removing children's games from the streets went back to the beginnings of urbanization in North America; it had been felt in Boston in 1657.[67] But at the opening of the twentieth century, street baseball increased this concern and provided a major impetus in the spread of the play movement in the urban centers of the United States. "Only in the modern city," Jane Addams emphasized in 1909, "have men concluded that it is no longer necessary for the municipalities to provide for the insatiable desire for play." Only ten cities had supervised playgrounds prior to 1900.[68] However, the pressure of children playing sandlot baseball changed all that, and on the eve of America's entry into the first World War, that number had risen to 414 cities with 3,270 play centers.[69]

While street baseball reaffirmed the social importance of play in the city, professional baseball followed "the individualistic tendencies of America" that left leisure to commerce, giving everyone who could buy a ticket the choice of watching the kind of sport he or she liked best, without making an effort to persuade a group of people to agree on playing one specific game, as an urban reformer of the age commented.[70] It ignored any urge to participate in the play and, like urban politics, followed representational lines. Professional experts took places on the field which from time to time many men in the grandstands dreamed of occupying themselves. The exclusiveness of the diamond recalled the operation of an exclusive club. In 1885, the Philadelphia *Sporting Life* compared major-league baseball clubs to closed corporations and political machines run by an "inside ring" that reaped steadily growing profits by keeping outsiders away from the inner sanctum of the enterprise.[71]

On the professional diamond itself, the physical dangers of baseball also helped keep bat and ball in the hands of a limited group of players. In 1905, an editorial in the New York *Times* stressed that "the peaceful citizen would as soon think of standing to be shot at by a small calibre rifle as by one of these new-fangled ballistas of a pitcher."[72] Almost twenty years earlier a court had declined to protect a fan from other perils of baseball when it found that even on the grandstand he must take all risk of accident. In that 1887 damage suit, a justice of the New York Supreme Court had taken the sale of a ticket as evidence of a contract signifying merely "that a seat would be provided and a game of ball played."[73]

The hazards of the game opened up baseball to gifted players from major immigrant groups. In addition to the many athletes of English and Irish ancestry who had always been present in major-league baseball, American Indians, Frenchmen, Germans, Jews, Poles, Italians, and Latin Americans entered the game. At the turn of the century some of these players had risen beyond any narrow immigrant identity to become some of the great heroes of the sport. Big Ed Delahanty, Louis Francis "Chief" Sockalexis, Napoleon "Larry" Lajoie, and John Peter "Honus" Wagner represented

these giants of the game.[74] However, black players remained
barred from major-league teams, perpetuating the discrimination
officially introduced in 1867 when the rules of the National Association of Base Ball Players barred black players and black clubs
from membership.[75] In this respect, too, baseball mirrored life in
the modern city.

Most residents ignored the gap between the harsh realities of
professional baseball and the glib assertions of one of its magnates:
"The genius of our institutions is democratic; Base Ball is a democratic game."[76] Their experience often contradicted the American
creed, but the fans managed to live with these inconsistencies
because the modern city provided a greater degree of personal
freedom than most of them could have found elsewhere. They
embraced the potential of American democracy for improving the
quality of life, but were loath to consider the rights of others as
long as many of their own expectations went unfulfilled or others
seemed to be threatening their positions.

City people, at the turn of the century, considered the ball park
not as a testing ground for the egalitarian promises of their society
but as a source of diversion. As with their limited role in urban
politics, they were satisfied with being represented on the field by
their sports idols. Only a few followed the flight of fancy of a commentator who in 1914 considered baseball the only institution
"that has been wholly built by our people, democratic to the last
degree, and vibrant with that peculiar enthusiasm which all the
world recognizes as characteristically American."[77] Most of them
responded to the appeal of baseball by taking their places in the
grandstand, the bleachers, or on the turf at the margin of the field.

In the ball park they watched a spectacle that responded to their
concerns. The game enriched their dreary urban existence by providing a few leisure hours in the outdoors. In the warmth of the afternoon sun, the spectators transcended temporarily the physical
limitations urban life imposed upon them and experienced relief
from the tension of their complex surroundings. They saw plays
that reduced their bewildering struggle for success to a game of

one-thing-at-a-time and to the measurable progress of a successful athlete mastering one obstacle after another. They detected few gray areas in the ball park. The game presented immediate and clear-cut wins and losses and pitted good guys against bad guys.

During a few hours in the ball park, city people saw plays that they could remember afterwards because of the way specific events built up to a memorable moment—the sudden skillful triumph over an adversary. By making intense competition against an opponent its essential feature, baseball seemed to legitimize and extoll each spectator's daily struggle for success. Watching the rivalry on the diamond introduced standards of competition into the spectators' lives. The game also reduced their daily tensions because its ups and downs seemed more momentous than their own lives.

The spectators learned to appreciate baseball's demonstrations of efficiency and excellence—qualities many of them took as keys to success in industrial America. They followed the dynamic between individual competition and cooperative triumph. Their involvement in the lessons of the diamond thrived on an appreciation of a faster throw, a better catch, or a longer hit. One of the classic attempts at the close of the nineteenth century to improve the working habits of laborers and the performance of industry was also inspired by the struggle for perfection on the baseball diamond. Frederick W. Taylor, who came to personify the search for a reasonable estimate of the production capacity of man and machine, as a boy playing baseball regularly impressed his friends, one of them recalled, with the necessity "that the rectangle of our rounders' court should be scientifically accurate."[78] Ultimately the way the distances between the bases and the position of the pitcher's mound came to be arranged in the ball park reflected the triumph of the search for the balance between the possible and the impossible play.

Rounders "made scientific," the *Encyclopedia of Sport* called baseball in the 1890's, and that property fascinated enthusiasts who saw in the game a manifestation of the problems of their lives of chance in what otherwise seemed a predictable age of technology.[79] Paradoxically, the outcome of the contest on the field became more uncertain the more scientific the game itself appeared to become. A timely base hit or an untimely error could now tip the scale, while in the days of the slugging batters of old the better team, more often than not, had won on its overwhelming superiority in batting and scoring. The sophisticated nuances of play were obviously lacking when a team won by twenty, thirty or fifty runs.[80]

The fans loved the order and efficiency of professional baseball, from the meticulous arrangement of the field to the critical moments of a play when split seconds counted. Life and work in the modern city had awakened them to an appreciation for economy of motion. They marveled at the reduction of a play on the field to a few swift movements and the perfection embodied in the flawless execution that decided a contest. "In baseball," Mark Twain noted in the 1880's, "you've got to do everything just right, or you don't get there."[81]

A generation exposed to the worship of perfection outside the ball park quickly accepted baseball as "the most perfect thing in America." This sharing of excellence demonstrated on the field converted the enjoyment of a diversion into an education and a conditioning agent. "Even to those who simply sit on the stands and watch," a rather condescending propagandist of the sport wrote in 1911, "there comes the inspiration that follows a thing well done."[82] In the ball park, momentarily removed from their struggle for a decent existence in the modern city, fans also learned to appreciate the game's examples of fairness and decency.

The spectators recognized baseball as their game. It appealed to their high-strung, eager temperaments. "Wearisome monotony . . . is utterly unknown in Base Ball," the leading English sports journal stressed on the occasion of an American All-Star team's visit to Great Britain in 1874, "as the attention is concentrated for but a short time, and not allowed to succumb to undue pressure of prolonged suspense."[83]

Mark Twain, in a "Welcome Home" speech to a team returning from a world tour in 1889, hailed baseball as "the very symbol, the outward and visible expression, of the drive and push and rush and struggle of the raging, tearing, booming nineteenth century." He went on to use baseball as a sign to delineate the "modern world," describing the game as a new, visible equator separating the part that mattered from the remainder of the globe where men did not steal "bases on their bellies."[84] The title "world champion," given to the most successful big-league team, confirmed this new geography. It came to designate the winner of the first seven World Series, played between the champions of the National League and the Association in the 1880's. Later, the title was awarded the victor in the annual World Series between the champions of the National League and the American League—established in the first decade of the twentieth century.

Basic to baseball's attraction was man's fascination with throwing and catching a ball. That predilection helped turn boys into enthusiastic players until they "began slowly to grasp the humiliating fact"—experienced by H. L. Mencken in the 1890's—that they were not "earmarked for a career of glory on the diamond."[85]

With the great expanse of greenery that it required, baseball also appeared to bring the countryside into the metropolis. It radiated the wholesome air of a timeless country sport which, each spring, cleansed anew the foul atmosphere of the modern city. From the 1880's on, a new feature of the baseball year strengthened the effect of conjuring up a bit of countryside. Big-league teams began to go into rural isolation, preferably a fashionable resort in the South, to get over the effects of a winter of loafing with "the hardest five weeks' grind in the world," thus seeming to extend baseball's links with country life and sunshine.[86] Big-time baseball now returned every year to the country, whence many enthusiasts assumed it had come, to recharge its energy.

Baseball's manipulation of reality extended to man-made time, too. Although its spectacular plays were the epitome of swift motion and speedy action, baseball rose above any ordinary concern for an economy of time. If the score was tied after nine innings, the game continued as long as it took to achieve victory. While mechanical time prevailed almost everywhere in the modern city, with the factory whistle and the time clock regulating laborers in factories and clerks in stores, natural time regulated baseball. Only nature itself, requiring postponement on account of rain or termination of play after sundown, could interfere with the course of play.

The game's close ties with nature were used to underscore its virtue. In order to make sure that the tangible blessings of baseball were recognized, apologists extolled those of its features that filled the needs of city people. Untouched by logic or evidence, they stressed that getting out into the fresh air of the ball park promised to open men's eyes to their "business interests" and to protect boys from "immoral association."[87] Despite news stories about dishonest games, umpire baiting, rowdy behavior on and off the field, and shady business deals, the importance of baseball as an inspiration for moral and upright behavior was rarely contested. Nothing was allowed to shatter the mystique of the popular game: upright young men fighting to excell on a green field under a clear sky in the big city. Clergymen of all denominations seemed to agree on the value of the game, and testified to their faith in baseball or used baseball as a testimony of their faith.

Cardinal Gibbons of Baltimore did the former; the Presbyterian minister William Ashley Sunday the latter. Although the Cardinal, by his own admission, knew little about baseball, in 1896 he stressed that he had never heard of baseball games being "used as vehicles for gambling," and for him that fact alone raised baseball "above the level of the average sporting event."[88] He might have understood men's weaknesses well or the general level of sports might have been low, but during the same decade the Orioles of his Baltimore achieved notoriety for winning three consecutive pennants by getting away with "much of their brow-beating and hooliganism."[89]

Evangelist "Billy" Sunday, in 1904, began weaving into his

meetings a story of how prayer saved a game when he played outfield for the Chicago White Stockings. He recalled that he had
chased the crucial hit through the crowd and over the benches at
the edge of the field. Praying all the way, he suddenly threw out
his hand, and the ball struck and stuck in the glove. While Sunday
was still reflecting on his "first great lesson in prayer," a spectator
slipped him a ten-dollar bill with the words: "Buy a new hat, Bill.
That catch won me $1,500."[90]

The increasing numbers of visitors to the ball park attested to
the attractions of baseball. In the 1870's, with encouragement by
reporters who frequently found public interest greater than they
had anticipated, attendance ranged from 800 to 1,500 spectators
per league game. In the following decade, the capacity of new ball
parks which many owners built with the profits of the prosperous
1880's reflected the increase in spectators.

Baltimore's park, constructed in 1883, had seats for 5,000 people, as did the new, well-enclosed grandstand in Buffalo. From
Chicago *Leslie's Illustrated* reported that "lovers of the sport
poured in from all the adjacent cities" to see the concluding series
of games between the Chicago White Stockings and the New York
Giants in 1885, "and from ten to twelve thousand spectators witnessed each game."[91] Chicago had the model field of the 1880's,
with space for 10,000 spectators, divided into 2,000 grandstand
seats, 6,000 open seats, and standing room.

The crowds of the 1890's came close to exhausting the technical
capacity of wooden stands and created a demand for bigger and
more substantial grandstands that stimulated the introduction of
brick-and-steel structures in the first decade of the twentieth century. Brooklyn and Chicago built ball parks in the 1890's that
seated more than 10,000 people. In 1896, the new Philadelphia
stadium, "the best athletic ground in the world," furnished 16,000
visitors with seats and 5,000 with standing room.[92]

Despite the setting, constantly more comfortable and lavish, the
athletic contest itself remained the major attraction. The enthusiasm of the fans crowding the Boston ball park, considered the

smallest of the 1890's by most observers of major-league baseball, seemed to support a lesson one of the club owners had learned from keeping both eyes on people's fascination with the game itself in order to find out how to ensure the attendance figures he wanted. His "common sense" taught him that baseball was "conducted primarily to make money," and that he could risk charging even his players' wives full admission when so many people clamored to get into the park.[93]

In 1890, the president of the Baltimore Orioles had gone one step further when he discounted any relationship between the quality of play and attendance figures. He put his team into a minor league to avoid what he thought might become a costly salary dispute with players. People will "come out to Union Park to drink beer, dance and have picnics just the same," he argued, confident that baseball and ball park had captured the loyalty of the residents of the modern city.[94] In 1908, *Spalding's Official Base Ball Guide* attested to the game's ever-broadening appeal for the steadily increasing groups of immigrants in the modern city: "The wonderful growth of the public's interest in Base Ball during the last half decade has attracted many hundreds of thousands of people to the game to whom its history previous to the last four or five years is unknown, or at least hazy."[95]

In case enthusiasm faltered, many of the promotional stunts that big business cultivated to market its products helped to sustain the degree of loyalty that baseball magnates considered essential for financial success. Signboards, streetcar posters, handbills, balloons, and newspaper advertisements informed the fans about the game schedule for the season. Inside the park, the music of a brass band often set the tone for the afternoon's enjoyment. Bars and tables offered beer and refreshments, and in the stands vendors sold chewing gum, peanuts, tobacco, pies, sandwiches, and soda water.

Children's Day and Ladies' Day, and an Amateur Day, which admitted ballplayers free if they appeared in the uniform of their clubs, represented variations of stunts that sold baseball as a bargain. This approach triumphed in the double-headers that clubs began staging in the 1880's. Sideshows, from Buffalo Bill to bicycle races, added thrills to the spectacle of the regular game, and owners kept squeezing in so many extras that the league prohibited changing the starting time of a game by more than one hour.

In addition to the anticipation of a good game, the enjoyment of the open air, and the lure of advertising, the ball park attracted residents of the modern city who watched the game as another step in the daily process of becoming Americans. As immigrants, they surrendered to the aura of the national game, which seemed to them indeed a "true expression of the American spirit."[96] Although some of them came from countries famous for national games, the memories of this faded in the new environment as had awareness of the debt that American sports owed in particular to Great Britain.

From the beginnings of English settlement in North America, colonists had played homeland sports, and "practically every phase of sporting life in America was tinged with English influence."[97] Later on, as the industrially most advanced country in the early nineteenth century, Great Britain pioneered the organization and staging of sports spectaculars; its influence refined the play of the young nation. Ideas about sportsmanship and rules made their way across the Atlantic with English, Scottish, and Irish immigrants whose attitude toward enjoying sports and teaching games helped to reduce prejudice against organized play and spectator sports.

Many other immigrants carried with them only a rather limited sports heritage because they had never experienced the opportunity to learn or the leisure to play a sport. In the United States, work and not play was their lot, too, and they were approaching an age at which their generation thought it senseless actually to take up playing a new game. Not schooled enough in English to follow a stage play or to read a book, they were natural sports spectators, bound to the ball park by forces similar to those that drew them to the metropolitan press.

The immigrants' age and poverty marked them as the chief supporters of spectator sports. When only privileged youngsters had the time to play sandlot baseball (evoking, as a German visitor noticed, the envy of children working in mills and factories), poor men automatically belonged in the stands where they could share temporarily at least one feature of leisure in the modern city.[98] This common experience forged a bond between diverse groups of people, and watching baseball took precedence over ethnic games because rooting for a big-city team also gave rootless people a sense of belonging. It also helped them acquire a better understanding of their new world.

In the ball park, exposure to the rules of the national game educated immigrants as Americans. Familiarity with the regulations, easily acquired for a game that had eliminated the gentleman's understanding as the basis for assessing the validity of a play, bestowed a certain brand of citizenship upon the spectators. Just knowing the difference between what did happen on the field and what could have happened permitted immigrants to become involved in the American game. The ball park furnished a sphere of public life where they could avoid rejection and loss of face because of misunderstanding or ignorance. Soon their growing knowledge of the subtleties of the game made them eligible to join the turbulent democracy of protesters who noisily expressed their dissent from the umpire's decision.

The spectacle of the ball park clarified some of the newcomers' confusion about control and authority in their new world. They had left behind countries governed by explicit rules and implicit prerogatives, and now were ignorant of the underlying rationale of the precepts and restrictions which shaped the free-for-all of the modern city. As yet, they did not understand the application of the democratic maxims protecting the humanity of many people that increasingly guided behavior in the marketplace and the job market, or etiquette in the department store and on the avenue. Bewildered, they faced a maze of individual and social practices that blunted the operation of regulations and obscured the exercise of authority. As a result they saw themselves, and others, handicapped by their ignorance of the canons of conduct that governed the race for riches. When they recognized how ballplayers used rules to win and how the umpire applied the rules to keep competition within certain bounds, immigrants also began to see how webs of control affected the American modern city.

The practical lessons of the ball park spoke directly about most spectators' basic concern: getting ahead in their urban world. The exciting plays seemed to end all too soon, having barely demonstrated late-nineteenth-century morality in action, but the spectators carried home with them the message of the ball park in the form of the players' statistics. The measure of success was plain. The most runs determined the winner of a game; in the table of team standings, the number of games won and lost separated the less successful clubs from the champion of the moment. In the context of averages spanning several seasons, the achievements of players and teams created a shared historical experience among people without a common history. Such plain statistics appealed to the American passion for counting as a way of mastering reality.[99]

People eagerly absorbed game statistics and scores, conveniently reduced to a formula that fitted the routine of urban communication. Their interest gave them an excuse, particularly if the home team was on the road, to slip away from work in the late afternoon to glimpse the score in a saloon. There a telegraph operator throning on a balcony above the bar chalked the details of the innings on a blackboard. For throngs of people downtown, unable to get to the ball park or sneak into a bar, the pointers and counters of a giant scoreboard on the facade of a landmark provided contact with the progress of the innings. These special message systems in the heart of the urban world further fostered the impression that there was a relationship between competition on the diamond and in the modern city.[100]

More often than not, the immediacy of a trip to the ball park tied people, city life, and baseball together. Ball parks came to be located along the routes of streetcar lines, in easy reach of large numbers of spectators, who learned to vist them rather casually, as a matter of course. Hard-nosed speculators assessed transit franchises and real estate values, which influenced the selection of sites.[101] Eager to accommodate changing needs, they rapidly built wooden structures; at times they were also inspired by the prospect for the sale of beer. "Young man, if you can get the City Council to give you a six months' license to sell beer . . . , I will build you a ball park," one of them with obvious interests promised a manager in the 1890's.[102]

On other occasions, baseball men took over fields, such as the New York Polo Grounds, originally used for sports too exclusive for city people. They laid out the diamond, put up wooden stands, and were in business. At times the grandstands burned down as quickly as they were built. But new ones rose in a hurry, and the many projects that were built made it possible to test the usefulness of various sites until a ball park came to be fixed in the setting that offered the best location for nourishing the local roots of a "worldwide" spectacle.[103]

The characteristics of each ball park depended on many circumstances, ranging from the spectators' willingness to tolerate local characters like Zane Grey's "Old Well-Well," whose roared approval identified spectacular plays and also earned him his nickname, to a given neighborhood's distinctive atmosphere.[104] In 1885, Chicago's new West Side Park featured a covered entrance for gentlemen going by carriage to the grandstand. In April 1909, in addition to the 35,000 spectators who crowded on opening day into Shibe Park in Philadelphia, the first concrete and steel ballpark, several thousand people inaugurated a special feature of the setting by buying space on the adjacent rooftops of the rowhouses of Twentieth Street that skirted the right-field wall.

The surrounding real estate occasionally determined the size of the outfield, which could differ from park to park, changing the conditions of play. Irrespective of the lay of the land, the ball parks blended into that incongruous harmony of contrasts which characterized the modern city. The street entrances of the classic parks that rose at the beginning of the twentieth such as Shibe Park and Fenway Park, Forbes Field and Ebbets Field, resembled the facades of downtown offices, department stores, or apartment houses.[105]

Despite various shapes and appearances, all ball parks conjured up ideas of leisure. "As an amusement enterprise," a ballplayer and a journalist argued in 1910, "baseball today is scarcely second to the theater," catering "to millions of spectators" and representing "an investment of perhaps $100,000,000 in property and players."[106]

Nature itself seemed to be in league with baseball to assure a successful spectacle. The opening of the baseball season in the spring marked the return of sunny days that could be enjoyed in the open. On the field young men signaled the triumph of youth by succeeding in fierce competiton. The green grass enlivened the monotony of the surrounding world of brick and stone. The carefree atmosphere, charged with the heady air of the modern city, increased the spectators' appetite for self-indulgence as they consumed beer and soda, hot dogs, peanuts, and Cracker Jacks, which had become culinary marks of mass leisure by the turn of the century. The ambience of the ball park enthralled the spectators, letting them forget everyday life forever—as suggested by one tune that became immediately popular when it was first heard in 1906—and turning the sharp edges of competition into an enjoyable spectacle.

Baseball offered a lesson in modern living in an imitation of a pastoral setting. Its features of intense rivalry as well as a limited amount of sportsmanship, general enthusiasm as well as rabid partisanship oriented crowds of people toward an acceptance of competition as a part of daily life, an awareness of a distinct urban vitality, and an appreciation for recreation. Spectators packing grandstands and bleachers intensified the pressure on factories and stores for a half-holiday once a week, lightening the routine of living and working.[107] Seeing others play ball for a living encouraged them to play sandlot baseball or to take up other sports. In the 1890's, the *Nation* called the growing interest in sports "the athletic craze" and likened its intensity to preceding crazes involving greenbacks, silver, and grangers.[108]

The magnetism of the ball park pulled together crowds of strangers who succumbed to a startlingly intense sensation of community created by the shared experience of watching a baseball game. One outsider, who unexpectedly came across this phenomenon during a study of the worldwide power of sport, saw this momentary unity as a religious bond. Visiting Chicago in the 1920's, this publicist of German sports, who later did his share to make the 1936 Berlin Olympic Games a communal spectacle serving an ideology, detected the links forged by the ball park even in the seventh-inning stretch: "All the spectators rise solemnly as if in church."[109]

The feeling of community that the ball park could evoke among crowds of city people struck a young Harvard graduate writing a newspaper column for a college pal in the late 1880's as incongruous with the diversity of the modern city. Ernest Lawrence Thayer set his baseball ballad, "Casey at the Bat," in Mudville, a rural heaven of shared sentiments. His lines about the luckless batter appeared in the Sunday edition of the San Francisco *Examiner*, next to the column of the avowed cynic Ambrose Bierce.[110] Together with "Casey's Revenge," which followed several weeks later, it might have been lost with the weekend, had it not found a stage larger than the ball park.

A few weeks later, a young vaudeville performer recited the poem, fortuitously clipped by a friend, as entr'acte in a comic opera at the baseball night of a New York theater, when he had to acknowledge the presence among the spectators of members of the New York Giants and the Chicago White Stockings. The audience "shouted its glee," De Wolf Hopper recalled, because it "had expected, as any one does on hearing 'Casey' for the first time, that the mighty batsman would slam the ball out of the lot."[111] With "Casey," baseball reached the stage of the popular theater that provided a setting where people could not only laugh about their own frustrated hopes and the shattered illusions of others but also learn to bridge some of the conflicts inherent in the modern city.

# VAUDEVILLE HOUSE

Their enthusiastic applause indicated that the thousands of spectators liked the variety bill presented in Boston's magnificent new
playhouse on Easter Monday, 1894. To assure that the significance
of the occasion would not be lost, however, a vaudeville actress
recited a long dedicatory poem commemorating the opening of
Keith's New Boston Theater. She lauded the throngs of men,
women, and children who crowded the house that day from eleven
in the morning until nearly eleven at night. "All are equals here,"
she told the audience; the theater knew "no favorites, no class."
Exhorting the spectators to enjoy the show, "ever to keep in view
things of the present—ever seek the new," she promised happiness "in that spice of life, Variety," with its motto, "ever to
please—and never to offend." The exciting performance and the
fabulous setting effectively supported her final claim about the new
theater, which she considered unequaled; "in Greece, in Rome, or
all the world around, no dome like this was ever to be found."[1]

The palatial theater, situated in the heart of Boston's shopping
district on Washington Street between another theater and a
famous hotel, represented vaudeville's symbiosis with the modern
city. A few weeks before its dedication, Henry Irving had called
the new building "superior so far as architectural effects go to any
in Europe." The enthusiastic reception of his Boston performances, which also included a lecture at Harvard on individuality,
no doubt influenced the verdict of the great English actor who, a

year later, became the first actor to be knighted. However, his judgment also expressed the instinctive response of thousands to the "combination of . . . Romanesque architecture [and] Louis XV decorations."[2]

The awed spectators moved from stately foyers into grandiose lobbies decorated with shimmering mirrors and ornate panels that purged them of the mundane activity of the street. They proceeded through three broad archways into the great auditorium, with its two galleries and scores of private boxes. A monumental proscenium arch with three "heroic paintings of draped female figures" symbolizing Comedy, Music, and Dance and a richly decorated ceiling displaying a "unique electrolier" with "one hundred and eighty incandescent lamps" helped set the mood for the 3,600 spectators settled in their luxuriously upholstered chairs.[3]

The variety show performers gliding over the boards of the stage on that Easter Monday heightened the impact of the setting. Alice Shaw, a whistling soloist "known on two continents as 'La Belle Siffleuse,'" gave way to "Mullenbach's troupe of Arab gymnasts." Club juggler Morris Cronin preceded a "truly mysterious act of thought transference" by Guibal and Greville. Les Frères Crescendos, "the queer French musical electriques," and Munroe and Mack, "the black-face comedians," ushered in Tom and Hattie Nawn's picture of "life in an Irish household." The "character vocalist" Lydia Yeamans Titus, with Fred J. Titus at the piano, provided popular songs.[4] All the acts blended with the gorgeous setting into one rare impression of delight. Instead of dwelling on the incongruous contrasts provided by whistling, acrobatics, singing, hocus-pocus, and comedy all appearing in what their generation regarded as a gem of architecture, the enthusiastic spectators happily recognized the variety show and the theater as integral parts of one unified experience—the vaudeville house.[5]

In the vaudeville house, a distinctly urban form of popular theatrical entertainment drew the residents of the modern city together and gave them a glimpse of themselves. The show dramatized the

spectrum of humanity in the city and the diversity of urban life
through its subject matter and variety. Consequently, it attracted
the entire range of city people and, after exposing them through
comedy and song to a diverse set of human problems, provided
them with a fleeting measure of harmony. During these hours the
audience also distilled models for everyday behavior and guides for
living in the modern city from the stage routines, the etiquette,
and the ambience of the vaudeville house.

The vaudeville house emerged as the source of amusement for
city people during the 1870's and 1880's. In his report of the grandiose opening of B. F. Keith's New Theater in Boston, built under
the supervision of Keith's associate E. F. Albee at a cost of
$600,000, a correspondent of the country's leading theatrical jour-
nal wryly recalled that "eleven years ago Mr. Keith started in the
amusement business in this city."[6] The laconic sentence fanned
fading memories of the small beginnings of the vaudeville magnate, who in 1883 opened his Washington Street Museum in a
store, displaying freaks and staging variety shows. It also emphasized the swiftness with which the vaudeville house had established itself in the modern city.

The success of Keith's vaudeville house rested on a solid foundation provided by two popular attractions: the theater, worshiped
by the residents of the modern city as a temple of culture; and the
variety show, whose diversity a heterogeneous people loved. The
adaptation of the theater building to the needs of a new form of
urban entertainment depended on money and technology, and
both resources became available as soon as entrepreneurs grasped
its business potential. The old-type variety show presented a problem of a different order. Its seedy setting and coarse content of-
fended those people who loathed the atmosphere of dives and
drunks, profanity and prostitutes, but cherished the array of comedy and song, acrobatics and dance. From time to time waves of
urban reform had engulfed some of the vile features of variety
without sweeping them away, but when the modern city began
inching towards maturity it also began shedding some of the

cruder features of mass entertainment in general. With this
change, the variety show, too, took on an appearance that most
people considered respectable.

The transformation came through an interaction between the
vast anonymous forces shaping urban life in industrial America and
individual impresarios pioneering new ways to make themselves
and other people happy. Women's growing desire to share some of
the diversions that just a few years previously had seemed exclusively the prerogative of men and the determined curiosity of
youngsters to discover what delighted their parents combined as
an influence. Tony Pastor and F. F. Proctor, B. F. Keith and E. F.
Albee as entertainers and businessmen recognized the artistic and
economic possibilities of a new variety show in a changing context,
and they set out to explore and develop its potential.

Much of the change hung in the city air, in a manner of speaking. Enjoyment of leisure, which had always found expression
among all segments of the population in forms of recreation ranging from idleness to hard play, came to be recognized as legitimate
by some of the most respected spokesmen of the age. In the
1850's, Henry Ward Beecher explained to his New York City
newspaper readers the pleasures of daydreaming and the "industri-
ous laying down" he cultivated frequently on his farm while his
neighbors worked diligently.[7] Most people had to search for relaxation closer to home, and they found it, increasingly, in the vaudeville house. They were just ordinary folk who flocked eagerly to a
wholesome show. They came from almost every walk of life and
considered themselves far removed from the dissolute loafers and
insolent debauchees who, they assumed, had been the patrons of
the old variety hall.

If they had thought about it, the new vaudeville enthusiasts
might have realized that the comedy routines, gymnastic acts, and
sentimental songs represented a popular application of an approaching gospel of relaxation. Herbert Spencer, playing John the
Baptist for the new creed in a banquet address in New York in
1882, prophesized its coming, saying that "we have had somewhat

too much of the 'gospel of work.' "[8] Washington Gladden, considering popular amusements from his perspective as a leader of the Social Gospel Movement, identified variety entertainment as a positive urban institution, effectively presented by capable managers in a large and cheerful hall at low prices. If wisely managed, he stressed, it would prove to be "an agency more potent than many laws in the preservation of peace and the reformation of public morals."[9]

The wide appeal of clean variety carried the show from the beer hall to the vaudeville stage. Stripped of their offensive setting and content, the acts of the new variety increased their drawing power when they began illuminating the audience's own urban experience. Hand in hand with this feature went the accommodation of the program schedule to the tempo of modern city life and to the city's reservoir of potential customers. Soon variety shows played "continuously," generally twice a day, thriving on the patronage of women and children who took in the early show. It was when these groups could join other spectators as a matter of course to enjoy the show that the new form of urban popular entertainment took hold. In due course this sort of show received a fashionably French name, vaudeville, to indicate its newly acquired respectability and class, some promoters thought. Tony Pastor, however, saw no reason for a special term; he kept insisting that vaudeville was just clean variety and avoided the new label.[10]

Although this specific application of the word "vaudeville" was new in the 1880's, the term itself had been used in America for many years, with the pronunciation "vodeveal" betraying its French origin.[11] The fifteenth-century French had called certain satires "songs of the Vau-de-Vire," after a minstrel who lived in the valley (vau or val) of the Vire in Normandy. When some of these tunes reached Paris, they were sung on the streets like any other voix de ville, "city songs"," and at times that expression was also taken as a source of the word vaudeville. By the eighteenth century the songs had found their way into farces staged by troupes of actors who struggled against the monopoly of the Comédie-

Française in the Paris theater. Now they were called *Vau-de-Ville*, "valley of the city," an appropriate corruption of the place of origin, and the plays, initially announced as *comédies avec vaudeville*, ended up being labeled simply *vaudeville*.[12] Its origin in satire, its connection with city streets, and its theatrical illegitimacy all combined to add spice to the word.

In nineteenth-century America the piquant association stuck and the word referred to smart and racy one-act plays, delightfully simple and simply delightful productions as their popularity attested. In August 1837, Philip Hone saw two of these "vaudevilles" with his daughters in Niblo's Garden, the New York haven of light diversions and gay music, and called them "the most attractive amusement of the season."[13] Such shows evoked, for some, the magical flair of Parisian entertainment and were irresistible to impresarios and men-about-town in female company. The productions succeeded in conjuring up a suggestion of the air of the great city. This connotation of vaudeville grew stronger, and the word began referring to shows presenting big-city life and not merely to popular stage songs and plays in general, as in early nineteenth-century England.[14]

Variety acts lent themselves particularly well to portrayal of the many-faceted modern city, and they became connected with the word vaudeville. Homesick men in the urban islands of the rural ocean of the Far West were receptive to entertainment that evoked the splendor of urban ways they had encountered during their migrations. In 1850, the "French Vaudeville Company" delighted audiences in San Francisco and Sacramento.[15] The attraction of the urban life-style for young men and women chafing in the isolation of the countryside made small towns particularly responsive to traveling variety shows staged by so-called vaudeville companies.

In June, 1852, in Portage City, Wisconsin, J. L. Robinson advertised his tent show as "the oldest established vaudeville company in the United States." His entertainment promised to be "moral, novel, and mirthful." The company "embraces near twenty-five ladies and gentlemen," the announcement explained, "many of whom stand at the head of their respective professions as Performers, Vocalists, Musicians, and Dancers." Robinson stressed that he had "the best vaudeville company ever organized" using the word to describe a touring variety show about three decades before John W. Ransome, who is at times credited with the first such usage, and before the appearance of the "Vaudeville Theatre" in San Antonio in the early 1880's.[16]

A good, and that meant clean, variety program consisted of "ballads, minstrel acts, comic songs, gymnastics, jugglery, fancy dancing and short sketches," Michael B. Leavitt recalled in recounting his beginnings as a theater manager. He too claimed to have been the first to apply the word vaudeville to a variety show, in 1880. In the early 1860's, he had followed the lead of established Philadelphia impresarios who entertained country people with touring troupes that exposed these audiences for an evening to the ways of the big city.[17] The versatile shows also amused city people in a wide range of establishments, one of which advertised itself as a "Vaudeville Saloon" in Boston in 1840.[18] The shows' appeal grew steadily, and by the 1880's vaudeville dominated all other forms of theatrical entertainment in the modern city.[19]

The popularity of minstrel shows and dime museums declined as vaudeville rose, due to their inability to adapt to rapidly changing ways of life and to speak directly to urban interests and concerns. The minstrel show, usually a troupe of white comedians made up as black men presenting songs, dances, jokes, and farces, experienced its heyday between 1850 and 1870, when American preoccupation with Negro slavery was at its peak. During the 1870's companies increased the number of performers, as well as their antics, in an attempt to compensate for the limited response they got from modern city audiences untouched by either the mystique of plantation life or the inhumanity of slavery.[20] In consequence, the minstrels killed that spontaneity of the early shows which might have attracted European immigrants searching for quick answers to the questions of their new urban world.

Similar weaknesses undermined the appeal of the dime museum. Like the minstrel show, it could not hold the attention of large urban crowds. City people were people on the make and they kept their eyes open for insights useful for their lives, as audiences have done since Thespis got his cart rolling. In the 1840's, P. T. Barnum's American Museum produced a few answers. It owed its success to halls of freaks and curiosities as well as a lecture hall where, in the words of the promoter, "instruction is blended with amusement."[21] However, over the decades, people's willingness to believe diminished, leaving the dime museum to depend increasingly on the appeal of its variety stage to bring in an audience. Divided between freak show and variety stage, the dime museum failed to sustain its popularity. It either abandoned the display of curiosities and turned into a variety house, or struggled along as a dime museum, a "sordid institution" ministering to "a public not renowned for sensitiveness."[22]

The shows of the riverboat and circus, enormously successful at mid-nineteenth century, matched the specialty acts of variety and the fantastic artificiality of minstrelsy. However, they failed to flourish in the modern city because they could not establish an urban base. In part, the changing technology of communication undercut the riverboat. The expanding railroad took people who sought stylish entertainment into the big cities, replacing the steamer as the mode of transportation and ending its role as a place of amusement. The circus train kept its menagerie rolling and became a mark of seasonal change. Soon the show had to be almost constantly on the road in order to compete effectively with other attractions, surprise one town after another, and move on as soon as the delight wore thin. Its three rings had some of "the last words in orchestrated splendor," but their diffused magnificence did not produce the "concentrated interest, attention, or pleasure" city people craved.[23]

No variation of the theater could stop the inroads of vaudeville into the modern city because the intellectual, social, and ethnic appeals of plays and operas violated its egalitarian creed. The masses of people remained unmoved by the classic repertoire of plays; nor did anyone consider them entitled to share the drama of social status staged by old and newly rich families in the boxes and on the parquet of big-city opera houses. Comedy, on the level attractive to the majority of residents, had the distinct ethnic identity of Edward Harrigan and Tony Hart's Mulligan Guard series. The easily recognizable urban milieu of these sketches, mostly Irish-American with touches of German and black elements, made them popular but also limited their appeal. Light opera, with its undercurrent of Central European sentimentality, suffered from similar limitations.

All these variants of the theater lacked sufficient versatility in form and content to attract large, broadly based audiences. From time to time they produced hybrids, new combinations of familiar artistic formulas, which created fleeting sensations. In 1866, the first successful American revue, *The Black Crook*, an "original magical and spectacular drama" in the words of its author, combined fabulous staging, enticing music, and an unaccustomed display of women in tights. This fashion had just been introduced by Adah Isaacs Menken in her tricot act on horseback in *Mazeppa* and by Lydia Thompson's troupe of English blondes. Charles Dickens considered *The Black Crook* "the most preposterous peg to hang ballets on that was ever seen. The people who act in it have not the slightest idea of what it is about, and never had." After taxing his intellect "to the utmost," he proclaimed the Black Crook "to be a malignant hunchback leagued with the powers of Darkness to separate two lovers, and . . . the Powers of Lightness coming (in no skirts whatever) to the rescue, he is defeated."[24]

In essence, *The Black Crook*, and similar extravaganzas, succeeded "mainly on the well-formed lower extremities of female humanity," in the view of George Templeton Strong. Despite this limitation, he considered the revue quite artistic, "in a meretricious sort of way," with its colorful decorations and changing lights.[25] Most city people reserved their strict opprobrium for the old-type variety show of concert saloons, burlesque houses, and beer halls. They identified these settings, called "free and easies," with dissolute men and lewd women, liquor, boxing matches, and prostitution. They suspected, quite correctly, that such company shaped the style of the song and dance, the content of the jokes and sketches, and the behavior on the stage and in the hall. Although women appeared as entertainers and waitresses, the show was for men only, for seasoned men who liked their entertainment raw.[26]

In spite of this, variety fascinated people because it pleased many different tastes. It inched toward respectability when saloons and gardens began to emphasize liquor and beer more and shows less. Its connection with burlesque ended, too, when burlesque moved away from the parody of plays and operas, and, with the decline of stock companies and "the coming of the English blondes," specialized in the display of the female body. Freed from the demands for spirits and flesh, the old-type variety show now began attracting a wide range of spectators.[27]

Variety retained variety as its strongest drawing card while appropriating features from other popular forms of entertainment. Its snappy specialty acts appealed strongly to urban audiences oriented to precision and concerned about performance. The mixture of various acts, or "olio," suited the diverse character of modern city life. The female performers foreshadowed the integration of women into the audience of the vaudeville house. To these variety elements the minstrel show contributed the classic vaudeville routine of the exchange between straight man and comedian, derived from the banter between the painstakingly adroit interlocutor and his two end men. It also provided blackface entertainment, which gave performers a dual identity and shielded them against being identified with their robust humor. Animal acts—trained dogs and seals expounding the irresistible lure of the big city by imitating human activities—and gymnasts extolling self-discipline and perfection as keys to success came from the circus.

Burlesque furnished hilarious plays shortened to sketches and farces reduced to pantomime. It also contributed the groups of dancers who furnished vaudeville with its *corps de ballet*.

The fusion of these elements created the general characteristics of vaudeville. Its bill went beyond a specific appeal to distinct groups or classes. It aimed at everyone in the modern city. The earlier forms of popular amusement had dealt primarily with specific aspects of American life or particular human predicaments. The images of blacks and plantations, frontiersmen and log cabins, as well as the fascination with the exotic and the love of animals had sustained many of them. But popular entertainment also included lewd jokes, the sale of cheap liquor, and the exposure of those parts of the female anatomy which most women kept covered. Vaudeville supplanted these time-honored features with distinctly modern attractions. Its urban orientation, scientific demonstrations, and general appeal to the mental attitudes of men and women eager to get ahead in life reflected most people's search for new activities appropriate to the modern city. In the amusement world, the vaudeville house was a phenomenon as novel as the modern city. It clearly belonged "to the era of the department store," as one observer of its emergence felt in 1899.[28]

Vaudeville appropriated the variety format, but eliminated the "coarse, slap-dash fun" considered "fit only for men, and men who were not over particular in their tastes at that" which had once been supplied in generous amounts by promoters "with whom refinement usually took second place when it came to . . . making a hit."[29] The wholesome vaudeville bill showed the influence of managers and impresarios whose censorship straightened out acts and kept them clean. "Vaudeville is censored as no other amusement field in America," one judgment read in 1910.[30] It also reflected the growing sophistication of modern city life, which increasingly admitted women and children to its amusements. Their presence supported an art form that may not have raised people's morality, but kept public immorality within bounds and away from stylish foreign influences pursued by the *haut monde* whose fashions, in turn, were imitated by students and clerks.

During the 1870's acceptance of the Parisian cancan, with high-kicking dancers momentarily exposing colorful garters and ruffled drawers, made the different nakedness of the first pair of hootchy-kootchy dancers seem an embarrassing affront. These dancers were stranded in Philadelphia when the Turkish Theatre, on the grounds of the Centennial Exposition of 1876, folded for lack of patronage.[31] Their shaking of body muscles, supposedly in Oriental style, appeared inappropriate in a cultural context that tolerated the Parisian dance. Having fallen on fertile ground, the cancan swept Broadway and thrived on official censure during the height of the 1874 Christmas season. It attracted large crowds of "young boys, clerks, and students, gathered from all quarters, to witness a disgusting exhibition . . . which was Parisian only in name."[32]

As a New York *Times* reporter had predicted, when the entire company was booked at the precinct house for creating a public nuisance, "not one of them was even of French extraction." However, most people knew the cancan to be of French origin and that seemed to justify its acceptance.[33] "When *The Black Crook* first presented its nude woman to the gaze of a crowded auditory," actress Olive Logan, who had turned from the stage to writing, reported in 1869, "men actually grew pale at the boldness of the thing," but "in view of the fact that these women were French ballet dancers after all, they were tolerated."[34]

Vaudeville, however, succeeded without resorting to its French connection. The show's combination of wholesomeness and urban sophistication, its "cheerful frivolity," one commentator felt in 1905, cast its respect for convention into a novel format, while still permitting "nothing that . . . would offend a strict morality."[35] Studied innocence shone brightly. At first glance, the presentation of the individual acts seemed to reflect the casual life of the modern city. In fact, the bill was meticulously planned, well balanced, and precisely executed. Its underlying structure built up to a well-defined climax, which the show reached without apparent effort. All encumbrances that clung to vaudeville as a result of its multiple heritage disappeared as impresarios learned to create an elegant bill. The afterpiece of the old variety, the final funny effort that had once brought all troupers together, fell by the wayside in the 1890's, not only because the performers loathed it but because the format of the vaudeville show, despite its individual acts, achieved a unity that made any belated group sketches superfluous.[36]

The tempo of the show, like that of the modern city, kept the audience spellbound. When the managers of vaudeville stumbled onto the concept of the "continuous show," they created a theatrical counterpart of the powerful rhythm of modern city life. One of the great advertising slogans of the closing years of the century drove home to New Yorkers vaudeville's claim to their total attention:

> AFTER BREAKFAST GO TO PROCTOR'S
> AFTER PROCTOR'S GO TO BED

F. F. Proctor had introduced the idea of the "continuous show" to New York in 1893, following the Boston lead of B. F. Keith and E. F. Albee, who had opened one of their new houses, the Bijou Theatre, with this innovation in 1885.[37] Keith, in later years, remembered the reluctance of the great comic Sam Bernard to follow the new format. "It's no use to go out there," the comedian argued with Keith in the wings, "they are all the same people and have been here for two hours now." But out he went again, "and that was the beginning of the second show of the 'continuous.' "[38]

Keith's motive was simple. He wanted to have an audience all the time. He knew that everyone left when the curtain came down and that "it was hard to get others in for the next performance," and so he began turning over his packaged attractions, again and again.[39] It meant staging successive shows, usually two, at times three, from a matinee at noon to an evening performance. In the course of the afternoon, the solitary piano player, who had started the program with his flourishes, gave way to an orchestra. If all went well managers faced the task of making room in the theater for waiting patrons who had not yet purchased tickets. For this purpose they wove so-called chasers into the bill at the end of each show, listless and boring acts intended to drive out of the house those visitors who seemed inclined to stay in their seats forever.

When the successful two-a-day format became standard vaudeville routine, several impresarios claimed to have invented it, but Keith and Albee's dime museum experience backed their claims to authorship. Both men had moved into vaudeville by staging variety and exhibiting freaks which people watched before and after the variety show. F. F. Proctor, the perceptive vaudevillian and shrewd innovator, himself suggested the analogy between this and vaudeville when he reminisced about his own experiments with the format.[40]

Other dime museum operators had in fact used the device of continuous shows before Keith and Albee. C. E. Kohl and George Middleton, who founded the first dime museum in Chicago in 1882, opened their Clark Street Museum in 1883, and "ran a variety show of about an hour's duration, which was repeated throughout the afternoon and evening." In 1884, they leased the Olympic Theatre and turned it into a continuous vaudeville house.[41] Exactly which managers were the "inventors" of the new variety format is immaterial, but it is significant that the concept of the continuous performance pointed the way to vaudeville's absolute rule over the residents of the modern city. That feat was accomplished by the standard nine-act bill.

The nine-act bill usually opened with a so-called "dumb act," a dancing routine, an animal group, or some other proven attention-getter that latecomers seeking seats could not ruin. This type of lead act reflected the old joke about the French theater manager who felt like beginning his plays with the second act because his house was invariably empty during the first.[42] A typical vaudeville act filled the number two position—at times a ventriloquist, more frequently a man and woman singing to settle the audience and ready it for the show. The following comedy sketch, holding "the audience every minute with a culminative effect that comes to its laughter-climax at the curtain," began the actual build-up of the show and had the audience excitedly anticipating what was to come. The fourth and fifth spots produced the "first big punch of the show," a "corker" in the argot of the trade, succeeded by a big dance act or a rousing musical number, both guaranteed successes that fully occupied the conversation of the spectators during the intermission.

The opening of the second half presented a unique problem. The sixth act had to restore the attitude of expectant delight and excitement, yet it had to stay at a level just below that of the subsequent routines. Comedy pantomime, jugglery, or magic often answered the need, while allowing the spectators to get back to their seats without unduly disrupting the house. Very likely a big playlet, the single problem of a story's chief character compressed into a single impression, hastened the show to its climax. That came with the grand comedy hit in the number eight spot, usually done by a great star for whom the audience had been waiting. A big "flash" closed the performance, such as the showy sight of a troupe of white-clad trapeze artists fying on a black background, capturing once more the attention of people anxious to leave after the big attraction and filling all spectators with the memory of a show that had been action-packed to the last moment.[43]

Repeated two or three times a day, the performances hardly seemed to differ. In the early 1910's, they provoked almost identical comments from reformers throughout the country who, in the absence of other objectionable features, concentrated on the intellectual level of vaudeville. "Its most striking characteristic is simply stupidity. . . . No person of moderate intelligence can attend a dozen vaudeville performances without being disgusted at their vapidity," a writer for the New York Child Welfare Committee declared.[44] The Drama Committee of the Twentieth Century Club regarded Boston vaudeville as a clean show, more often than not "inexcusably dull and mediocre," yet also presenting headliners "comparing favorably with many of the alleged stars appearing in productions at the regular theaters." The Commonwealth Club of California accepted vaudeville as a "substitute for amusements that do positive harm," but advocated limiting "its coarseness and vulgarity." [45]

In 1903, in one of the wittiest pieces of *Harper's* "Editor's Easy Chair," a visitor to the editorial sanctum elaborated on his wish "to elevate the vaudeville," until the editor guided him to the realization: "You mean to kill it." [46] Reformers could not undermine the popularity of vaudeville. Israel Zangwill found it far more probable that "the artlessness of the public and the artfulness of the managers will long keep the present pabulum unaltered, save in increasing staleness." [47] The two-a-day performances marked variety's conquest of the modern city, heralded by the establishment of a regular vaudeville department in the leading theatrical trade journal. [48] The rapacious demands of continuous performance ultimately had disastrous effects, when at times bills came to be repeated four or five times a day in the 1910's, draining the novelty of the acts, straining the originality of the show, and exhausting the performers, although these had originally seized the opportunity of additional work as one way to cope with the hardships caused by the depression of the early 1890's. [49]

Audiences generally liked the studied casualness of the "continuous," which softened the formality of the theater. People moved in and out of the house at their leisure, after they had learned to find their seats in the section of the auditorium that corresponded to the tickets they had purchased for fifty, thirty-five, or fifteen cents. The freedom of movement and the disappearance of reserved seats encouraged the same independent and egalitarian spirit that the modern city had fostered. Vaudeville's aggressive format, repeated each afternoon and evening, brought the momentum of the modern city from the sphere of work into that of amusement.

Only a special type of performer, the vaudeville artist, was suited to the unique format of the show. Its timing and tempo required, in a manner of speaking, that the trouper start with a sprint, condensing all his versatility into one act. In order to sustain the rhythm of the entire show, each performer needed emotional and physical reserves to increase the intensity of his routine so that the mounting momentum held the audience captive until the curtain rose for the next act. A vaudevillian needed the energy to create the magic that unified the separate acts like the continued vibration of a tone linking the breaks between the notes of a staccato phrase in a piece of music. In contrast to an ordinary actor or actress, the vaudeville performer had to generate the magnetism to attract a large audience, year after year, in a world of entertainment that knew no season.

Constantly pressured to meet these taxing tests, vaudevillians respectfully referred to accomplished professionals as "performers." Everyone on stage could be an artist, but "performer" applied only to "finished, resourceful, technically expert men and women." It was a plain word reflecting "the sobriety, orderliness, and dullness" of their private lives as a group, according to Hutchins Hapgood.[50] A New York *Times* reporter considered it a "great compliment, when a veteran refers to a younger artist as a performer, . . . always to be relied upon as a tower of strength and as able to meet any emergency."[51] At times instant failure, reflected in a stage manager's signal to walk off, exposed the strain of meeting these standards. In other cases, sudden stardom rewarded the performer for his extraordinary accomplishment.

Some famous vaudevillians used their success as an entree into the legitimate theater, the world of the full-evening play or musical. Vaudeville performers occupied an ambiguous position among other actors. They were of the stage, but their "companion players, the trained seals, the amusing monkey, the docile elephant," as one famous actor recalled of his excursion into vaudeville, seemed to place them on different boards—those covered with sawdust.[52] Jugglers and gymnasts may have considered themselves artists without applying the word to their profession, but the self-styled escape artists made certain that the billing of their acts told the audience where they belonged, and these identifications consequently carried little weight among real actors and actresses. The legitimate stage retained its aura and its magnetism.

Despite the enormous popularity of vaudeville, some of its brightest stars found the lure of the dramatic theater irresistible. From Lillian Russell, who in 1880 as Nellie Leonard got her start and quite literally her name while singing in the variety show at Tony Pastor's New Broadway Theatre, to the comedian Willie Howard, who in 1897 as a boy soprano of eleven sang refrains of hits in the balcony or from the wings of one of Proctor's New York theaters, a steady flow of talent went from the vaudeville house to other theaters.[53]

Celebrated stage stars, in turn, succumbed to the indiscriminate adulation of the vast vaudeville audiences and the enticing salaries offered by shrewd managers. A famous American singer told reporters that she did not mind "appearing between a cat circus and an aggregation of trained monkeys; since the animal artists are the best of their kind."[54] Some, like Sarah Bernhardt or Ethel Barrymore, may have just played on the crowd's fascination with a famous name. The regular variety bill accompanying their appearance consisted of first-class acts to provide entertainment as vaudeville audiences understood it, or the celebrities might insist on a garland of high-class troupers as the suitable frame for a grand dame of the theater. In any case, their passage behind the footlights of the vaudeville house, although understandably much discussed and described, taxed the variety show more than their presence added to it as mass entertainment.

The entrance of Eva Tanguay into vaudeville demonstrated the difference between a genuine vaudeville performer able to meet an audience on its level of expectation and a guest star requiring people to accept a special set of standards. As ruling queen of the musical comedy theater in 1906, she brought to the vaudeville house a "dynamic personality, all nerves and excitement." This attribute identified her as a true performer for an audience that never lost consciousness that Sarah Bernhardt or Ruth St. Denis were "exotics" and that demanded "a certain adjustment to its point of view," as Caroline Caffin in her classic vignettes on vaudeville explained in 1914. Eva Tanguay's ability to electrify a vaudeville audience depended not on a great voice or brilliant acting but on her ability to establish an immediate rapport with city people. Her voice had "no music in it," her dancing steps made "no attempt at rhythmic movement," but her vivacity seemed spontaneous. "It's all been done before, but not the way I do it," she sang, and her assurance looked so convincing, and her good humor sounded so frank, that they formed "foundation enough on which to raise a perfect sky-scraper of illusion."[55]

The gigantic skyscraper of make-believe erected by vaudeville stood on the realistic foundation of a modern business organization.[56] The economic development of vaudeville followed the general American trend toward the combination of enterprises as one answer to the task of distributing products profitably in a national market. Vaudeville managers circulated their shows by means of traveling companies, circuits of theaters, and booking offices. They followed the lead of the national theater business, which had emerged at mid-century in response to the rising star system. It made a "group of speculators . . . virtual dictators of all theatrical policies." It also turned the theaters into distribution centers for a well-advertised product—the star—and led to the disintegration of the stock companies that had relied on their own talents.[57] In vaudeville, Michael B. Leavitt, manager of a San Francisco theater, pioneered the idea of organizing a circuit of theaters between Omaha and San Francisco into a single booking unit, when he found that he could not get East Coast vaudeville shows because they lacked the mechanism to book themselves into theaters between New York and San Francisco—the most convenient way to pay their way west.[58]

The number of circuits increased rapidly in the 1880's, and in the following decade a network covered the country. They reinforced the tight discipline of staging and the smooth system of presenting vaudeville shows, but they stripped managers and performers of their economic and artistic independence. In place of the actor-manager or manager-businessman, powerful booking agents in a few key cities took charge, dictating the content of the bill, censoring the individual acts, and determining the salaries of the performers. Their activities controlled growth and competition because they sought only the best bills for their chains of theaters.

The struggle of agents for acts and theaters also produced the fabulous expansion of vaudeville at the turn of the century. In 1896, New York City counted seven vaudeville theaters; in 1910, it had thirty-one. During the same time span the count jumped from six to twenty-two in Chicago and from twelve to thirty in Philadelphia.[59] Outwardly, the vaudeville era peaked in 1913, with the opening of the Palace Theater in New York as *the* most prestigious vaudeville house and the temple of American show business. From then on, "playing the Palace" constituted the height of success in the minds of both performers and spectators.

While the momentum of vaudeville as the most popular form of entertainment created the illusion of a golden age of variety in the opening decades of the twentieth century, the same years also brought the stranglehold of oligopoly to the industry. Vaudeville as big business came to be controlled almost entirely by two booking offices—the United Booking Office in New York and the Western Vaudeville's Manager Association in Chicago. Modeled after the Theatrical Syndicate, which had established its virtual monopoly over the legitimate stage within seven years after its founding in 1896, these offices provoked and then quickly settled a strike of performers who had formed the White Rats Actors Union in 1900. The managers made just enough concessions to reduce the tension about booking schedules and salary arrangements that their operation produced, but they carefully kept their control of the vaudeville industry intact, and with that formula managed to weather subsequent difficulties.

The vaudeville czars shrewdly recognized their precarious position in a business where artists were both labor and product. During disputes they asserted their power by showing movies—in-

troduced into vaudeville bills under the name "cinematograph" by
B. F. Keith in 1896—but for the most part they relied on a policy
of appeasing the performers with minor concessions such as a company union. The threat of blacklisting was an ever-present deter-
rent to rebellious performers.[60] The final paragraph of a detailed
survey of the vaudeville field, conducted in response to a unani-
mous resolution by Equity's members in the early 1920's, summed
up the relationship: "On the cover of 'Vaudeville News' there appeared each week a picture of two clasped hands. One was labelled
'Manager,' the other 'Artist.' A true representation of the situation
would show the artist standing at attention with his hand at salute
receiving orders from his officer."[61]

Under the control of B. F. Keith and E. F. Albee there
emerged a combination of the New York and Chicago booking offices that exploited the vulnerability of vaudeville to monopoli-
zation. Vaudeville lacked the balancing influence of banks, which
as outside financial interests would have checked the effectiveness
of the monopoly, because each specialty took care of its own production costs, but then required booking in a unit with other acts.
The Keith-Albee organization weathered challenges from other
would-be monopolists within the industry and undercut independent operators by tying the stars to its many theaters through paying them fabulous salaries. Keith and Albee, and their associates,
amassed fortunes. "As recently as ten years ago the vaudeville
business of this country was yet undeveloped," an insider marveled in 1911, "but in these few years many men have become
millionaires in that field."[62] These millionaires made vaudeville
into a big business, characterized by *Equity* in 1923 as "highly
organized on a commercial basis, widely developed, scientifically
exploited, with control vested in the hands of a small centralized
and concentrated group of entrepreneurs and capitalists."[63]

Vaudeville differed markedly from newspaper syndicates, department store chains, and major-league baseball teams as an
emerging big-business enterprise. From an economic perspective,
one feature distinguished the vaudeville monopoly. When the sys-

tem of circuits reached the level of integration that made any performer a star who played the large vaudeville palaces successfully,
vaudeville as an industry controlled labor as well as supply and
demand in its field of production. From the vantage point of daily
life, the monopoly could flourish because the modern city kept
feeding vaudeville with devoted and enthusiastic spectators to
whom it gave an opportunity to see themselves and others as part
of a large community.

The free and ambitious air of the modern city, forthright for all
its grossness, shaped the composition of the vaudeville audience.
Vaudeville made women feel welcome and assisted their integration into the heart of the modern city, just as the department store
had done. It provided females with an opportunity to seek pleasure and relaxation downtown without being forced to camouflage
their purpose with the pretense of shopping. In 1910, one woman
considered the vaudeville house "essentially the people's and the
family theatre," as expressed by a hoary slogan with a feminine
slant: "Any young girl can take her mother there with perfect
propriety."[64]

A generation earlier, vaudevillians had begun exploring the potential of cheap variety shows as an attraction for a mixed audience
because "a child could take his parents there." Most people understood that if a child were to take anyone, it would be its mother,
because the father would be there already. Some impresarios gave
away dress patterns and sewing kits in an effort to erase more rapidly the memory of the less wholesome old-style variety. By the
beginning of the 1890's, the managers seem to have resolved the
issue, offering "attractive entertainment that women and children
can enjoy."[65] In 1914, a survey in Portland, Oregon, showed that
over 70 percent of the children below high-school age visited
vaudeville houses and that 24 percent attended a show "once a
week or oftener."[66]

The experience of the family audience, albeit in a rather extreme form, was immortalized by Frank Norris in McTeague's visit
with Trina's folks to the San Francisco Orpheum. Now that he had

finally got Trina, as his friend put it, McTeague faced the task of entertaining her properly, which meant, of course, with members of her family along. The logic of social conduct pointed further to attending *the* theater as the answer. Living up to this obligation turned into a formidable enterprise for the California miner-turned-dentist. The course of events surrounding the visit to the vaudeville house bordered on disaster, both imagined and real. At the outset the purchase of the tickets, complicated in McTeague's mind by his lack of words, ignorance of the theater, and insistence on sitting away from and at the same time on the side of the house facing the drums, provided a memorable lesson in modern city life. At the conclusion the little brother's mishap, brought on by eating an orange and a banana and drinking a glass of lemonade during the intermission, showed that the spell the show cast over the audience was a factor contributing to the accident. Despite all incidents the performance itself produced nothing but wonder, contentment, and happiness.[67]

For the managers creating a family audience required not only staging a clean and entertaining bill but also upgrading the audience itself. That was made easier by the fact that in large American cities, the "exuberant, restless, explosive, irrepressible mass of humanity that crowds the cheaper places of a West-end London theatre had found its way into other theaters, as one traveler related in 1879.[68] Some of the recent newcomers, still tied to the languages and dialects of their homelands, also shied away from vaudeville. They responded to the nostalgia for distant scenes and the security of cultural community generated by the ethnic stage. "Ein Yid bleibt ewig ein Yid" ("A Jew is always a Jew"), the leading character in *Rabbi Shabshi's Daughter* emphasized, in a theater that "swarmed with men, women, and children largely from the sweat-shops."[69]

However, the experience of a "Yiddish mother" among the spectators of an ethnic theater presaged the general movement of the urban mass audience into the vaudeville house. Explaining to a journalist that at home she liked to talk about the old country, she also stressed that her children made fun of her and called her a "Dutchman," while her husband confessed that he preferred the vaudeville house to the ethnic theater any time.[70] And once these immigrants had learned enough English from their children, they flocked into the vaudeville house. It provided amusing entertainment, but it also stimulated aspirations for an ampler life that transformed downtrodden men and women into rising people and convinced ambitious people that they were indeed on their way up. The gap between dream and reality narrowed over the years. "Every town of consequence in the country," one journalist noted in 1902, has a vaudeville house, "and the patronage of these establishments is not likely to be distinguished from the audiences that uphold grand opera."[71]

The self-identification of the vaudeville audience as people on the make received support from managers and impresarios who sensed the spectators' desire to learn manners that would help them secure their status as residents of the modern city. Wealth touched some of them, but most depended on reserved behavior and a modest appearance to demonstrate their identity as city people. With that frame of mind, the audience eagerly absorbed the mores of the vaudeville house, which refined howls of approval into enthusiastic applause, shrill dislike into deadly silence, and exuberant participation into rapt attention. Large signs asking openly for the kind of behavior that specific moments required, small cards politely but noticeably presented to embarrased spectators who had stepped out of line, floormen in the parquet, and bouncers in the gallery reinforced the proper etiquette.

Printed requests, discreetly handed out by uniformed employees, suggested: "Gentlemen will kindly avoid carrying cigars or cigarettes in their mouths while in the building. . . . Gentlemen will kindly avoid the stamping of feet and pounding of canes on the floor. . . . Applause is best shown by clapping of hands."[72] Pep talks from the stage reinforced the messages: "Our theaters are for women and children and, we hoped, gentlemen."[73] When women responded to another managers' campaign and took off their fashionable hats during the performance, vaudeville received additional proof that its audience had come to be refined as well as entertained.[74] The spectators observed the clues diligently and tolerated the managers' didactic hand, always gloved but rather heavy at times, because as people who hoped to ascend the social ladder, they saw vaudeville as a school of etiquette, intimately related to the satisfaction of their hunger for improvement as well as entertainment.

The palatial theaters themselves, whose splendor easily outstripped most spectators' desire for evidence of success, combined with the anticipation of an enjoyable show, built up expectations and inspired images which occupied the audience's imagination until vaudeville's most powerful attractions began. These scenes portrayed directly the reality and fantasy of many spectators and seemed to give more than an evening's experience of life without its having to be lived, just as the legitimate stage satisfied a specific kind of dramatic hunger. Song and humor softened the dramatic impact of the show and intensified the intimate contact with daily life that was vaudeville's outstanding characteristic.

The robust nature of vaudeville humor penetrated the entire show and spoke to its crowds, explosively expressing the terror and the magnificence, the pity and the cruelty of their experience. For an audience not only conscious of sufferings but also exposed to them, humor was achieved through outrageous distortions. Mad comedy, noisy satire, and the physical ordeal of the fall guy slapped across the stage by the elegantly dressed brute reduced to a zany act the story of the underprivileged that most spectators knew by heart. George M. Cohan, listing "a few of the hundred-odd things" constantly laughed at on the stage, thought his readers would "probably be ashamed in doing so" if they saw them "in cold type."[75] Vaudeville humor forsook subtlety, but gained sophistication through its dogged pursuit of verisimilitude. The comedian's answer to the question of why he had not gone to his mother-in-law's funeral as he intended, but instead to a ballgame, indicated the intensity of the desire for realism: "I did want to, but she isn't dead yet."[76]

The frequently brutal humor of vaudeville departed from the traditional American approach of laughing *with* people. The residents of the modern city lacked the natural intimacy of a rural setting that fostered that form of cogeniality. They did not know the format of a slowly told story that repeated the shared experience of an agricultural community gathered around the stove of a country store or on the porch of a farmhouse. City people also lacked the leisure to wait expectantly for that meeting of minds which generated fun to be shared and enjoyed by all. Toughened by constant exposure to the mass of humanity, people readily laughed *at* others because the reaction came naturally and created a common sentiment as well as a feeling of superiority in a highly competitive milieu. Their aggressive form of humor bound together groups of heterogeneous people in a moment of harmony that for them justified laughing at the plight of a harassed minority.

It all seemed "lots of fun," in the perspective of a visiting member of the French Academy, to whom "all these caricatures" suggested "the sharp and grim acerbity of our humorists." He was enchanted by the reply of a young girl to an ardent admirer who had complained bitterly that she would marry him at once if he were only rich: "You have often praised my beauty, but until now I did not know how much you recognized my good sense." In the "chaffing of young girls" on stage, "which might so easily be cruel, there is much jovial good-humor," Paul Bourget felt, as also in "the caricatures of the lower classes—notably, the tramps, the negroes, and the Irish."[77]

Any embarrassment the players may have felt due to the base nature of the humor was often hidden behind the burnt cork or charcoal of the performer's blackface makeup, inherited from the minstrel show and the old-type variety. But vaudeville rotated an ever-changing kaleidoscope of victims—Irish and blacks, Germans and Jews, as well as Italians and Poles, interspersed with the "rube," the rejected suitor, or the tramp. Such subjects could become laughing matter only in a world that, by restricting the humanity of large numbers of people, drove many to disparage the humanity of a few groups in order to feel better about themselves.

The songs of vaudeville, in contrast to its humor, engendered a universal uplift and heartfelt exaltation. Timely as well as timeless in their subject matter, they addressed the plight and pleasure of urbanites, expressing the feelings of employers and laborers, housewives and maids. Inspired by news stories in the metropolitan press or by people's longing for the familiarity of a distant scene, the songs softened acidulous humor with unfailing empathy. "The great Tony Pastor, the talk of the town, the famed comic singer, wit, jester, and clown," as the New York *Herald* promoted him in 1862, considered the newspaper the most valuable source of inspiration for popular songs.[78] Other songwriters expressed the same feeling. In 1895, one of them dedicated to the New York *Sunday World* "The Band Played On," the popular tune about Matt Casey's stylish social club in a rented hall where on payday each week he and his cronies greased the floor with wax, donned Sunday clothes on Saturday night, and waltzed with their strawberry blondes.[79]

Pastor, who loved to sing until his memory faded and he had trouble recalling the lyrics, in his later years as impresario and manager continued to appear on the stage of his New York theater. Thus he demonstrated his conviction that songs "on some of the most commonplace themes will often entertain" such a mixed crowd "as a fellow's best girl, the old man's boss, the mother-in-law, the scolding wife, and so forth."[80] His songs reported the laying of "the Great Atlantic Cable," told "Where Tweed Is Gone," explained "The Great Civil Service Reform," discussed the "Waterfall" hairstyle of women and the fashionable "Grecian Bend." Many of his more than a thousand tunes found their way into his popular songsters. Two in particular stayed with him as his standard repertoire until he went on stage for his last anniversary in 1908: "Sarah's Young Man" and "Down in a Coal Mine."[81]

The sentiments expressed in these favorites underline the time-less element of vaudeville songs: they spoke of the joy and anguish of love in the springtime of life and the drudgery and loneliness of toil "underneath the ground, where a gleam of sunshine never can be found."[82] Such songs attested to the lure of the big city, in-formed newcomers about urban etiquette, popularized the tele-phone and policeman. They glorified success, advised women on their public and private roles in city life, and responded to the yearning of immigrants for the old country and of other people for the countryside. Some of their titles—such as "Give My Regards to Broadway," "Go On and Coax Me," "Hello Central, Give Me Heaven," "The Little Lost Child," "The Man Who Broke the Bank in Monte Carlo," "Little Annie Rooney," "In the Good Old Sum-mer Time," "Down Where the Wurzburger Flows," and "On the Banks of the Wabash"—expressed the interests of newly urbanized people.[83] Some of the devices used to bring the audience fully in tune with the spirit of the songs were described by Theodore Dreiser based on knowledge he had gained from his brother Paul Dresser, a successful songwriter and publisher. Hired boys in the gallery often took up the chorus during a show and hundreds of organ grinders, covering the streets under the direction of padroni, spread the melodies throughout the cities.[84]

The emotional appeal of song and humor was strengthened by the intimate relation between the show and urban life. Although lyrics and sketches dealt with a vast range of human affairs, they commonly did this in terms of city existence. Whether a tune sen-timentalized the uses of leisure or a sketch parodied the rela-tionship between the sexes, the dominant chord or the punch line touched on specific urban thoughts or conditions. Commonly, each bill dealt with the questions of success, ethnic diversity, sex, and urban behavior, issues that occupied most spectators.

Among these the quest for success stood out. "It doesn't matter if it rains or snows, my one ambition is to get the dough": at the opening of the twentieth cedntury a popular tune spelled out city people's preoccupation.[85] Not only the subject matter of the show urged the audience on to the pursuit of success, however; the major stimulation came from the vaudeville troupers themselves, who pranced across the boards two or three times a day. Their unending rivalry for the limelight and their perpetual drive to excel set the example for all.

The presentation of an act whose studied casualness culminated in achieving the most difficult feat without apparent effort allowed most spectators, who craved success without being spectacularly successful, to share vicariously the performer's accomplishment. The star's mastery of the routine, which effectively disguised the drudgery of big-time vaudeville, seemed to make success a result of luck, inviting the audience to partake in the good fortune. When the illusion reached the point of giving way to reality, the next trouper emerged from the wings to revive it. Enthusiastic ovations rewarded consummate performances and the approval as well as the accomplishment revived the spirits of skeptics disheartened by misfortune. The applause converted the performer's success, initially distant because of the aura of mystery surrounding the feat, into a noisy reality created by the spectators themselves. This delightful experience enabled city people to equate success with a pleasurable moment.

The reduction of success to a moment's enjoyment, the product of the symbiosis between headliner and audience, linked heterogeneous groups of spectators. The entire show reinforced the bond with its appeal to concerns shared by all city people eager to rise above their station in life. The common ground momentarily found in the vaudeville house provided a vantage point for spectators to recognize the tensions of ethnic diversity as presented in individual vaudeville acts. Sketches from the homes or workplaces of immigrant groups and newcomers to the city exposed the range of humanity and revealed the similarities between people's behavior, often ignored and frequently hidden.

A sketch like "Lady Bountiful Visits the Murphys on Wash Day" transplanted the spectators into the kitchen of an Irish household. They saw an Irish washerwoman at work, oblivious to a boy snitching a pie cooling on the sideboard. The woman, catching him taking a bite, rubs the pie into his face and kicks him out, only to find herself immediately forced to clean the kitchen because of clouds of dust sweeping through the window. A policeman enters, hugs the laundress, and is offered food and drink. When he joins the woman in an embrace on a bench under the window, a sack of coal is emptied on the couple, producing the ultimate confusion that the audience expected to see.[86]

Similar slapstick humor and ethnic stereotyping permeated another sketch, "Ein Bier," which finds a German laborer resting on a barrel. Opening a basket lunch, he notices a sign on the opposite wall that offers beer for sale. Motivated by a presumed national characteristic, he exits to get his lager. A passing boy up-ends the barrel and covers the opening with the towel from the food basket, and the returning workman, hoping to enjoy his beer on the barrel, promptly falls in.

"A Frontier Flirtation" played on the hayseed-in-the-city theme. A heavily veiled young woman sitting on a park bench is accosted by a country bumpkin who seeks her acquaintance. Encouraged, he sits down beside her, but her veil parts, exposing a mask with the face of a billy goat that frightens the rube away. A gentleman takes his place and removes the mask, and the two laugh and embrace.[87]

These crude vignettes presented cultural traits, real or imagined, of certain groups. But this expressiosn of many people's prejudices actually brought some people closer to each other, because the blatant stereotypes paraded on stage contradicted the experience men and women acquired daily in their encounters with members of other groups on the street, in the store, or on the job. Further, the ridicule heaped mercilessly upon fist-fighting Irishmen, lazy blacks, beer-drinking Germans, sharp-witted Jews, tight-fisted Scots, ignorant farm folks, and song-loving Italians fortified the individual spectator's self-esteem sufficiently to enable him or her to detect and to accept the elements of a common humanity in other life-styles. The members of the audience occasionally recognized their own drive, anxiety, or rationality in the sketches of other people who were different yet similar to themselves in their quest to get ahead.

The variety show also provided inspiration for women, who responded to the urge to enter areas of life the modern city opened to them or tried to make their way in the general movement for success. The vaudeville actresses who appeared in great numbers on the stage represented a new type of woman that served as a model for the women in the audience. On the neutral stage of the vaudeville house, they demonstrated a novel pattern of behavior that stripped away much of the demeaning sexual overtones characteristic of the old-type variety show.

Their careers, from chorus line to headliner, demonstrated the significance of a cool head and the ability to use it to advance in life. They showed that for them beauty was merely the "ladder reaching to the heights." They were willing "to listen to a discipline" of constant training "that keeps a girl in the background," hidden behind the neutral image of the performer," until she isn't a girl" any longer. Singing and dancing lessons, schools of elocution and business assisted them in their enormous drive to succeed and defy the stereotype of the chorus girl who "attempts nothing which she has not the power to attain" through her looks alone.[88] Their talent and minds identified self-possession as a base for the interaction between women and men, and their appearances identified glamor as woman's avenue into modern city life.

Inevitably, the entrance of the glamorous star on stage constituted a big scene in itself, quite independent of her act. The standing ovation that at times greeted her before she seemed to have done anything but walk on reflected the audience's involvement with her appearance. From her black picture hat with white egret feathers to the winking rhinestone buckles of her modish shoes, her dress revealed the wisdom of the adage that clothes make the man and demonstrated the appropriate way for a woman to strip the proverb of its narrow connotation. Her gloves, her jewelry, her hair style and her makeup contributed to the picture of poise she created. Her image, ingeniously adapted by a legion of troupers to suit the carriage and agility of a chorus girl or a lady juggler, furnished a model for many other women as well. Caroline Caffin found this image duplicated on "the main thoroughfare of almost any city in the Union."[89] According to their means and tastes, women imitated the star's clothes and coiffure, her adornment and her bearing, as a clear-cut way to appear as attractive as modern city life demanded without attracting undesirable forms of attention.

The example of the alluring star affected directly a new relationship that developed between women and men, abetted by the conditions of downtown life. It guided women in their increasing contacts with men, such as those that occurred as the result of a necessary ride on the streetcar or a casual stroll down the avenue. It also helped them clarify their roles as shoppers or employees in department stores, and in the numerous daily encounters that once would have been bewildering, but now were matter-of-course. The self-possession which the star radiated because of her striking ability as a performer, and which other women imitated, reduced the difference between the sexes. An emphases on poise and appearance generated a matter-of-fact attitude pervading the meeting of men and women on the urban scene. The celebrated star and the mixed audience which allowed women to appear in the vaudeville house shaped attitudes of urban behavior that facilitated contact but maintained independence, mingling the opportunity for pleasure with the freedom of choice.

Vaudeville's rules of etiquette extended into modes of speaking. The tempo of the show, recasting the rhythm of city life into the whirl of waltz or the syncopation of ragtime, placed a premium on the facile phrase and snappy repartee. "Conversation is becoming a lost art," a teacher lamented in 1917, "largely through the influence of the vaudeville stage."[90] Aggressively delivered, the smart talk frequently gave the impression that the speaker knew what he was talking about. It was at times abrasive and callous, but it enabled the vaudeville artist to hold his mental ground in most encounters with which his script presented him. Moreover, the argot of his profession, constantly producing new expressions, kept the seasoned performer from "dying on his feet."

The slang of the vaudeville artist was rigorously up to date, as two articles in the New York *Times* showed in 1917. Like bursts of laughter that culminated in one hilarious explosion, triggered by a comedian who by "topping laughs" produced a show-stopping hit, the words crowded each other in a "condensed system of rapid-fire expression." Although an act could fail, more often it "flopped," "did a Brodie," was a "bust," "flivved," or "blacked out." To be "walked out on" seemed harmless compared with "getting the bird" or "the raspberry."[91] The spirit of the argot permeated the delivery of a line, as much as the sense of line itself, touched the audience, accompanied the crowd into the streets, and enabled city people to communicate in concentrated forms of speech.

The style of urban speech that vaudeville fostered among patrons suited the general habits of dress inspired by the performers. If their roles did not require disguises, they always seemed to walk on stage in their Sunday best, sometimes three times on a workday. Their fashionable attire, in turn, added to the spectators' festive mood, and encouraged them to think about their Sunday finery as their city best or to erase the distinction between the good and the old suit in favor of one stylish suit worn every day.

Together with its influence on speech and dress, the vaudeville stage fostered other social conventions that touched people's relations with their fellows. The precision of the acts, the split-second timing essential to the success of the routines, and the air of punctuality at curtain time impressed the spectators strongly with the importance of the rule of the clock, particularly those fresh off the farm who were still wedded to the natural cycle of the day. Run by the clock on the factory tower and the timetable of the railroad, the vaudeville house conveyed the regimen of industrial time to city people in the guise of a social practice that eased their access to pleasure.

Men and women acting out their daily routine against the backdrop of the downtown scene began adhering assiduously to the respect for time cultivated on the vaudeville stage. On the street and in the streetcar, in the store and in the park, they learned to deal with the fleeting urban moment. On stage, venerable acts such as "Riding in a Street Car," "Central Park After Dark," and "Waiting at the Church" elaborated the lesson.[92]

Vaudeville identified on stage a set of urban problems and, in the absence of generally accepted solutions, also suggested ways of coping with them. The show stressed efficiency and discipline as foundations for modern city life. Its acts reiterated these messages continuously; in particular the routines of acrobats, jugglers, and animals spelled them out in detail. The flying rings and parallel bars of trapeze artists heightened the suspense that accompanied the struggle for timing and perfection and impressed the spectators with their significance. The comic among the three trick-bicycle riders, who fell and crashed while the others jumped rope or rode on one pedal, achieved a similar effect. So did the agility of jugglers, and some performers added special touches. When the acrobat who balanced himself on top of a column of chairs came tumbling down with the pyramid he had purposely upset and landed on his feet, all smiles, discipline of body and mind shone brightly.

Trained animals added nuances. Leaping dogs and ball-balancing seals indicated that even animals could learn self-control. Temporarily compelled to ape human occupations, the groups of animals playing instruments, treading mills, firing cannons, riding bicycles, promenading as well as shopping suggested the powerful magnetism of city life that drew into its midst not only people but other creatures as well, dressed like them in pants, jackets, hats, and skirts. They accentuated the special place of humans in an environment people had created and learned to master.

People asserting their freedom from domineering surroundings watched escape artists and magicians with fascination. Harry Houdini, who had gained his mastery of theatrical magic and feats of dexterity from books, circuses, and sideshows, at the beginning of the twentieth century emerged as one of vaudeville's superb show-

men, constantly walking, wriggling, or swimming his way to freedom through walls, out of handcuffs, safes, or coffins at the bottom
of big fish tanks. A great trickster, he left far behind colleagues
who still pulled a rabbit from a hat or sawed a woman in half.
Houdini's insistence that he owed his success only to himself, and
not to supernatural phenomena, intensified his enormous appeal to
the vaudeville audience. Edmund Wilson thought in 1925 that
Houdini seemed "to have become more interested in understanding how effects are produced than in astonishing people with
them." [93]

Magic came to city people not only from magicians, but also
from numerous artists dubbed "professors," who added proof to
the daily experience of many people who affirmed control over
their environment by throwing a magic switch or opening an enchanted faucet. The scientific experiments conducted on stage,
demonstrating the flow of electricity or the pressure of a column of
water, entertained more than they enlightened. Although the principles inherent in such feats may not have been understood by
many people, the exhibitions of the "professors" furnished scientific support for their desire to take the illusions of vaudeville as reality. And the moving pictures of the kinescope topped all expectations of scientific progress. " 'What will they do next.' observed
Trina, turning in amazement to McTeague. 'Ain't that wonderful,
Mac?' " [94]

Irrespective of illusion or reality, the vaudeville show always
managed to produce its most desired effect: happiness. Each act
contributed, but the tunes and lyrics of the songs added a special
share of good feeling. The words blended old and new values, the
nostalgia for faraway places and the joys and sorrows of city life,
and totally captured the public fancy. "Sung, whistled and
hummed by the great American 'unmusical' public," the composer
of "Break the News to Mother" and "After the Ball" argued, the
songs' enormous popularity proved their merit beyond question;
"many a sad and weary heart has been made glad by the strains of
these 'popular' songs." [95] The contentment they spread through

the vaudeville house put each spectator at ease with himself and in sudden harmony with the rest of the audience.

The great popular chord of happiness struck anew by each song merged with the glorification of urban life which the entire bill engineered.[96] The vaudeville house ameliorated the anguish born of the dichotomy between country and city. It gave some spectators confidence that they would learn the ways of the city. Others regained the incentive to pursue the promises of modern life and good fortune.

Visible to all in the downtown section of the modern city, the ornate facade of an Orpheum, Olympic, or Alhambra reinforced the message of the show. Whatever name the local fancy might actually have dictated, any of these magnificent palaces carried confidently the humble designation of vaudeville house. The richly carved marble, colorful streamers, and glittering lights of the imposing structure tellingly expressed the strenth of its magic that could turn despair into hope and ugliness into beauty. Its location made it accessible to all people. Irrespective of rank or family, the purchase of a mere ticket admitted any one through the open portal.

In order to keep the stream of patrons at a constant flow, the general construction, equipment, and operation of a vaudeville house, from the selection of a site to the running of a nursery, from staff management to advertising policy, became the subject of careful study. Thoughtful comments reveal the practical mind benefiting from accumulated experience: "If any untoward event happens while the performance is on, such as fire or anything that threatens panic, the orchestra should immediately play a lively march, preferably something like 'Dixie.' "[97] Practicality, however, had its limits. In 1899, a consulting engineer for a sanitary project argued that "we have a right to demand theater buildings with less outward and inside gorgeousness, but in which the paramount subjects of comfort, safety, and health are . . . generously provided for." However, elegance, meticulously pursued by the management, seemed the most effective policy for vaudeville.[98]

From the sidewalk, swept and washed regularly, to the red-carpeted engine room in the basement, Keith's general manager E. F. Albee turned the New Boston Theater into a show that almost stole the show. In true vaudeville fashion, the basement incarnated his intentions. At the main entrance, a marble stairway led through a long cream-colored corridor to the reception hall of the power station below the street level. There the soft reflection of globe lights enhanced the practical beauty of the white marble switchboard, covering an entire wall, and guided attention to the engines and generators in the main room. From a gallery, guarded by a tall nickel-plated railing, the visitors saw a "wondershop of marble and swiftly moving steel" which, in the eyes of one expert, "for elegance, utility, beauty, and artistic worth" surpassed any of its kind.[99] The dynamo, which in Henry Adams's world rivaled the Virgin, in Keith's rivaled the stage for attention.

On the stage of the vaudeville house, the performers presented man's constant search for success, but the theater itself furnished the setting for the spectators to apply the lessons and to experience modern life directly. On the sidewalk and at the entrance, in vestibule, lobby, parquet, and gallery, men and women explored the luxury of an enchanted space in which to rehearse their small acts for the big stage of the world waiting outside. For them community was created there, where rationality and imagination applied the suggestions of make-believe to the reality and dreams of urban life. They emerged from the encounter as city people—urban men and women on the point of acquiring social skills and sharing cultural values that enabled them to cope with the complexities of modern city life. Their new life-style identified them as urbanites, each able to find, or to create, islands of survival in a turbulent sea of people.

# EPILOGUE:
# RESILIENT CITY

During the nineteenth century new forms of culture emerged in America in response to problems created by the modern city. Fashioned freely by and for large numbers of people, they marked the culmination of the process of creating ways of life out of new social and economic institutions. Modern city culture boldly answered the mounting need of diverse people for a common urban identity that also left enough room for each individual's dreams and aspirations. Its expressions spoke to and for the average individual, without putting artists and writers, architects and philosophers, on pedestals.

Straightforward and egalitarian at the core, the restless spirit of American city culture contrasted with the attitude toward culture that prevailed in nineteenth-century Europe. There, the great lights of each generation sedately shouldered the burden of the inherited values of their civilization, accumulated over centuries. Haunted by the feeling of being *epigone*, mere offspring of famous ancestors who had created the culture, thinkers and artists tried diligently to embellish the great tradition. When success evaded them, they strove to transmit their heritage safely to another generation. Unable to measure up to the requirements of an idealized past, the heirs faced the danger of witnessing the end of all art— predicted by the philosopher Georg F. W. Hegel—or at least the closing of the epoch of classicistic art—envisioned by the poet Henrich Heine.

One of the pillars of nineteenth-century European culture, Matthew Arnold, felt keenly the obligation to protect the lofty edifice of his civilization. During his first expedition across the Atlantic, in 1883–84, he considered Americans too attached to the common and ignoble. In the culture of the United States his English eyes saw no objects of distinction or beauty—his great sources of inspiration in seeking the splendor and refinement of highly cultivated life. Chilled by the practical air of the American modern city, he shuddered at the thought of what England might have become without cathedrals, churches, and castles.

Americans, anxious to define culture more in terms of struggling people than of inherited artifacts, found their field of creativity in the modern city. They approached human predicaments in a manner prescribed by their outstanding eighteenth-century urbanite, Benjamin Franklin, who found the answer to both the quest for the happiness of the greatest number and the task of protecting the humanity of crowds of people lost in the urban wilderness in ordinary but useful achievements. In the modern city, nineteenth-century Americans of radically different origins forged cultural patterns along these lines which helped them cope with the complex demands of a strange cityscape.

The task of preserving private space loomed large in a city filling up with people. The territorial division of the urban chaos into districts of work and residence provided a basic framework of planned space supported by the gridiron of real estate parcels. The reality of rising land values killed the dream of the single-family house. When boarding houses and tenements proved to be rather inadequate substitutes, Americans adopted the flats of the apartment house as units they could consider their own. The apartment eased their adjustment to crowded surroundings, familiarized them with the labor-saving devices of a new technology of living, and accustomed them to the steadily enlarging vertical dimension of urban life.

The metropolitan press answered the need for communication among the inhabitants of these fragments of private space. The dailies bridged people's isolation by bringing news about others and their surroundings, taking the place of the flow of gossip that the tempo of life had reduced to a trickle. Newspaper reports and stories provided people adrift in the modern city with a sense of direction and rudiments of urban behavior. Additionally, advertisements furnished crucial information about opportunities for work and leisure, and above all told how to shop smartly and buy less expensively. These messages in particular established a link between women tied to domestic chores and the world outside that beckoned them.

Through the department store, women found their way into the heart of the modern city. The concentration of many shops under one roof and management created a downtown center for their activities. The facilities of the big store expanded the social features of shopping into cultural patterns. The store's egalitarian air and pleasant atmosphere brought women from all walks of life together. These daily contacts, which generated self-assurance, and the fashion cycle, which encouraged consumption, gave etiquette and appearance a special significance. The department store vastly expanded the interaction of all people and located the center of urban elegance downtown, in a district once dominated by the business activities of men only.

The athletic events in the ball park proclaimed the codes of intense competition which characterized men's struggle for success. In a summer setting reminiscent of country life, baseball introduced urbanites unfamiliar with the rules of their seemingly erratic world to the importance of restraints within countless activities of a free society. Sharing the pageant of the first urban spectator sport also conveyed essential American attitudes to thousands of immigrants. That experience qualified many of them for citizenship in the modern city, with its privilege of people-watching as the elementary form of urban leisure.

The vaudeville house gave expression to some of the bonds fostered by metropolitan press, department store, and ball park. Its variety show attracted an audience of men, women, and children who sought relaxation, but also found instruction. The program addressed everyday problems, commenting on the struggle for success, the relation between the sexes, the meeting of ethnic and racial groups, and the task of living in the modern city. In the guise of entertainment, the scenes of the vaudeville house outlined the emergence of patterns of life that eased relationships among groups as well as most people's contact with their environment.

The new ways of life identified city people who shared a growing awareness of a distinctly urban world. Out of the conformity of daily behavior these men and women created common links that enabled them to accept and to overcome the contrasts and divisions in their surroundings. As a result they moved with growing confidence through the strange setting of the modern city, their progress assured by the styles of thinking and acting they derived from the culture created out of new social and economic institutions. The world of city people thrived on their ability to use the apartment house, metropolitan press, department store, ball park, and vaudeville house for cultural ends, and that ability gave their ways of life distinctly American features.

Resourcefulness, resilience, and drive marked these urbanites as people on the make. Occasionally, when they were able to step back for a moment from the rush of getting ahead, they could recognize themselves as individuals in a multitude. These moments of self-discovery brought forth new modes of getting along with others, as city people managed to discard old assumptions about the relationship between men and women by living the new ones of modern city culture. Their new identity gained cultural significance from the fact that it assured a modicum of human dignity.

Modern city culture sought to assure the future of the ordinary person. It was sustained by the cultural diversity of great numbers of people. Freedom to participate openly in the continuous transformation of ways of life integrated these masses of people into the cityscape. Law and custom encouraged individuals to seek answers to personal concerns, while the egalitarian assumptions of democracy gave people confidence to liberate themselves from the rule of conventions that had outlived their usefulness, thus enriching contacts between men and women in advance of political democracy, which was slower to realize some of the goals of equality.

The fusion between utility and human kindness, an outstanding American trait, made this urban culture the national way of life. From coast to coast people embraced the major aspects of modern city culture and adapted them to local needs. In a nation composed of many different groups of immigrants, the extension of this culture bestowed a measure of uniformity and stability. City life followed similar patterns east and west, north and south, and also penetrated the countryside, bringing urban ways into areas that knew no cities. The formation of a national system for communicating ideas and marketing products hastened the expansion for the social structures and business organizations on which the urban life-style was based.

Railroad lines and telegraph wires served as major arteries for spreading patterns of city life everywhere. Pullman cars, coaches, and sleepers whisked businessmen, baseball players, and vaudeville performers from coast to coast, and to many stops in between. Freight trains moved cargo that added a touch of reality to dreams of comfort and fashion in out-of-the-way places. Telegraph wires hummed the latest news, conveyed orders or canceled contracts, and relayed to fans in New York the outcome of the final inning played in Chicago.

While telegraph and railroad diffused urban ways, the significance of the city as a distinct territorial focus of life diminished. Within the framework of the national urban culture, suburban developments grew up and flourished without needing to surrender to the city. Their residents relied on the automobile to give them independence from train tracks and streetcar lines, which for decades had directed the flow of people into the heart of the city. This increased mobility enabled them to earn a living in the city while living urbanely in the country, without interaction with the diverse groups of people in the city.

The automobile and the modern city were incompatible. A new

technology dictated different patterns of life. The ways of big-city life derived from apartment house, metropolitan press, department store, ball park, and vaudeville house now gave way to novel forms developed to meet new issues. Their decline led to the rise of an urban culture of tabloids and movies, radio and television, shopping centers and condominiums, as well as buses and trucks.

The rise and decline of the modern city appeared as a phase in a cultural process of change. Culture furnished answers to everyday needs until the problems it addressed disappeared in the face of new realities. The culture of the modern city in nineteenth-century America proved the city to be, as in other moments in history, a lasting ground for social organization. In diversity, city people found order. In moments of doubt about the future of the city, the example renews faith in the ability of the urban setting to create satisfying forms of human life.

# NOTES

## I. MODERN CITY CULTURE

1. Jane Addams, *Twenty Years at Hull House* (New York, 1961), 80–81, and *The Spirit of Youth and the City Streets* (Urbana, Ill., 1972), 4–5, 8, 62. The books first appeared in 1910 and 1909 respectively.
2. Jacob Riis, *How the Other Half Lives: Studies among the Tenements of New York* (New York, 1957), 16. The book was first published in 1890.
3. Theodore Dreiser, *A Book about Myself* (New York, 1922), 64, 100–101, 219–20.
4. Helen Farr Sloan, ed., *John Sloan: New York Etchings (1905–1949)* (New York, 1978), vii–viii.
5. David Graham Phillips, "The Union of Sixth Avenue and Broadway," *Harper's Weekly*, XXXV (March 21, 1891), 210.
6. Allan Nevins and Milton Halsey Thomas, eds., *The Diary of George Templeton Strong*, 4 vols. (New York, 1952), II, 251.
7. Joseph Alexander von Huebner, *A Ramble Round the World, 1871* (New York, 1874), 17.
8. Edward T. Devine, "The Shiftless and Floating City Population," *Annals of the American Academy of Political and Social Science* (September, 1897), 5; Riis, *How the Other Half Lives*, 52–59.
9. Edgar Allan Poe, "The Man of the Crowd," in *The Complete Tales and Poems* (New York, 1975), 475, 476. The story was first published in 1840.
10. Walt Whitman, *New York Dissected: A Sheaf of Recently Discovered Newspaper Articles by the Author of Leaves of Grass*, ed. Emory Holloway and Ralph Adiman (New York, 1936), 55, 127.
11. Edwin Hubbell Chapin, *Humanity in the City* (New York, 1854), 17.

12. [James Dawson Burn], *Three Years Among the Working-Classes in the United States during the War. By the Author of "The Autobiography of a Beggar-Boy"* (London, 1865), 117.

13. K[ate] M. B[ishop], "Rus in Urbe," *Overland Monthly*, II (September, 1883), 335.

14. Abraham Cahan, *Yekl: A Tale of the New York Ghetto* (New York, 1896), 70–75.

15. Isabelle Lowe, *Lillian: The Beautiful Typewriter. A Thrilling Tale of Modern City Life* (Baltimore, 1907), 26.

16. Arnold B. Wolfe, *The Lodging House Problem* (Boston, 1906), quoted in Sheila M. Rothman, *Woman's Proper Place: A History of Changing Ideas and Practices, 1870 to the Present* (New York, 1978), 43.

17. "The Girl Who Comes to the City: A Symposium," *Harper's Bazaar*, XLII (June, July, December, 1908), 594, 693, 1227.

18. Joseph Kirkland, "Among the Poor of Chicago," in Robert A. Woods, et al., *The Poor in Great Cities: Their Problems and What Is Doing to Solve Them* (New York, 1895), 238.

19. William Dean Howells, *The Rise of Silas Lapham* (New York, 1963), 6, 61. The novel was first published as a book in 1885.

20. Charles Wentworth Dilke, *Greater Britain: A Record of Travel in English-speaking Countries during 1866 and 1867*, 2d ed., 2 vols. (London, 1869), I, vii.

21. Junius Henri Browne, *The Great Metropolis: A Mirror of New York* (Hartford, Conn., 1869), 339.

22. Frederick Douglass to Harriet Beecher Stowe, March 8, 1853, in Philip Foner, ed., *The Life and Writings of Frederick Douglass*, 4 vols. (New York, 1950–55), II, 232.

23. Otto von Bismarck, speech in the German Reichstag, May 18, 1889, quoted in Willy Hellpach, *Mensch und Volk der Grosstadt*, 2d rev. ed. (Stuttgart, 1952), 6.

24. John Collier and Edward M. Barrows, *The City Where Crime Is Play* (New York, 1914), 2–3.

25. T. L. Nichols, *Forty Years of American Life*, 2d ed. (London, 1874), 206, 207. The account appeared first in 1864.

26. Joel Tyler Headley, *The Great Riots of New York, 1712–1873* (New York, 1873), 17.

27. Washington Gladden, "Is It Peace or War," *Century Magazine*, XXXII (August, 1886), 565–76.

28. Robert E. Park and Herbert A. Miller, *Old World Traits Transplanted* (New York, 1921), 276.

29. Lander MacClintock, trans., *Orpheus in America: Offenbach's Diary of His Journey to the New World* (Bloomington, Ind., 1957), 70.

30. Hutchins Hapgood, *Types from City Streets* (New York, 1910), 16.

31. F. Bret Harte, "San Francisco, by the Poets. Number Two. South Park—After Gray," *Californian*, September 24, 1864, p. 9; Gunther Barth, "Metropolism and Urban Elites in the Far West," in Frederic Cople Jaher, ed., *The Age of Industrialism in America: Essays in Social Structure and Cultural Values* (New York, 1968), 159, 162.

32. Nicholas B. Wainwright, ed., *A Philadelphia Perspective: The Diary of Sidney George Fisher Covering the Years 1834–1871* (Philadelphia, 1967), 218.

33. A Non-Resident American, "City Life in the United States," *Contemporary Review*, XL (November, 1881), 711.

34. "The Girl Who Comes to the City: A Symposium," *Harper's Bazaar*, XLII (January, 1908), 54.

## II. DIVIDED SPACE

1. William Dean Howells, "By Horse-car to Boston," *Suburban Sketches*, new and enl. ed. (Boston, 1877), 105–7, 112–13, 114.

2. Richard M. Hurd, *Principles of City Land Values* (New York, 1903), 18.

3. "Commissioners' Remarks," in William Bridges, ed., *Map of the City of New York and Island of Manhattan* (New York, 1811), 24–25, quoted in John W. Reps, *The Making of Urban America: A History of City Planning in the United States* (Princeton, N.J., 1965), 297.

4. J[ohn] C. Myers, *Sketches of a Tour Through the Northern and Eastern States, the Canadas & Nova Scotia* (Harrisonburg, Va., 1849), 51; *American Review*, II (November, 1845), 536–38, quoted in Emory Holloway, comp., *The Uncollected Poetry and Prose of Walt Whitman*, 2 vols. (Garden City, N.Y., 1921), I, 92.

5. "Editor's Easy Chair," *Harper's New Monthly Magazine*, XIII (July, 1856), 272.

6. Phoebe B. Stanton, *The Gothic Revival & American Church Architecture: An Episode in Taste, 1840–1856* (Baltimore, 1968), 7, 29, 319.

7. George L. Hersey, "Godey's Choice," *Journal of the Society of Architectural Historians*, XVIII (October, 1959), 111.

8. Alan Burnham (ed.), *New York Landmarks: A Study & Index of Architectually Notable Structures in Greater New York* (Middletown, Conn., 1963), 357, 358, 359, 360, 363.

9. Montgomery Schuyler, "The New York City Hall: A Piece of Architectural History," *Architectural Record*, XXIII (May, 1908), 387.

10. Henry W. Cleveland and William Samuel Backus, *Village and Farm Cottages* (New York, 1856), 47.

11. Winston Weisman, "Commercial Palaces of New York: 1845–1875," *Art Bulletin*, XXXIV (December, 1954), 289, 290.

12. "The Park and the Work Done Upon It," *San Francisco Real Estate Circular*, XII (August, 1873), 4.

13. Edith Wharton, *A Backward Glance* (New York, 1934), 55.

14. Quoted in "Origins of the Municipal Park Movement," in Frederick Law Olmsted, Jr., and Theodora Kimball, eds., *Frederick Law Olmsted: Landscape Architect, 1822–1903*, 2 vols. (New York, 1922), II, 12.

15. William Cullen Bryant, "A New Park," New York *Evening Post*, July 3, 1844, quoted in Allan Nevins, *The "Evening Post": A Century of Journalism* (New York, 1922), 193–94, and in Henry Hope Reed and Sophia Duckworth, *Central Park: A History and a Guide* (New York, 1967), 3.

16. "A Review of Recent Changes, and Changes Which Have Been Projected, in the Plans of the Central Park," in Olmsted and Kimball, *Olmsted*, II, 248; Geoffrey Blodgett, "Frederick Law Olmsted: Landscape Architecture as Conservative Reform," *Journal of American History*, LXII (March, 1976), 877, 878.

17. "Municipal Park Movement," in Olmsted and Kimball, *Olmsted*, II, 14.

18. J. P. Quincy, "Social Life in Boston," in Justin Winsor, ed., *Memorial History of Boston*, 4 vols. (Boston, 1881), IV, 9.

19. Marshall Pinckney Wilder, "The Horticulture of Boston and Vicinity," in *ibid.*, 613.

20. Quoted in "The Beginnings of a Park for New York," in Olmsted and Kimball, *Olmsted*, II, 22.

21. "The Winning Design by Olmsted and Vaux," in *ibid.*, II, 46.

22. John H. Rauch, *Public Parks: Their Effects upon the Moral, Physical and Sanitary Conditions of the Inhabitants of Large Cities; with Special Reference to the City of Chicago* (Chicago, 1869), 31.

23. [James Dawson Burn], *Three Years Among the Working-Classes in the United States during the War. By the Author of "The Autobiography of a Beggar-Boy"* (London, 1865), 127, 129.

24. Frederick Law Olmsted, "Public Parks and the Enlargement of Towns," *Journal of Social Science*, III (1871), 19.

25. Frederick Law Olmsted, Jr., "Neighborhood Pleasure-Grounds in Boston," *Harper's Weekly*, XLI (December 25, 1897), 1920.

26. Frederick Law Olmsted., Jr., "The Town-Planning Movement in

America," *Annals of the American Academy of Political and Social Science*, LI (January, 1914), 178.

27. Galen Cranz, "Changing Roles of Urban Parks: From Pleasure Garden to Open Space," *Landscape*, XXII (Summer, 1978), 12–13.

28. Charles Mulford Robinson, *The Improvement of Towns and Cities, or the Practical Basis of Civic Aesthetics* (New York, 1907), 158.

29. "Chicago Parks and Their Landscape Architecture," *Architectural Record*, XXIV (July, 1908), 19.

30. Lawrence H. Larsen, "Nineteenth-Century Street Sanitation: A Study in Filth and Frustration," *Wisconsin Magazine of History*, LII (Spring, 1969), 239–47.

31. Allan Nevins and Milton Halsey Thomas, eds., *The Diary of George Templeton Strong*, 4 vols. (New York, 1952), II, 396.

32. F. L. Olmsted, Vaux & Co., *Preliminary Report upon the Proposed Suburban Village of Riverside, Near Chicago* (New York, 1868), 7.

33. Robert Treat Paine, Jr., "Homes for the People," *Journal of Social Science*, XV (September, 1881), 116.

34. Richard Nelson, *Suburban Homes for Business Men, on the Line of the Marieta Railroad. A Description of the North-Eastern Suburbs, the Scenery, Soil, Cost of Property, Conveniences of Living, Churches, Schools and Societies* (Cincinnati, 1874), 143–44.

35. H. C. Bunner, *The Suburban Sage: Stray Notes and Comments on His Simple Life* (New York, 1896), 156.

36. Kenneth T. Jackson, "The Crabgrass Frontier: 150 Years of Suburban Growth in America," in Raymond A. Mohl and James T. Richardson, eds., *The Urban Experience: Themes in American History* (Belmont, Calif., 1973), 199, 206–7.

37. Mrs. Samuel McCune Lindsay, "The Suburban Child," *Pedagogical Seminary*, XVI (1909), 498.

38. Emory Holloway and Ralph Adimari, comps., *New York Dissected: A Sheaf of Recently Discovered Newspaper Articles by the Author of Leaves of Grass* (New York, 1936), 96.

39. Thomas Butler Gunn, *The Physiology of New York Boarding-Houses* (New York, 1857), 12, 299, 300.

40. Henry Morgan, *Boston Inside Out: Sins of a Great City: A Story of Real Life*, 2d ed. (Boston, 1880), 101.

41. Addison B. Burk, "The City of Homes and Its Building Societies," *Journal of Social Science*, XV (September, 1881), 121.

42. Charles Barnard, "A Hundred Thousand Homes: How They Were Paid For," *Scribner's Monthly*, XI (February, 1876), 477–87.

43. Octavia Hill Association, "Certain Aspects of the Housing Problem in

Philadelphia," *Annals of the American Academy of Political and Social Science*, XX (July, 1902), 117.

44. Robert W. DeForest and Lawrence Veiller, eds., *The Tenement House Problem*, 2 vols. (New York, 1903), I, 69.

45. Jane Adams, "The Housing Problem in Chicago," *Annals of the American Academy of Political and Social Science*, III (July, 1902), 100.

46. "Americanisms," *Notes and Queries*, IX (February 10, 1866), 118.

47. John H. Griscom, "The Sanitary Conditions of the Laboring Population of New York with Suggestions for Its Improvement," quoted in Gordon Atkins, *Health, Housing, and Poverty in New York City* (Ann Arbor, Mich., 1947), 19.

48. Robert H. Bremner, "The Big Flat: History of a New York Tenement House," *American Historical Review*, LXIV (October, 1958), 54.

49. Edith Wharton, *The Age of Innocence* (New York, 1962), 32. The novel appeared first in 1920.

50. Charlotte Perkins Gilman, "The Passing of the Home in Great American Cities," *Cosmopolitan*, XXXVIII (December, 1904), 139.

51. George Augustus Sala, *London Up to Date* (London, 1894), x, 212.

52. I. N. Phelps Stokes, "Appendix," in James Ford, *Slums and Housing: History, Conditions, Policy*, 2 vols. (Cambridge, Mass., 1936), II, 867.

53. Charles H. Israels, "New York Apartment Houses," *Architectural Record*, XI (June, 1901), 477.

54. Hubert, Pirsson & Hoddick, "New York Flats and French Flats," *Architectural Record*, II (July–September, 1892), 55.

55. *Ibid.*

56. "Some Apartment Houses in Chicago," *Architectural Record*, XXX (February, 1907), 122.

57. Ernest Flagg, "The Planning of Apartment Houses and Tenements," *Architectural Review* (Boston), X (July, 1903), 89.

58. "The Problems of Living in New York," *Harper's New Monthly Magazine*, LXV (November, 1882), 918.

59. "The New Homes of New York: A Study of Flats," *Scribner's Monthly*, III (March, 1874), 76.

60. Andrew Alpern, *Apartments for the Affluent: A Historical Survey of Buildings in New York* (New York, 1975), 3, 108.

61. "Problems of Living in New York," 922.

62. William Dean Howells, *A Hazard of New Fortunes* (New York, 1960), 46, 50–51, 53. The novel was first printed in *Harper's Weekly* in 1889.

63. W. G. Hoskins, "The Rebuilding of Rural England, 1570–1640," *Past and Present*, no. 4 (November, 1953), 55.

64. Ernest Flagg, "The New York Tenement-House Evil and Its Cure," *Scribner's Monthly*, XVI (July, 1894), 108.
65. Howells, *A Hazard of New Fortunes*, 80.
66. Henry James, *The Bostonians*, (New York, 1886), 28.
67. Frank R. Stockton, *Rudder Grange* (New York, 1879), 1.
68. A. C. David, "A Cooperative Studio Building," *Architectural Record*, XIV (October, 1903), 293; W. W. Wheatly, "Transporting New York's Millions," *World's Work*, VI (May, 1903), 3423.
69. John Anderson Miller, *Fares, Please* (New York, 1941), 3–4.
70. "Street Railroads," *San Francisco City Directory 1875*, p. 20; George Rogers Taylor, "The Beginning of Mass Transportation in Urban America, Part II," *Smithsonian Journal of History*, I (Fall, 1966), 36, 39, 43, 49.
71. Marcus T. Reynolds, "The Housing of the Poor in American Cities," *Publications of the American Economic Association*, VIII (March–May, 1893), 109.
72. Kenneth T. Jackson, "Urban Deconcentration in the Nineteenth Century: A Statistical Inquiry," in Leo F. Schnore, ed., *The New Urban History* (Princeton, N.J., 1975), 140.
73. George W. Hilton, "Transport Technology and the Urban Pattern," *Journal of Contemporary History*, IV (July, 1969), 126.
74. Robert Treat Paine, "The Housing Conditions in Boston," *Annals of the American Academy of Political and Social Science*, III (July, 1902), 124; Sam B. Warner, Jr., *Streetcar Suburbs: The Process of Growth in Boston, 1807–1900* (Cambridge, Mass., 1962), 157.
75. Hilton, "Transport Technology," 127.
76. W. W. Wheatly, "Transporting New York's Millions," 3422.

## III. METROPOLITAN PRESS

1. Horace Greeley, *Recollections of a Busy Life. A New Edition, with a Memoir of Mr. Greeley's Later Years and Death* (New York, 1873), 83–85.
2. S. N. D. North, "History and Present Condition of the Newspaper and Periodical Press of the United States, with a Catalogue of the Publications of the Census Year," in U.S., Department of the Interior, Bureau of the Census, *Tenth Census* (Washington, 1884), VIII, 51.
3. Frederic Hudson, *Journalism in the United States, from 1690 to 1872* (New York, 1873), 243, 559.

4. James D. McCabe, "The Metropolitan Press," in *New York by Sunlight and Gaslight* (Philadelphia, 1881), 592–601.

5. Whitelaw Reid, *Some Newspaper Tendencies: An Address Delivered Before the Editorial Associations of New York and Ohio* (New York, 1879), 21.

6. Frank Luther Mott, *American Journalism: A History of Newspapers in the United States through 260 Years, 1690 to 1950*, rev. ed. (New York, 1950), 229, 431, 519, 526.

7. Edward Warren, *The Life of John Collins Warren, M.D., Compiled Chiefly from His Autobiography and Journals*, 2 vols. (Boston, 1860), I, 14.

8. P. T. Barnum, *The Art of Money Getting, or Golden Rules for Making Money*, appeared frequently as an addition to his *Life*, first published in 1855. The quote is from a later edition of *The Life of Barnum, the World-Renowned Showman* (New York, 1899), 506.

9. North, "History and Present Condition of the Newspaper," 51.

10. Marvin Trachtenberg, *The Statue of Liberty* (New York, 1976), 183–84.

11. New York *World*, May 11, 1883.

12. Abraham Cahan, *Yekl: A Tale of the New York Ghetto* (New York, 1896), 2–14.

13. William S. Rossiter, "Printing and Publishing," in U.S., Department of the Interior, Bureau of the Census, *Twelfth Census* (Washington, 1902), IX, 1048. North, "History and Present Condition of the Newspaper," 126–31.

14. Rossiter, "Printing," 1032, 1048.

15. New York *Sun*, September 3, 1833.

16. Charles Dickens, *Martin Chuzzlewit* (New York, 1965), 260–61. "The Life and Adventures of Martin Chuzzlewit" appeared first in twenty monthly installments from January 1843 to July 1844.

17. James D. McCabe, Jr., *Lights and Shadows of New York Life* (Philadelphia, 1872), 14.

18. Max O'Rell [pseud. of Paul Blouët], *A Frenchman in America: Recollections of Men and Things* (New York, 1891), 115, 118.

19. Edward Winslow Martin, *The Secrets of the Great City: A Work Descriptive of the Virtues and the Vices, the Mysteries, Miseries and Crimes of New York City* (Philadelphia, 1868), 15.

20. Otto Groth, *Die unerkannte Kulturmacht: Grundlegung der Zeitungswissenschaft (Periodik)*, 7 vols. (Berlin, 1960–72), I, 175.

21. Knut Hamsun, *The Cultural Life of Modern America*, trans. Barbara Gordon Morgridge (Cambridge, Mass., 1969), 25.

22. Theodore Dreiser, *A Book about Myself* (New York, 1922), 467, 485.

23. Philadelphia *Inquirer*, January 3, 1890.

24. "Characters about Town: The 'Bohemian,' " San Francisco *Golden City*, January 26, 1868.

25. For a succinct discussion of "journalese" turn to Wilson Follett, *Modern American Usage*, ed. Jacques Barzun (New York, 1974), 240–42.

26. *Inquirer*, January 3, 1890.

27. San Francisco *Call*, January 3, 1874.

28. *Golden City*, January 26, 1868.

29. Alexis de Tocqueville, *Democracy in America*, ed. J. P. Mayer, and trans. George Lawrence (Garden City, N.Y., 1979), 519.

30. Lambert A. Wilmer, *Our Press Gang: or, A Complete Exposition of the Corruptions and Crimes of the American Newspaper* (Philadelphia, 1860), 18–19.

31. Bernard Weisberger, *The American Newspaperman* (Chicago, 1961), 75; Mott, *American Journalism*, 193–98, 257–62.

32. North, "History and Present Condition of the Newspaper," 46–47.

33. Hudson, *Journalism in the United States*, 394; Alan R. Miller, "America's First Political Satirist: Seba Smith of Maine," *Journalism Quarterly*, XLVII (Autumn, 1970), 488–92.

34. Hudson, *Journalism in the United States*, 411.

35. Frank Presbrey, *The History and Development of Advertising* (Garden City, N.Y., 1929), 196; Mott, *American Journalism*, 228–41.

36. New York *Herald*, May 6, 1835.

37. *Ibid.*, April 11, 12, 13, 1836.

38. *Ibid.*, June 2–10, 1836. See also James L. Crouthamel, "James Gordon Bennett, the New York *Herald*, and the Development of Newspaper Sensationalism," *New York History*, LIV (July, 1973), 303–7.

39. Crouthamel, "Bennett," 298, 306–7, 314–16.

40. Allan Nevins, ed., *The Diary of Philip Hone, 1828–1851*, 2 vols. (New York, 1927), I, 275.

41. *Ibid.*, II, 518.

42. Alain René Le Sage, *Le Diable boiteux* (Paris, 1707).

43. Candace Stone, *Dana and "The Sun"* (New York, 1938), 385–93, 403–4; Mott, *American Journalism*, 376–77.

44. "Trying Tramping," San Francisco *Daily Evening Post*, August 3, 6, 8, 10, 16, 24, September 7, October 12, 1878.

45. *Sun*, September 3, 1833.

46. Presbrey, *History of Advertising*, 195.

47. *Ibid.*, 198, 208.

48. Daniel Frohman, *Hints to Advertisers* (New York, 1869), quoted in *ibid.*, 255–56.

49. *Ibid.*, 210.

50. Reid, *Some Newspaper Tendencies*, 13.

51. George P. Rowell & Company, *American Newspaper Directory* (New York, 1869).

52. Neil Harris, *Humbug: The Art of P. T. Barnum* (Boston, 1973), 118–20, 121–34, 141; "The Late Robert Bonner," New York *Times*, July 8, 1899; James Melvin Lee, "Robert Bonner," *Dictionary of American Biography*, s.v. II, 437 (hereafter cited as *DAB*).

53. William Cullen Bryant, in the New York *Evening Post*, March 20, 1832.

54. Rossiter, "Printing," 1048.

55. Alfred M. Lee, *The Daily Newspaper in America: The Evolution of a Social Instrument* (New York, 1937), 83.

56. "The Classification of News," *The Journalist*, July 9, 1887, p. 4.

57. George Juergens, "A Newspaper for Women," in *Joseph Pulitzer and the New York World* (Princeton, 1966), 132–73.

58. Edward Bok, *The Americanization of Edward Bok: The Autobiography of a Dutch Boy Fifty Years After* (New York, 1924), 168.

59. Hamilton Holt, *Commercialism and Journalism* (Boston, 1909), 83.

60. John Rickards Betts, "Sporting Journalism in Nineteenth-Century America," *American Quarterly*, V (Spring, 1953), 53.

61. Mott, *American Journalism*, 298, 397, 496.

62. U.S., Department of the Interior, Bureau of the Census, *Aggregate Value and Produce, and Number of Persons Employed in Mines, Agriculture, Commerce, Manufactures, &c., Exhibiting a Full View of the Pursuits, Industry, and Resources of the United States of America* (Washington, 1841), 408.

63. North, "History and Present Condition of the Newspaper," 58–59.

64. U.S., Department of the Interior, Bureau of the Census, *Report on Manufacturing Industries in the United States at the Eleventh Census, 1890. Part III. Selected Industries* (Washington, 1895), VI, 651, 654.

65. North, "History and Present Condition of the Newspaper," 52–53, 56–58, 75, 78.

66. *Eleventh Census*, VI, 649.

67. Rowell & Co., *American Newspaper Directory*, 3, 4, 171–77; George P. Rowell, *Forty Years an Advertising Agent, 1865–1905* (New York, 1906), title page.

68. Reid, *Some Newspaper Tendencies*, 30–32.

69. *Ibid.*, 30–31.

70. "A Decade of American Journalism," *Westminster Review*, CXXVIII (October, 1887), 854–55.

71. North, "History and Present Condition of the Newspaper," 51.

72. *The New York Tribune: A Sketch of Its History* (New York, 1883), 12–13; Winston Weisman, "New York and the Problem of the First Skyscraper," *Journal of the Society of Architectural Historians*, XII (No. 1, 1953), 21; Juergens, *Pulitzer*, 7n.

73. Frank M. O'Brien, "Benjamin Henry Day," *DAB*, V, 155.

74. "Report of the Commissioner of Patents for the Year 1843," *House Doc. 177*, 28 Cong., 1 Sess., 5.

75. Charles Sanford Diehl, *The Staff Correspondent: How the News of the World Is Collected and Dispatched by a Body of Trained Writers* (San Antonio, 1931), 75–76.

76. *The New York Tribune*, 25.

77. North, "History and Present Condition of the Newspaper," 85, 90.

78. *World*, September 27, 1883.

79. Don Carlos Seitz, *Joseph Pulitzer: His Life and Letters* (New York, 1924), 214.

80. *Herald*, April 11, 16, 1836.

81. *Leslie's Illustrated Weekly Newspaper*, August 2, 1856, p. 124.

82. Rossiter, "Printing," 1086–87.

83. John R. G. Hazzard, *The Wonders of the Press* (New York, 1878), quoted in North, "History and Present Condition of the Newspaper," 100n.

84. *Ibid.*, 89.

85. Rossiter, "Printing," 1099.

86. North, "History and Present Condition of the Newspaper," 103.

87. Rossiter, "Printing," 1024–26; Lyman Horace Weeks, *A History of Paper-Manufacturing in the United States, 1690–1916* (New York, 1916), 297.

88. Rossiter, "Printing," 1092–94.

89. *Ibid.*, 1100.

90. Presbrey, *History of Advertising*, 250, 358; Lee, *Daily Newspaper*, 129–30.

91. Juergens, *Joseph Pulitzer*, 94–111.

92. "Things Talked Of," *Harper's Weekly*, XXXVII (April 22, 1893), 367.

93. North, "History and Present Condition of the Newspaper," 105.

94. T. L. Nichols, *Forty Years of American Life*, 2d ed. (London, 1874), 216.

95. Hudson, *Journalism in the United States*, 608–10.

96. Richard A. Schwarzlose, "Early Telegraphic News Dispatches: Forerunner of the AP," *Journalism Quarterly*, LI (Winter, 1974), 600.

97. William S. Rossiter, "News-Gathering Organizations," in *Twelfth Census*, IX, 1102–04.

98. Sidney H. Aronson, "Bell's Electrical Try: What's the Use? The Sociology of Early Telephone Usage," in Ithiel de Sola Pool, ed., *The Social Impact of the Telephone* (Cambridge, Mass., 1977), 23.

99. Charles H. Levermore, "The Rise of Metropolitan Journalism, 1800–1840," *American Historical Review*, VI (April, 1901), 446, traces modern journalism to an "aggressive democracy."

100. *Herald*, March 2, 1836.

101. New York *Herald*, June 2, 1840; James Parton, *Famous Americans of Recent Times* (Boston, 1867), 277.

102. Chicago *Times*, June 8, 1861.

103. *Ibid.*, November 27, 1875.

104. Justin E. Walsh, *To Print the News and Raise Hell! A Biography of Wilbur F. Storey* (Chapel Hill, N.C., 1958), 6–8, 138.

105. Will Irvin, "The American Newspaper: A Study of Journalism in Its Relation to the Public. II: The Dim Beginnings," *Collier's*, XLVI (February 4, 1911), 18.

106. H. L. Mencken, *Newspaper Days, 1899–1906* (New York, 1945), 147.

107. Greeley, *Recollections*, 139; *The New York Tribune*, 5.

108. *Tribune*, June 20, 1845.

109. J. Parton, *The Life of Horace Greeley, Editor of the "New York Tribune"* (New York, 1855), 414–16, 420.

110. Juergens, *Pulitzer*, 270–86.

111. Leon Nelson Flint, *The Editorial: A Study in the Effectiveness of Writing* (New York, 1920), 61.

112. Walt McDougal, *This Is the Life!* (New York, 1926), 103, 137.

113. W. A. Swanberg, *Citizen Hearst: A Biography of William Randolph Hearst* (New York, 1961), 101–69.

114. *The Journalist*, January 26, 1889, p. 2; Susan E. Dickerson, "Woman in Journalism," in Annie Nathan Meyer, ed., *Woman's Work in America* (New York, 1891), 128–29.

115. Ida M. Tarbell, *All in the Day's Work: An Autobiography* (New York, 1939), 86.

116. Alexander Black, *Miss Jerry: With Thirty-seven Illustrations from Life Photographs by the Author* (New York, 1895), vii, ix, 152–53.

117. Marion Marzolf, *Up from the Footnote: A History of Women Journalists* (New York, 1977), 13–39.

118. *Herald*, April 12, 1836.

119. Nils Gunnar Nilsson, "The Origins of the Interview," *Journalism Quarterly*, XLVIII (Winter, 1971), 707–13.

120. "Forepaugh's Parade," Philadelphia *Inquirer*, April 20, 1890.

121. *World*, October 30, 1884; McDougal, *This Is the Life!*, 95–98, 100; Juergens, *Pulitzer*, 100, 103. For reprints of the cartoon see William Murrell, *A History of American Graphic Humor 1865–1938*, 2 vols. (New York, 1938), II, 82, plate 68; Stephen Hess and Milton Kaplan, *The Ungentlemanly Art: A History of American Political Cartoons*, rev. ed. (New York, 1975), 121.

122. *World*, June 23, 1883; Juergens, *Pulitzer*, 269.

123. "Eureka Masquerade," *Call*, February 19, 1874.

124. Max Weber, "Geschaeftsbericht," *Verhandlungen des ersten deutschen Soziologentages* (Tübingen, 1911), 49.

125. New York *Times*, January 11, 1920.

## IV. DEPARTMENT STORE

1. Henry James, *A Small Boy and Others* (New York, 1913), 64–66.

2. For general discussions of department store history see Frank M. Mayfield, *The Department Store Story* (New York, 1949); H. Pasdermadjian, *The Department Store: Its Origins, Evolution, and Economics* (London, 1954); John Williams Ferry, *A History of the Department Store* (New York, 1960); Daniel J. Boorstin, *The Americans: The Democratic Experience* (New York, 1973), 101–9.

3. Allan Nevins, ed., *The Diary of Philip Hone, 1828–1851*, 2 vols. (New York, 1927), II, 772.

4. *Ibid.*

5. Winston Weisman, "New York and the Problems of the First Skyscraper," *Journal of the Society of Architectural Historians*, XII, no. 1, (1953), 13.

6. Hans Sedlmayr, *Art in Crisis: The Lost Center*, trans. Brian Battershaw (Chicago, 1958), 32. For a reproduction of the design see *ibid.*, between pp. 68–69. Leo Colze, *Berliner Warenhaeuser* (Berlin, 1907), 16–17; Johannes Wernicke, *Warenhaus, Industrie und Mittelstand* (Berlin, 1911), 14–15.

7. The following discussion of changes in French retailing practices has profited from the work of Michael Barry Miller, "The Department Store and Social Change in Modern France: The Case of the Bon Marché, 1869–1920" (Ph.D. thesis, University of Pennsylvania, 1976), 3–30, 33, 43–46.

8. David H. Pinkney, "The City Grows," in *Napoleon III and the Rebuilding of Paris* (Princeton, N.J., 1958), 151–73.

9. Émile Zola, *Au bonheur des dames* (Paris, 1927), 467. The novel was first published in 1883.

10. This discussion of the Bon Marché as a new building type has gained perspective from a dissertation by Meredith Leslie Clausen, "Frantz Jourdain and the Samaritaine of 1905" (Ph.D. thesis, University of California, Berkeley, 1975), 19–38, 183–92.

11. Zola, *Au bonheur des dames*, 248.

12. For views of the stairs turn to "Le grand escalier du Bon Marché," in Henri Mitterand and Jean Vidal, comps., *Album Zola* (Paris, 1963), 197; Monika Steinhauser, *Die Architektur der Pariser Oper* (Munich, 1969), plate no. 238, "Louis Charles Boileau, Treppenanlage des Kaufhauses 'Au Bon Marché,' Paris, 1872."

13. Steinhauser, *Pariser Oper*, 174.

14. George Augustus Sala, *Twice Round the Clock, or the Hours of the Day and Night in London* (Leicester, Eng., 1971), 175–85. The sketches were first published in 1858. For a view of the Burlington Arcade, one specifically referred to by Sala, see Johann Friedrich Geist, *Passagen, ein Bautyp des 19. Jahrhunderts* (Munich, 1969), plates 11–14.

15. This discussion of William Whiteley and his store has profited from Richard S. Lambert, *The Universal Provider: A Study of William Whiteley and the Rise of the London Department Store* (London, 1938), particularly 21–120. See also Thomas Seccombe, "William Whiteley," *Dictionary of National Biography*, Supplement, III, 652–53 (hereafter cited as *DNB*).

16. "Seasonable Topics from England," New York *Daily Graphic*, May 12, 1876.

17. Bayswater *Chronicle*, December 2, 1876, quoted in Lambert, *Universal Provider*, 86.

18. "William Whiteley," *Encyclopaedia Britannica* (1911), XXVIII, 605.

19. W. P. Frith, *My Autobiography and Reminiscences*, 2d ed., 2 vols. (London, 1887), II, 38–40.

20. *Ibid.*, 39.

21. [George Augustus Sala], "Young London. I. Westbourne-Grove and Thereabouts," London *Daily Telegraph*, June 2, 1879.

22. Anthony Trollope, *North America* (New York, 1951), 212. The original edition appeared in 1862.

23. [Sala], "Young London. I.," *Daily Telegraph*, June 2, 1879.

24. Anna A. Rogers, *Why American Marriages Fail, and Other Papers* (Boston, 1909), 22–23.

25. Alfred D. Chandler, Jr., *The Visible Hand: The Managerial Revolution in American Business* (Cambridge, Mass., 1977), 226.

26. A Late Retailer, *A Peep into Catharine Street, or the Mysteries of Shopping* (New York, 1846), 23–24. See also the comment in New York *Herald,* September 26, 1846.

27. "Method in Trade Carried to Perfection," *Hunt's Merchants' Magazine,* XVII (October, 1847), 441–42.

28. "New-York Daguerreotyped," *Putnam's Monthly,* I (February, 1853), 129.

29. "Editor's Easy Chair," *Harper's New Monthly Magazine,* XLIX (June, 1854), 122.

30. "New-York Daguerreotyped," *Putnam's Monthly,* I (April, 1853), 356.

31. San Francisco *Call,* July 5, 1894; May 24, July 5, 1896; Forest Crissey, *Some Forty Years Ago* (Chicago, 1915), [21].

32. New York *Daily Advertiser,* September 2, 1825.

33. Eliza Leslie, *The Behaviour Book: A Manual for Ladies,* 4th ed. (Philadelphia, 1854), 77.

34. *Ibid.,* 80.

35. *Herald,* September 26, 1846.

36. George Dutton, "An Exposition of the Crisis of 1857," *Hunt's Merchants' Magazine,* XXXVIII (January, 1858), 19–35.

37. "New-York Daguerreotyped," *Putnam's Monthly,* I (April, 1853), 358; *Frank Leslie's Illustrated Newspaper,* October 6, 1860.

38. "Men Who Have Assisted in the Development of Architectural Resources. No. 1. John B. Cornell," *Architectural Record,* I (October–December, 1891), 245. For a tribute to the building written just after its destruction in 1956, turn to Alan Burnham, "Last Look at a Structural Landmark," *Architectural Record,* CXX (September, 1956), 273–79.

39. Elbert Hubbard, "A. T. Stewart," *Little Journeys to the Homes of Great Businessmen,* 2 vols. (New York, 1909), II, 116.

40. "Development of Architectural Resources," 245.

41. Hubbard, "Stewart," 118.

42. William J. Fryer, Jr., "Iron Store-Fronts," *Architectural Review and American Builders' Journal,* I (April, 1869), 621.

43. *Herald,* September 18, 1846; Harry E. Resseguie, "A. T. Stewart's Marble Palace—the Cradle of the Department Store," *New York Historical Society Quarterly,* XLVIII (April, 1964), 146–49; Donald A. Smalley, Introduction to Frances Trollope, *Domestic Manners of the Americans* (New York, 1949), xl–xlix. For a perspective of the Cincin-

nati Bazaar, drawn from a conjectural restoration by Clay Lancester, see his "Egyptian Hall and Mrs. Trollope's Bazaar," *Magazine of Art* (March, 1950), 97.

44. For a picture of the Tiffany dome turn to Lloyd Wendt and Herman Kogan, *Give the Lady What She Wants!* (Chicago, 1952), 2.

45. "Editor's Easy Chair," *Harper's New Monthly Magazine*, IX (July, 1854), 261.

46. *Herald*, September 18, 1846; "Architecture in the United States," *North American Review*, LVIII (April, 1844), 436–80. For a discussion of the *palazzo* mode turn to Winston Weisman, "Commercial Palaces of New York: 1845–1875," *Art Bulletin*, XXXIV (December, 1954), 285–302.

47. "Development of Architectural Resources," 245.

48. "New-York Daguerrotyped," *Putnam's Monthly*, I (April, 1853), 358; *Herald*, September 18, 1846.

49. For a reproduction of an interior view of Stewart's New Store see Resseguie, "A. T. Stewart's Marble Palace," 161.

50. Edward Bellamy, *Looking Backward: 2000–1887* (New York, 1960), 207. The book was first published in 1888.

51. "Alexander T. Stewart," *Harper's New Monthly Magazine*, XXXIV (March, 1867), 523.

52. "Stewart, and the Dry Goods Trade of New York," *Continental History*, II (October, 1862), 528–34; "Stewart," *Harper's Magazine*, XXXIV (March, 1867), 522–25; Matthew Hale Smith, *Sunshine and Shadow in New York* (Hartford, Conn., 1868), 57–59; James Grant Wilson, "Alexander T. Stewart," *Harper's Weekly*, XX (April 29, 1876), 345–46; Hubbard, "Stewart," 97–126. See also Charles S. Sydnor, "Alexander Turney Stewart," *DAB*, XVIII, 4; Harry E. Resseguie, "The Decline and Fall of the Commercial Empire of A. T. Stewart," *Business History Review*, XXXVI (Autumn, 1962), 255–86, "A. J. Stewart's Marble Palace," 131–62, and "Alexander Turney Stewart and the Development of the Department Store, 1823–1876," *Business History Review*, XXXIX (Autumn, 1965), 301–22.

53. New York *Evening Post*, September 22, 1846.

54. "Announcing the Death of Mr. Stewart—Scene in Front of the Tenth Street Store—Drawn by C. S. Reinhart," *Harper's Weekly*, April 29, 1876, p. 345. For Charles Stanley Reinhart see William Howe Downes, "Benjamin Franklin Reinhart," *DAB*, XV, 490–91.

55. Reginald Pond, *Selfridge: A Biography* (London, 1960), 107.

56. Elizabeth Cady Stanton, *Eighty Years and More: Reminiscences 1815–1897* (New York, 1971), 205–9. The book appeared first in 1898.

57. William Cole and Florett Robinson, eds., *Women Are Wonderful! A History in Cartoons of a Hundred Years with America's Most Controversial Figure* (Cambridge, Mass., 1965), 173.

58. Theodore Dreiser, *Sister Carrie* (New York, 1961), 299. The novel was first published in 1900.

59. Jesse Rainsford Sprague, *The Making of a Merchant* (New York, 1928), 30–31.

60. Philadelphia *Inquirer*, January 3, 1888; Edward Filene, *More Profits from Merchandising* (Chicago, 1926), 129–31.

61. *Golden Book of the Wanamaker Stores: Jubilee Year, 1861–1911* (Philadelphia, 1911), 12.

62. Amos W. Wright, "Marshall Field," *Harper's Weekly*, XXXV (March 21, 1891), 211; Ralph M. Hower, *History of Macy's of New York: 1858–1919* (Cambridge, Mass., 1943), 49; Chandler, *Visible Hand*, 227.

63. For a good description of department stores in the 1890's turn to Samuel Hopkins Adams, "The Department Store," *Scribner's Magazine*, XXI (January, 1897), 1–27. See also "The Department Store in the East," *Arena*, XXII (August, 1899), 165–86; "The Department Store in the West," *ibid.* (September, 1899), 320–41.

64. John Wanamaker, "The Evolution of Mercantile Business," *Annals of the American Academy of Political and Social Science*, XV, Supplement (1900), 133; Louis E. Schlèber, *The Modern Store* (Boston, 1916), 5. I am indebted to Raymond Hillman and the Pioneer Museum and Haggin Galleries in Stockton, California, for a copy of the second publication.

65. Ernest Poole, *Giants Gone: Men Who Made Chicago* (New York, 1943), 115.

66. Thorstein Veblen, "Pecuniary Canons of Taste," in *The Theory of the Leisure Class* (Boston, 1973), 87–118. The book was first published in 1889.

67. Hugh Dalziel Duncan, *Culture and Democracy: The Struggle for Form in Society and Architecture in Chicago and the Middle West During the Life and Times of Louis H. Sullivan* (Totowa, N.J., 1965), 127.

68. Thomas Wakefield Goodspeed, "Marshall Field," in *The University of Chicago Biographical Sketches*, 2d ed. (Chicago, 1924), 28.

69. Adams, "Department Store," 14.

70. U.S., Department of Commerce, Bureau of the Census, *Statistics of Women at Work: Based on Unpublished Information Derived from the Schedules of the Twelfth Census: 1900* (Washington, D.C., 1907), 92.

71. Hower, *Macy's*, 65–66.

72. For the average working conditions of women clerks in department stores see Consumers' League of New York, "Standards of a Fair House," in Adams, "Department Store," 24–25; "Some Features of Department Store Management," *Annals of the American Academy of Political and Social Science*, XIX (March, 1902), 156–58; and for poor conditions turn to the expose by Annie Marion MacLean, "Two Weeks in Department Stores," *American Journal of Sociology*, IV (May, 1899), 721–41. See also C. Wright Mills, "The Great Salesroom," in *White Collar: The American Middle Classes* (New York, 1951), 161–88.

73. William Sidney Porter, "A Lickpenny Lover," *The Complete Works of O. Henry*, 2 vols. (Garden City, N.Y., 1953), II, 1261– 62.

72. Porter, "The Ferry of Unfulfillment," *ibid.*, 1471; "The Purple Dress," *ibid.*, 1424–28.

75. These comments on shopping have profited from Dorothy Davis, *A History of Shopping* (London, 1966), 288–95.

76. For a reprint turn to the St. Louis *Republic*, November 5, 1892.

77. Wendt and Kogan, *Give the Lady What She Wants!*, 24, 218, 308; John H. Appel, *The Business Biography of John Wanamaker, Founder and Builder: America's Pioneer Merchant from 1861 to 1922* (New York, 1930), 102, 192.

78. James Playsted Wood, *The Story of Advertising* (New York, 1958), 184–85. Herbert Adams Gibbons, "Advertising Pioneer," in *John Wanamaker*, 2 vols. (New York, 1926), II, 14–27.

79. Frank Presbrey, *The History and Development of Advertising* (Garden City, N.Y., 1929), 245–48.

80. Appel, *John Wanamaker*, 389.

81. Gibbons, *Wanamaker*, II, 6. Hubbard, "A. T. Stewart," 118, gives
       JOHN WANAMAKER
       SUCCESSOR TO
       A. T. STEWART.

82. Robert W. Twyman, *History of Marshall Field & Co., 1852–1906* (Philadelphia, 1954), 173.

83. Hower, *Macy's*, 43.

84. Robert Muellerheim, *Die Wochenstube in der Kunst* (Stuttgart, 1904), 207.

85. Carl Bridenbaugh, *Cities in the Wilderness: The First Century of Urban Life in America, 1625–1742* (New York, 1938), 97.

86. Jane Addams, "The Subtle Problems of Charity," *Atlantic Monthly*, LXXXIII (February, 1899), 168.

87. St. Louis *Republic*, April 16, 1893; Philadelphia *Inquirer*, April 2, 1890.

88. *Republic*, February 19, 1893.

89. *Inquirer*, January 3, 5, 26, February 13, March 16, 1888; *Republic*, April 16, 1893.

90. *Herald*, September 26, 1846. For a reproduction of the cut see Resseguie, "Stewart's Marble Palace," 134.

91. Rogers, *American Marriages*, 25–26.

92. Karl Marx and Friedrich Engels, *Manifesto of the Community Party*, in Robert Maynard Hutchins, ed., *Great Books of the Western World*, 54 vols. (Chicago, 1952), L, 421. The *Manifesto* was first published in 1848.

93. Dreiser, *Sister Carrie*, 88.

94. James, *A Small Boy*, 66.

95. Percival and Paul Goodman, *Communitas: Means of Livelihood and Ways of Life* (New York, 1960), 127.

## V. BALL PARK

1. New York *Times*, May 31, 1888.

2. For general baseball history turn to Harold Seymour, *Baseball: The Early Years* (New York, 1960), and *Baseball: The Golden Age* (New York, 1971); David Quentin Voigt, *American Baseball: From Gentleman's Sport to the Commissioner System* (Norman, Okla., 1966), and *American Baseball: From the Commissioners to Continental Expansion* (Norman, Okla., 1970).

3. For a theory of play and games see Roger Caillois, *Man, Play, and Games* (New York, 1961), 3–10, as well as his critique of Johan Huizinga's theory of play (in *Homo Ludens* [New York, 1950], 13, 28) in his *Man and the Sacred* (New York, 1959), Appendix II, "Play and the Sacred," 152–62.

4. Roland Auguet, *Cruelty and Civilization: The Roman Games* (London, 1972), 49–50, 51.

5. Keith Thomas, "Work and Leisure in Pre-Industrial Society," *Past and Present*, no. 29 (December, 1964), 52.

6. For general histories of sports and spectator sports in the United States turn to John Allan Krout, *Annals of American Sport* (New York, 1929); Jennie Holliman, *American Sports (1785–1835)* (Durham, N.C., 1931); John Durant and Otto Bettmann, *Pictorial History of American Sports: From Colonial Times to the Present* (New York, 1952); John

Rickards Betts, *America's Sporting Heritage: 1850–1950* (Reading, Mass., 1974).

7. Quoted in Herbert Manchester, *Four Centuries of Sport in America, 1490–1890* (New York, 1931), 129.

8. William Henry Nugent, "The Sports Section," *American Mercury,* XVI (March, 1929), 329–31; Albert G. Spalding, *America's National Game: Historic Facts Concerning the Beginning, Evolution, Development and Popularity of Base Ball. With Personal Reminiscences of Its Vicissitudes, Its Victories and Its Votaries* (New York, 1911), 442.

9. Robert W. Malcolmson, *Popular Recreations in English Society, 1700–1850* (Cambridge, 1973), 90–91; Daniel T. Rodgers, *The Work Ethic in Industrial America* (Chicago, 1978), 102–3; Voigt, *Baseball: From Gentleman's Sport,* 87–89; Dale A. Somers, "The Leisure Revolution: Recreation in the American City, 1820–1920," *Journal of Popular Culture,* V (Summer, 1971), 113–39.

10. Nicholas B. Wainwright, ed., *A Philadelphia Perspective: The Diary of Sidney George Fisher Covering the Years 1834–1871* (Philadelphia, 1969), 333.

11. Allan Nevins, ed., *The Diary of Philip Hone, 1828–1851,* 2 vols. (New York, 1927), II 600–1.

12. David Graham Phillips, "The Delusion of the Race-Track," *Cosmopolitan,* XXXVIII (January, 1905), 262.

13. *Times,* October 14, 1853.

14. Edward W. Townsend, "A Sporty Boston Boy," *Fadden Explains: Max Expounds* (New York, 1895), 33.

15. *Times,* July 9, 1889; New York *National Police Gazette,* July 27, 1889; Dale A. Somers, *The Rise of Sports in New Orleans, 1850–1900* (Baton Rouge, 1972), 170–73.

16. Quoted in Krout, *American Sport,* 199.

17. Robert W. Henderson, *Ball, Bat and Bishop: The Origin of Ball Games* (New York, 1947), 174.

18. *Ibid.,* 132–69; Arthur Bartlett, *Baseball and Mr. Spalding: The History and Romance of Baseball* (New York, 1951), 1–11; Seymour, *Baseball: Early Years,* 8–11. For an illuminating discussion of baseball myths see David Q. Voigt, *America Through Baseball* (Chicago, 1976).

19. "The Centennial Season's Campaign," New York *Clipper,* November 6, 1875.

20. Henderson, *Ball,* 161–65; Krout, *American Sport,* 117.

21. Carl Wittke, "Baseball in Its Adolescence," *Ohio State Archeological and Historical Quarterly,* LX (April, 1952), 120–21.

22. New York *Spirit of the Times,* January 31, 1857.

23. Seymour, *Baseball: Early Years*, 35–37.

24. Somers, *Sports in New Orleans*, 50; Cecil O. Monroe, "The Rise of Baseball in Minnesota," *Minnesota History*, XIX (June, 1938), 162; Fred W. Lange, *History of Baseball in California and Pacific Coast Leagues, 1847–1938* (Oakland, 1938), 6–7.

25. Krout, *American Sport*, 119; Frederick G. Lieb, *The Baseball Story* (New York, 1950), 34.

26. Spaulding, *America's National Game*, 95–96.

27. Henry Chadwick, "Old Time Baseball," *Outing*, XXXVIII (July, 1901), 420.

28. "The Championship Record," *Clipper*, September 11, 1875. For Chadwick's role among the emerging baseball reporters see Voigt, *Baseball: From Gentleman's Sport*, 91–96.

29. *Spirit of the Times*, November, 1856.

30. John Rickards Betts, "Sporting Journalism in Nineteenth-Century America," *American Quarterly*, V (Spring, 1973), 41, 43, 49, 50.

31. For an example see "Close of the Game. Game Riddled with Corruption," *Clipper*, November 6, 1875.

32. Hugh Fullerton, "The Fellows Who Made the Game," *Saturday Evening Post*, CC (April 21, 1928), 18.

33. "Perils of the Baseball Lingo," reprinted in *Literary Digest*, XLVII (September 6, 1913), 379–80.

34. "English and Baseball," *Nation*, XCVII (August 21, 1913), 161.

35. Fullerton, "The Fellows," *Saturday Evening Post*, CC (April 21, 1928), 19. Hugh Fullerton's article also provided the lead to the follow-up story about the "Cross of Gold" speech. For Peter Finley Dunne's baseball language turn to H. L. Mencken, *The American Language*, 3d ed., (New York, 1933), 404–5.

36. Mrs. Fremont Older, *William Randolph Hearst: American* (New York, 1936), 82; Betts "Sporting Journalism," 56.

37. Bill Shannon and George Kalinsky, *The Ballparks* (New York, 1975), 4–5.

38. Seymour, *Baseball: Early Years*, 48–48, 51–52.

39. *Ibid.*, 56.

40. Joseph S. Stern, Jr., "The Team That Couldn't Be Beat: The Red Stockings of 1869," *Cincinnati Historical Society Bulletin*, XXVII (Spring, 1969), 25–41; Robert Knight Barney, "Of Rails and Red Stockings: Episodes in the Expansion of the 'National Pastime' in the American West," *Journal of the West*, XVII (July, 1978), 61–70.

41. Will Irwin, "Baseball. IV. The Business Side of the Game," *Collier's*, XLIII (June 5, 1909), 11.

42. Robert B. Weaver, *Amusements and Sports in American Life* (Chi-

cago, 1934), 102; David Quentin Voigt, "Baseball's Lost Centennial," *Journal of Popular Culture*, V (Summer, 1971), 60–64.

43. Spalding, *America's National Game*, 207.
44. Seymour, *Baseball: Early Years*, 76–85.
45. John W. Stayton, "Baseball Jurisprudence," *American Law Review*, XLIV (May–June, 1910), 374.
46. Quoted in Seymour, *Baseball: Early Years*, 80.
47. Peter A. Demens [Tverskoy], "Sketches of the North American United States," published in 1895; quoted in Oscar Handlin, comp., *This Was America* (Cambridge, Mass., 1949), 361.
48. Bruce Catton, "The Great American Game," *American Heritage*, X (April, 1959), 18.
49. Lewis Mumford, *Ethics and Civilization* (New York, 1963), 303.
40. Will Irwin, "Baseball. II. Working Out the Game," *Collier's* XLIII (May 15, 1909), 14.
51. Spalding, *America's National Game*, 6–8; David Lamoureaux, "Baseball in the Late Nineteenth Century: The Source of Its Appeal," *Journal of Popular Culture*, XI (Winter, 1977), 603–4; Walter Camp, "The American National Game: Professional and College Base-Ball in the Making," *Century Magazine*, LXXIX (April, 1910), 948.
52. Voigt, *Baseball: From Gentleman's Sport*, 184–85.
53. *Clipper*, November 27, 1884.
54. Voigt, *Baseball: From Gentleman's Sport*, 187–92.
55. In the early 1880's the title read: "New York *Clipper*. The Spirit of the Times Shall Teach Me Speed. *King John*, Act IV."
56. James L. Steele, "How the National Game Developed: Some Baseball Reminiscences," *Outing*, XLIV (June, 1904), 334.
57. William Chambers, *Things as They Are in America* (Philadelphia, 1854), 178.
58. Quoted in Irwin, "Baseball. II," 14.
59. *Ibid.*, 15.
60. Adrian C. Anson, *A Ball Player's Career: Personal Experience and Reminiscences* (Chicago, 1900), 33.
61. "Amherst 73, Williams 32—Eighty Years Ago," *Amherst Graduates' Quarterly*, XXVIII (May, 1939), 219–25; Stern, "The Red Stockings of 1869," 37; Anson, *Ball Player's Career*, 36.
62. Robert H. Boyle, "The Unreal Ideal: Frank Merriwell," *Sport—Mirror of American Life* (Boston, 1963), 241–71.
63. Carl H. Scheele, "Baseball—A Shared Excitement," in Peter C. Marzio, ed., *A Nation of Nations: The People Who Came to America as Seen Through Objects and Documents Exhibited at the Smithsonian Institution* (New York, 1976), 461.

64. Frederic L. Paxson, "The Rise of Sport," *Mississippi Valley Historical Review*, IV (September, 1917), 152–53.

65. Charles Phelps Cushing, "The Baseball of the City Urchin: The Game Has Been Modified So That It May Be Played in the Streets of the City," *Collier's*, XLVII (June 10, 1911), 20, 30, and "Back-Lot Baseball: The Real Baseball, Where Grit Is Learned and Wits Are Sharpened, Is the Baseball of the Back Lots," *ibid.* (August 12, 1911), 21. For variations of the game see Stewart Culin, "Street Games of Boys in Brooklyn, N.Y.," *Journal of American Folklore,* IV (1891), 231–33.

66. *Frank Leslie's Illustrated Newspaper*, October 30, 1869.

67. Alice Earle, *Customs and Fashions in Old New England* (New York, 1894), 18.

68. Jane Addams, *The Spirit of Youth and the City Streets* (New York, 1909), 5.

69. Wilbur P. Bowen and Elmer D. Mitchell, *The Theory of Organized Play: Its Nature and Significance* (New York, 1928), 24–25.

70. Frederic C. Howe, *The Modern City and Its Problems* (New York, 1915), 317.

71. Philadelphia *Sporting Life*, February 4, 1885, quoted in Seymour, *Baseball: Early Years*, 190.

72. "Modern Baseball," *Times*, October 11, 1905.

73. "An Important Suit [J. E. Dolen *v.* Metropolitan Exhibition Company]," *Clipper*, March 26, 1887.

74. Scheele, "Baseball—A Shared Excitement," 462–77.

75. Seymour, *Baseball: Early Years*, 42. For "Negro baseball" turn to Robert Peterson, *Only the Ball Was White* (Englewood Cliffs, N.J., 1970).

76. Spalding, *America's National Game*, 6.

77. Edwin Davies Schoonmaker, "Baseball and the Theater," *Harper's Weekly*, LVIII (January 17, 1914), 31.

78. Frank Barkely Copley, *Frederick W. Taylor: Father of Scientific Management*, 2 vols. (New York, 1923), I, 56.

79. R. G. Knowles, "Baseball," in *Encyclopedia of Sport*, 2 vols. (London, 1897–98), I, 73. John J. Evers and Hugh S. Fullerton, *Touching Second: The Science of Baseball* (Chicago, 1910), 119–39, expounded the geometry of the game.

80. Clarence Deming, "Old Days in Baseball," *Outing*, XL (June, 1902), 360.

81. Samuel Clemens, "Welcome Home to a Baseball Team Returning from a World Tour by Way of the Sandwich Islands (1889)," *The Writings of Mark Twain. Definitive Edition*, 37 vols. (New York, 1922–25), XVIII, 145.

82. M'Cready Sykes, "The Most Perfect Thing in America," *Everybody's Magazine*, XXV (October, 1911)), 446.
83. London *Field*, quoted in Spalding, *America's National Game*, 186.
84. Clemens, "Welcome Home," 145, 149.
85. H. L. Mencken, *Happy Days, 1880–1892* (New York, 1940), 231.
86. Christy Mathewson, *Pitching in a Pinch: or Baseball from the Inside* (New York, 1912), 211; Seymour, *Baseball: Early Years*, 182–85.
87. Seymour, *Baseball: Early Years*, 345–49; Roger Angell, *The Summer Game* (New York, 1972), 4, 295.
88. Spalding, *America's National Game*, 442.
89. Fred Lieb, *The Baltimore Orioles* (New York, 1953), 20.
90. Spalding, *America's National Game*, 400–41.
91. *Frank Leslie's Illustrated Newspaper*, October 10, 1885; *Clipper*, September 11, 1975; Henry Hall, ed., *The Tribune Book of Open-Air Sports: Prepared by the New York Tribune with the Aid of Acknowledged Experts* (New York, 1887), iii.
92. Seymour, *Baseball: Early Years*, 194–95.
93. *Ibid.*, 193.
94. John H. Lancaster, "Baltimore, a Pioneer in Organized Baseball," *Maryland Historical Magazine*, XXXV (March, 1940), 32.
95. Quoted in Betts, *America's Sporting Heritage*, 118.
96. Allan Nevins, "Preface" to Voigt, *Baseball: From Gentleman's Sport*, vii.
97. Holliman, *American Sports*, 10.
98. Wilhelm Liebknecht, *Ein Blick in die neue Welt* (Stuttgart, 1887), 124–25.
99. Michael Novak, *The Joy of Sports: End Zones, Bases, Baskets, Balls, and the Consecration of the American Spirit* (New York, 1976), 62.
100. For an example of a downtown scoreboard see the full-page photo on the front page of the Sunday picture section, *Times*, October 20, 1912.
101. Seymour, *Baseball: Early Years*, 203.
102. Edward Grant Barrow, with James M. Kahn, *My Fifty Years in Baseball* (New York, 1951), 25.
103. Frederick S. Tyler, "Fifty-Five Years of Local Baseball, 1893–1947," *Records of the Columbia Historical Society of Washington, D.C.* XLVIII–XLIX (1946–47), 269.
104. Zane Grey, " 'Old Well-Well'!," New York *Success Magazine*, XV (July, 1910), reprinted in *The Redheaded Outfield and Other Base- -ball Stories* (New York, 1920).
105. *Times*, April 13, 1909; *Harper's Weekly*, LIII (May 2, 1909), 389;

Shannon and Kalinsky, *Ballparks*, 59, 90, 91, 180, 183, 197; Lawrence S. Ritter, *The Glory of Their Times: The Story of the Early Days of Baseball Told by the Men Who Played It* (New York, 1966), 104–5.

106. Johnnie Evers and Hugh S. Fullerton, *Baseball in the Big Leagues* (Chicago, 1910), 24.

107. Allen Guttmann, *From Ritual to Record: The Nature of Modern Sport* (New York, 1978), 115–16; Blake McKelvey, *The Urbanization of America: 1860–1915* (New Brunswick, N.J., 1965), 184–85.

108. "The Athletic Craze," *Nation*, LVII (December 7, 1893), 423.

109. Carl Diem, "Das Baseballspiel," *Olympische Flamme: Das Buch vom Sport*, 3 vols. (Berlin, 1942), II, 830.

110. "Casey at the Bat. A Ballad of the Republic, Sung in the Year 1888," San Francisco *Examiner*, June 3, 1888.

111. DeWolf Hopper, *Once a Clown, Always a Clown: Reminiscences* (Boston, 1927), 72, 76–77, 80–81; Tristram Potter Coffin, *The Old Ball Game: Baseball in Folklore and Fiction* (New York, 1971), 154–61.

## VI. VAUDEVILLE HOUSE

1. Boston *Evening Transcript*, March 27, 1894; New York *Herald*, March 27, 1894.

2. New York *Dramatic Mirror*, March 24, 31, 1894.

3. William H. Birkmire, *The Planning and Construction of American Theatres* (New York, 1901), 50, 52.

4. *Evening Transcript*, March 27, 1894.

5. For the general history of vaudeville turn to Douglas Gilbert, *American Vaudeville: Its Life and Times* (New York, 1940); Joe Laurie, Jr., *Vaudeville: From the Honky-Tonks to the Palace* (New York, 1953); Bernard Sobel, *A Pictorial History of Vaudeville* (New York, 1961); Albert F. McLean, Jr., *American Vaudeville as Ritual* (Lexington, Ky., 1965); John E. DiMeglio, *Vaudeville, U.S.A.* (Bowling Green, Ohio, 1973).

6. *Dramatic Mirror*, March 31, 1894; Albert F. McLean, Jr., ed., "Genesis of Vaudeville: Two Letters from B. F. Keith," *Theatre Survey*, I (1960), 90.

7. Henry Ward Beecher, *Star Papers: or, Experiences of Art and Nature* (New York, 1855), 263–70.

8. *Herbert Spencer on the Americans and the Americans on Herbert*

*Spencer. Being a Full Report of His Interview, and of the Proceedings of the Farewell Banquet of Nov. 11, 1882* (New York, 1883), 34–35.

9. Washington Gladden, "Christianity and Popular Amusements," *Century Magazine*, XXIX (January, 1885), 392.

10. Gilbert, *American Vaudeville*, 4.

11. Katherine G. Busbey, *Home Life in America* (London, 1910), 187.

12. Phyllis Hartnoll, ed., *The Oxford Companion to the Theatre* (London, 1951), 822.

13. Allan Nevins, ed., *The Diary of Philip Hone, 1828–1851*. 2 vols. (New York, 1927), I, 271.

14. *The Compact Edition of the Oxford English Dictionary*, 2 vols. (New York, 1971), *s.v.* "vaudeville."

15. San Francisco *Daily Pacific News*, December 21, 1850.

16. Charles Pike Sawyer, "Mirrors of Variety. Not One Century, But Five, Is Behind the Two-a-Day," *Evening Transcript*, October 2, 1926; Gilbert, *American Vaudeville*, 4.

17. Michael B. Leavitt, *Fifty Years in Theatrical Management* (New York, 1912), 183–84, 189, 382.

18. Arthur M. Schlesinger, *The Rise of the City: 1878–1898* (New York, 1933), 301.

19. For an overview of theatrical entertainment in nineteenth-century America turn to Robert C. Toll, *On With the Show: The First Century of Show Business* (New York, 1976).

20. For the minstrel show see Carl Wittke, *Tambo and Bones: A History of the American Minstrel Stage* (Durham, North Carolina), 1930; Robert C. Toll, *Blacking Up: The Minstrel Show in Nineteenth-Century America* (New York, 1974).

21. Frederic Logan Paxson, "Barnum, Phineas Taylor," *DAB*, I, 637; Ruth Crosby Dimmick, *Our Theatres To-day and Yesterday* New York, 1913), 32.

22. Rollin Lynde Hartt, *The People at Play: Excursions in the Humor and Philosophy of Popular Amusements* (Boston, 1909), 110.

23. Marsden Hartley, "Vaudeville," *Dial*, LXVII (March, 1920), 336.

24. Quoted in Christopher Morley, *Born in a Beer Garden or, She Troupes to Conquer* (New York, 1930), 44.

25. Allan Nevins and Milton Halsey Thomas, eds., *The Diary of George Templeton Strong*, 4 vols. (New York, 1952), IV, 183.

26. Joe Laurie, Jr., "The Early Days of Vaudeville," *American Mercury*, LXII (February, 1946), 223–34.

27. Laurence Hutton, "The American Burlesque," *Harper's Monthly*, LXXXI (June, 1890), 73; Bernard Sobel, *Burleycue: An Underground History of Burlesque Days* (New York, 1931), 3–17.

28. Edwin Milton Royle, "The Vaudeville Theatre," *Scribner's Magazine*, XXVI (October, 1899), 495.
29. Leavitt, *Fifty Years*, 185.
30. Busbey, *Home Life*, 187.
31. Gilbert, *American Vaudeville*, 15–16.
32. New York *Times*, December 24, 25, 1874.
33. *Ibid.*
34. Olive Logan, *Apropos of Women and Theatres: With a Paper or Two on Parisian Topics* (New York, 1869), 134.
35. Hartley Davis, "In Vaudeville," *Everybody's Magazine*, XIII (August, 1905), 231, 232.
36. *Dramatic Mirror*, December 24, 1898.
37. William Moulton Marston and John Henry Feller, *F. F. Proctor: Vaudeville Poneer* (New York, 1943), 50.
38. McLean, "Genesis of Vaudeville," 86.
39. *Ibid.*, 91.
40. F. F. Proctor, "A Pre-Historic 'Continuous Performance,'" *Dramatic Mirror*, December 24, 1898.
41. Alfred Bernheim, comp., "The Facts of Vaudeville," *Equity*, VIII (October, 1923), 15. I am indebted to John Browning for a copy of the several installments of the detailed survey of the field.
42. Charles Hervey, "The Foyer of the Vaudeville (Place de la Bourse)," *Theatre*, I (May 1, 1882), 266.
43. Brett Page, *Writing for Vaudeville: With Nine Complete Examples of Various Vaudeville Forms by Richard Harding Davis, Aaron Hoffmann, Edgar Allan Woolf, Taylor Granville, Louis Weslyn, Arthur Denvir, and James Madison* (Springfield, Mass., 1915), 6–10, 155–56.
44. Michael M. Davis, Jr., *The Exploitation of Pleasure: A Study of Commercial Recreations in New York City* (New York, 1912), 32.
45. Quoted in William Trufant Foster, *Vaudeville and Motion Picture Shows: A Study of Theaters in Portland, Oregon* (Portland, 1914), 34–35.
46. "The Decline of the Vaudeville," "Editor's Easy Chair," *Harper's Monthly*, CVI (April, 1903), 811–15.
47. Israel Zangwill, "The Future of Vaudeville in America," *Cosmopolitan*, XXXVIII (April, 1905), 639.
48. *Dramatic Mirror*, June 29, 1895.
49. "Continuous Performances. Against the 'God,'" *ibid.*, April 21, 1894.
50. Hutchins Hapgood, *A Victorian in the Modern World* (Seattle, 1972), 185–86. The autobiography was first published in 1939.
51. *Times*, December 16, 1917.
52. Nat C. Goodwin, *Nat Goodwin's Book* (Boston, 1914), 179.

53. Parker Morell, *Lillian Russell: The Era of Plush* (New York, 1940), 27–28; Parker Zellers, *Tony Pastor: Dean of the Vaudeville Stage* (Ypsilanti, Mich. 1971), 63–65; Hugh Leamy, "You Ought to Go on the Stage: An Interview with Edward F. Albee," *Collier's*, LXXVII (May 1, 1926), 10; Albert F. McLean, "Howard, Willie," *DAB*, Supplement Four, 400–1.

54. Norman Hapgood, "The Life of a Vaudeville Artiste," *Cosmopolitan*, XXX (February, 1901), 393.

55. Caroline Caffin, *Vaudeville* (New York, 1914), 25, 36–40; Gilbert, *Vaudeville*, 327–31; Dorothy Kish, "Tanguay, Eva," *DAB*, Supplement Four, 814–15.

56. The following discussion of the business organization of vaudeville has benefitted from conversations with John Browning and from his honors thesis, "American Vaudeville as Industry: A Monopoly of Stars" (University of California, Berkeley, Department of History, 1978).

57. John Ranken Towse, *Sixty Years of the Theater: An Old Critic's Memories* (New York, 1916), 87.

58. Leavitt, *Fifty Years*, 198–206; Alfred Bernheim, *The Business of the Theater* (New York, 1933), 37.

59. Toll, *On with the Show*, 272.

60. McLean, "Genesis of Vaudeville," 95. For details about the beginnings of the union see the account of its founder, George Fuller Gordon, *My Lady Vaudeville and Her White Rats* (New York, 1909).

61. Bernheim, comp., "Facts of Vaudeville," *Equity*, VIII (March, 1924), 43–44.

62. Robert Grau, "The Amazing Prosperity of the Vaudeville Entertainers," *Overland Monthly*, LVII (June, 1911), 608.

63. Bernheim, comp., "Facts of Vaudeville," *Equity*, VIII (September, 1923), 9.

64. Busbey, *Home Life*, 187.

65. "At the Park," *Dramatic Mirror*, September 3, 1892; Gilbert, *Vaudeville*, 10.

66. Foster, *Vaudeville*, 14.

67. Frank Norris, *McTeague: A Story of San Francisco* (New York, 1950), 67–80. The book was first published in 1899.

68. Bronson Howard, "The Audiences of New York," *Theatre*, II (August 1, 1879), 26.

69. John Corbin, "How the Other Half Laughs," *Harper's Monthly*, XCVIII (December, 1898), 38; Marion Winthrop, "The Transplanted Teuton and His Amusements," *Craftsman*, XIV (June, 1908), 395–96.

70. Corbin, "How the Other Half Laughs," 47–48.
71. Charles R. Sherlock, "Where Vaudeville Holds the Boards," *Cosmopolitan*, XXXII (February, 1902), 413.
72. Royle, "Vaudeville Theatre," 488.
73. Gilbert, *American Vaudeville*, 205.
74. McLean, "Genesis of Vaudeville," 92–93.
75. George M. Cohan, "The Mechanics of Emotion," *McClure's Magazine*, XLII (November, 1913), 75.
76. *Wehman Bros. Combination Prize Joker* (New York, 1896), p. 9, quoted in McLean, *American Vaudeville as Ritual*, 116; Gilbert, *American Vaudeville*, 251.
77. Paul Bourget, *Outre-Mer: Impressions of America* (New York, 1895), 345, 347.
78. *Herald*, June 1, 1862, quoted in Zellers, *Tony Pastor*, 17.
79. Robert A. Fremont, ed., *Favorite Songs of the Nineties: Complete Original Sheet Music for 89 Songs* (New York, 1973), 15–19.
80. "Mirror Interviews: Tony Pastor," *Dramatic Mirror*, July 27, 1895.
81. Zellers, *Tony Pastor*, 20, 105, 108.
82. *Ibid.*, 20.
83. Fremont, *Favorite Songs*, 90, 157, 174, 183, 230; Paul Charosh and Robert A. Fremont, eds., *More Favorite Songs of the Nineties: Complete Original Sheet Music for 62 Songs* (New York, 1975), 55, 92, 149.
84. Theodore Dreiser, "Birth and Growth of a Popular Song," *Metropolitan Magazine* (November, 1898), cited from a reprint in Charosh and Fremont, *More Favorite Songs*, xiv.
85. "Mother, Pin a Rose on Me," in Fremont, *Favorite Songs*, 204.
86. Kemp R. Niver, "Vaudeville Acts," in *Motion Pictures from the Library of Congress Paper Print Collection, 1894–1912*, ed. Bebe Bergsten (Berkeley, 1967), 346.
87. *Ibid.*, 343, 344.
88. Alan Dale, "Stage Beauty and Brains," *Cosmopolitan*, L (March, 1911), 520, 522; Hjalmar Hjorth Boyesen, 2d, "Beauty in the Modern Chorus," *ibid.*, XXXIV (March, 1903), 487.
89. Caffin, *Vaudeville*, 30.
90. James Peyton Sizer, *The Commercialization of Leisure* (Boston, 1917), 61.
91. "The Argot of Vaudeville," *Times*, December 16, 23, 1917.
92. Gilbert, *American Vaudeville*, 94; Niver, "Vaudeville Acts," 341, 354.
93. Edmund Wilson, "Houdini," in *The Shores of Light: A Literary Chronicle of the Twenties and Thirties* (New York, 1952), 176.

94. Norris, *McTeague*, 78.

95. Charles K. Harris, *How to Write a Popular Song* (New York, 1906), 10.

96. This simile emerged while I was reading an excerpt from the *Music Trade Review*, July 14, 1900, p. 25, found in the succinct and instructive "Introduction" by Paul Charosh to Charosh and Fremont, *More Favorite Songs*, ix–xii.

97. Edward Renton, *The Vaudeville Theatre: Building, Operation, Management* (New York, 1918), 298.

98. William Paul Gerhard, "Needed Improvements in Theater Sanitation," *Popular Science Monthly*, LVI (November, 1899), 85.

99. Birkmire, *American Theatres*, 54–56; Frank B. Copley, "The Story of a Great Vaudeville Manager: E. F. Albee, who helped Keith found his vaudeville circuit, became his heir, and is now the leader in that field of entertainment," *American Magazine*, XCIV (August, 1922), 154.

# SOURCES

A great variety of sources document the life of city people in the nineteenth century. They range from the physical remnants of that world, which survive here and there in big cities, to attitudes toward urban living that occasionally still exist today. These documents are therefore better described in a bibliographic essay than a formal list. Full references are given for works not cited in the chapter notes.

In the early 1950's, I came across the remnants of the American modern city in New York. I spent weeks just staring at the traces of newspaper palaces along Park Row and Printing House Square, at the iron facade of what once had been Stewart's New Store on Broadway and East Ninth Street, and at the French elegance of the Stuyvesant apartment house on East Eighteenth Street. I recognized variants of these vanishing landmarks in subsequent years in Philadelphia and Boston, Chicago and St. Louis, as well as San Francisco and Portland.

However, most of my visual impressions came from prints and photographs. I found these frequently in archives and museums, but conveniently some had been incorporated into good picture books covering various sources and subjects. John A. Kouwenhoven, comp., *Adventures of America, 1857–1900: A Pictorial Record from Harper's Weekly* (New York, 1938), utilizes the illustrations of *Harper's Weekly;* Edward Van Every, comp., *Sins of America as "Exposed" by the Police Gazette* (New York, 1931), those of the *Police Gazette*. John Maass, comp., *Gingerbread Age: A View of Victorian America* (New York, 1957), and Lucius Beebe and Charles Clegg, comps., *San Francisco's Golden Era: A Picture Story of San Francisco before the Fire* (Berkeley, 1960), indicate the range of topics.

For New York City itself, the wealth of the material is immense. In addition to the magistral work of I. N. Phelps Stokes, *Iconography of Man-*

*hattan,* 6 vols. (New York, 1915–28), there are the extraordinary photographic surveys from the turn of the century by Moses King, comp., *King's New York Views* and *King's Brooklyn Views,* most recently reprinted in 1977 in New York, and the model publication of the Municipal Art Society of New York, Alan Burnham, ed., . . . *Landmarks* . . . (Middletown, Conn., 1963). Other approaches to pictures were employed by John Grafton, comp., *New York in the Nineteenth Century: 321 Engravings from "Harper's Weekly" and Other Contemporary Sources* (New York, 1977), Edward B. Watson and Edmund V. Gillon, Jr., comps., *New York Then and Now: 83 Manhattan Sites Photographed in the Past and in the Present* (New York, 1976), and Helen Farr Sloan, ed., *John Sloan . . . Etchings* (New York, 1978). These are but three of the dozen books on New York scenes produced by one publisher in recent years.

The spirit of historical research attempting to fathom distant scenes speaks clearly in the admirable work of Grace M. Mayer, *Once upon a City* (New York, 1958). There are many good investigations covering the history of the physical components of city life, from apartment houses to tenements, and from streets to parks. The articles in the *Architectural Record* and in the *Journal of the Society of Architectural Historians* bristle with insights on the subject. The richness of literature in one area alone is indicated by the extent of the bibliographies in James Ford, *Slums and Housing . . . ,* 2 vols. (Cambridge, Mass., 1936), II, 973–1002. Many of these studies incorporate observations of people who actually saw the modern city rise, and these comments further enhanced my appreciation of their world.

One set of comments, written at mid-nineteenth century, stood out brightly: the sequence of papers on new buildings beginning with "New-York Daguerreotyped," *Putnam's,* I (February, 1853), 121–36. At the opening of the twentieth century, Richard M. Hurd, . . . *City Land Values* (New York, 1903), lucidly discussed the effect of real estate values on the structure of buildings and streets. Major features of this entire topic are thoughtfully summarized in bibliographical essays by David R. Goldfield, "Living History . . . ," *History Teacher,* VIII (August, 1975), 535–81, and Thomas J. Schlereth, "City as Artifact," *AHA Newsletter,* XV (February, 1977), 6–9.

City people spoke to me most directly in their newspapers. News reports, human interest stories, and advertisements abounded with clues about the quality of life. I wished I could read all accounts, but I quickly realized that I would be lucky if I could make my way through some, while actually understanding a few of them. The New York *Herald* (cov-

ered from 1835 to 1855), the New York *Tribune* (1841–65), and the New
York *World* (1870–95), the Boston *Evening Transcript* (1870–1910), the
Philadelphia *Inquirer* (1870–95), the Chicago *Times* (1865–75) and the
Chicago Daily *News* (1880–97), the St. Louis *Republican* (1887–93), the
San Francisco *Chronicle* (1865–1900) and the San Francisco *Examiner*
(1885–1910), furnished the outlines of life in the modern city. My pursuit
of specific items relied on the New York *Times Index*, a bibliographic mar-
vel. As a record of evolving techniques of advertising I used Frank Presbrey, *History . . . of Advertising* (Garden City, N.Y., 1929). Profusely illustrated, this volume also contains the texts of many messages that
defined modern life, of the type that usually can only be found scattered
through volumes of newsprint or reels of microfilm.

Articles in general magazines brought out urban trends. *Harper's
Monthly* offered running comments on the urban scene, and I profited
particularly from the "Editor's Easy Chair." *Putnam's* and *Knickerbocker*
helped generally in the beginning, while the *North American Review* answered special questions in such articles as "American Architecture,"
XLIII (October, 1836), 356–84. The growth of magazines in the second
half of the century extended coverage of city people, as was evident in
*Harper's Bazaar, Scribner's, Lippincott's, Overland Monthly, Collier's
Cosmopolitan, Outlook*, and *McClure's*. The range is well illustrated by an
excellent survey of the rise of America's major spectator sport, Will Irwin,
"Baseball," *Collier's*, XLIII (May 8, 1909), 12–13, 32–34; May 15, 1909,
14–15, 16–30; June 5, 1909, 11–12, 25–26; June 12, 1909, 11, 31–33, and by
a determined attempt to elucidate one aspect of the urban experience of
women, "The Girl Who Comes to the City: A Symposium," *Harper's
Bazaar*, XLII (January, 1908), 54–55; February, 1908, 170–72; March,
1908, 277–79; April, 1908, 394–99; May, 1908, 500–3; June, 1908, 591–95;
July, 1908, 692–95; August, 1908, 774–77; September, 1908, 888–91; October, 1908, 1005–7; November, 1908, 1139–42; December, 1908,
1226–30.

Two magazines, *Harper's Weekly* and *Leslie's Illustrated*, offered sum-
maries of protracted news stories and, in their many illustrations, welcome
relief from the reams of fading newsprint. The familiar guides to the periodical literature were indispensible. In addition I relied on the second,
revised and enlarged edition of Robert C. Brooks, comp., "A Bibliography
of Municipal Problems and City Conditions," *Municipal Affairs*, V
(March, 1901). The subject index of that monument of scholarship, published by the New York Reform Club Committee on City Affairs, lists
about 12,000 different entries, and its author index gives the names of

4,500 writers of some 8,000 titles, with abundant cross references thrown
in for good measure. I also cherished the bibliography for its references to
urban developments in European countries.

The expansion of newspaper journalism in nineteenth-century America
spawned a branch of literature purporting to expose the ways of the
wicked city. Loose publishing procedures, enormous pretension, and rep-
etition characterize the products of this genre. One author, James D. Mc-
Cabe, issued his . . . *Secrets* . . . (Philadelphia, 1868) in the same place
and year under both his name and a pseudonym, Edward Winslow Martin. Other illustrated tomes, at times published anonymously or under a
pseudonym, related any intimate details that struck the writers' fancy.
Frequently expanded and reissued, they relied for circulation heavily on
the ingenuity of subscription agents. I valued the so-called facts of the exposés less than the descriptions of the physical and human settings of the
lurid tales.

In order to give examples of this type of writing, a few books are listed
here according to the date of their original publication, although I have
used whatever edition I could lay my hands on and cited in my notes
whatever I found on the title page: *Matrimonial Brokerage . . . By a Reporter* . . . (New York, 1859); Junius Henri Browne, *Great Metropolis*
. . . (Hartford, 1869); George Ellington [pseud.], . . . *Women* . . . (New
York, 1869); Matthew Hale Smith, *Sunshine and Shadow* . . . (Hartford,
1869); B. E. Lloyd, *Lights and Shades* . . . (San Francisco, 1876); Henry
Morgan, *Boston Inside Out* . . . (Boston, 1891). Almost at the beginning
and at the end of the genre of exposure literature there appeared its clas-
sics: Thomas Butler Gunn, *The Physiology of New York Boarding Houses*
(New York, 1857), and Jacob Riis, *How the Other Half Lives* (New York,
1890). Both transcend mere or sordid curiosity about people with compassion for their sufferings.

I learned more about people and life from stories and novels. James
Fenimore Cooper, William Dean Howells, Edgar Allan Poe, and O.
Henry proved particularly helpful. Besides these men, Frank Norris,
Theodore Dreiser, Edith Wharton, Abraham Cahan, Henry B. Fuller,
William Graham Phillips, and H. C. Bunner furnished a wealth of infor-
mation. The observations of Walt Whitman became a special resource,
thanks to the work of Emory Holloway and various collaborators, who
published Whitman's *Uncollected Poetry and Prose* . . . , 2 vols. (Garden
City, N.Y., 1921), . . . *Editorials from the Brooklyn "Daily Times"* (New
York, 1932), and . . . *Recently Discovered Newspaper Articles* . . . (New
York, 1936).

Many years ago, when I first came across Vicki Baum, *Grand Hotel*, I thought its success might spawn an entire branch of fiction devoted to forms of big-city life, but apartment or vaudeville house novels have not yet experienced a vogue. However, there are many ball park and baseball stories, registering the impact of the sport on the American mind, and they tell a lot about spectators. "Old Well-Well!," the story by Zane Grey first published in the New York *Success Magazine* in July, 1910, and afterwards in his collection, *Redheaded Outfield* . . . (New York, 1920), opened my eyes to the genre.

The significance of so-called lesser literary figures for my investigation may be illustrated with a reference to Edward W. Townsend. His stories about "Chimmie Fadden," as well as *Daughter of the Tenements* (New York, 1895) and *Near a Whole City Full* (New York, 1897), proved valuable precisely because they substituted actual observation for artistic imagination. The type of writing loosely called city novel has been discussed in various contexts. However, completeness of description, augmented with detailed references to sights and many pictures, still distinguishes a study published many years ago by Arthur Bartlett Maurice, "New York in Fiction," *Bookman*, X (September, 1899), 33–49; October, 1899, 128–43; November, 1899, 224–33; December, 1899, 348–58.

The records of three great diarists of nineteenth-century urban America substantiated the description of city ways in novels and stories. Their wealth of detail and the span of their record is impressive, covering the period when most American fiction had not yet entered the phase of realistic observation. The interests of each diarist complemented those of the others in the general picture they create of the decades between 1830 and 1870. Allan Nevins, ed., *Diary of Philip Hone*, 2 vols. (New York, 1927), features as urban statesman a leading citizen who could notice that the large new windows of a department store might be easily broken by a stone thrown by a boy. Nevins and Milton Halsey Thomas, eds., *Diary of George Templeton Strong*, 4 vols. (New York, 1952), shows an incisive mind shrewdly assessing the intellectual and artistic scene of the metropolis without losing sight of its human components. Nicholas B. Wainwright, ed., . . . *Diary of Sidney George Fisher* . . . (Philadelphia, 1967), presents the Philadelphia perspective of a self-willed observer who never felt the need to do anything else for a living.

The interaction of diarists, writers, and journalists with the modern city created literary gems in the form of autobiographies. Henry James, *Small Boy* . . . (New York, 1913), and Theodore Dreiser, . . . *About Myself* (New York, 1922), perceive the experience from opposite poles. Hutchins Hapgood, *Victorian* . . . (New York, 1939), exposes conflicts inherent in intensified urbanization by showing them being lived intensely. The com-

plexities of Americanization mark Jacob Riis, *Making of an American* . . .
(New York, 1901), and Edward Bok, . . . *Dutch Boy* . . . (New York,
1924). Jane Addams, *Twenty Years at Hull House* (New York, 1910), adds
the perspective of a woman, but I relied on what seems to have been her
favorite book, *Spirit of Youth* . . . (New York, 1909), to see the life
behind the legend that grew around the autobiography.

The physical and human complexity of the modern city struck visitors
from abroad strongly. In the rich body of travel literature, I concentrated
on books that detailed or stressed the distinctly American nature of the
urban experience. As so often, the great foreign commentators on nineteenth-century America, from Alexis de Tocqueville to James Bryce, from
Harriet Martineau to Paul Bourget, did not disappoint. However, there
were many others, increasingly well known through good translations. A
reference to I[srael] J[oseph] Benjamin, *Three Years in America*,
*1859–1862*, trans. Charles Reznikoff, 2 vols. (Philadelphia, 1956), and
Knut Hamsun, . . . *Modern America*, trans. Barbara Gordon Morgridge
(Cambridge, Mass., 1969), will also indicate the range of the commentators. Many compilations lightened that phase of research. Bessie Louise
Pierce, comp., *As Others See Chicago* . . . (Chicago, 1933), exemplifies
them well.

The emergence of the metropolitan press is, of course, best docu-
mented by the newspapers themselves. The wealth of information available increased my profound respect for the preservation of insights by a
profession at times called "history in a hurry." Two detailed, well-
organized census reports placed many facts into a clear framework: S. N.
D. North, "History and Present Condition . . . ," U.S. Department of
the Interior, Bureau of the Census, *Tenth Census* (Washington, 1884),
VIII, and William S. Rossiter, "Printing and Publishing," *ibid.*, *Twelfth
Census* (Washington, 1902), IX. A voluminous history of the American
press, Frederic Hudson, *Journalism* . . . (New York, 1873), written by
one of the leading practitioners of the new journalism, contains so much
evidence that only its sheer size can explain the neglect the book has suffered. The broad sweep it lacks is provided roughly a generation later by
another newspaperman, Will Irwin, "American Newspaper . . . ," *Collier's*, XLVI (January 14, 1911), 12; January 21, 1911, 15–18; February 4,
1911, 14–17; February 18, 1911, 14–17, 24, 27; March 4, 1911, 18–20, 36;
March 18, 1911, 16–18; April 1, 1911, 18–19, 28; April 22, 1911, 21–22,
35–36; May 6, 1911, 17–19, 30; May 27, 1911, 15–16, 23–25; June 3, 1911,
17–18, 29–31; June 17, 1911, 17–18; July 1, 1911, 17–18, 30; July 8, 1911,
15–16, 25; July 22, 1911, 22, 25–26; July 29, 1911, 15–16, 23, 25.
Comments of other insiders are typified by Lambert A. Wilmer, *Our*

*Press Gang* . . . (Philadelphia, 1860), James Parton, *Famous Americans* . . . (Boston, 1867), Horace Greeley, *Recollections* . . . (New York, 1873), and Whitelaw Reid, . . . *Newspaper Tendencies* . . . (New York, 1879). Among autobiographers, none surpass the perceptivity of H. L. Mencken, *Newspaper Days* (New York, 1945), as reporter and editor in Baltimore, or the graphic sketches of one of the first newspaper cartoonists, Walt McDougal, *This Is the Life* (New York, 1926). P. T. Barnum, *Art of Money Getting* (New York, 1855), drives home the significance of the newspaper in modern life; George P. Rowell, . . . *Advertising Agent* (New York, 1906), makes the importance of advertising his theme.

Recent histories of journalism are well represented by Frank Luther Mott, *American Journalism* . . . , rev. ed. (New York, 1950). Equally useful are the pertinent articles in the *Journalism Quarterly* and two by James L. Crouthamel, "Newspaper Revolution . . . ," *New York History*, XLV (April, 1964), 91–113, and ". . . Bennett . . . ," *ibid.*, LIV (July, 1973), 294–316. Justin E. Walsh, . . . *Storey* . . . (Chapel Hill, N.C., 1958), W. A. Swanberg, . . . *Hearst* . . . (New York, 1961), and George Juergens, . . . *Pulitzer* . . . (Princeton, 1966), are good biographies of publishers. Bernard Weisberger, . . . *Newspaperman* . . . (Chicago, 1961), probes well the work of journalists as a group. A succinct introduction to the vast literature of their activities is a bibliographical essay by Joseph Patrick McKerns, ". . . American Journalism . . . ," *American Studies International*, XV (Fall, 1976), 17–34.

An introduction to the mysteries of shopping at mid-nineteenth century, so crucial for an understanding of the growing role of the department store in the life of city women, came from newspapers and magazines, as well as trade pamphlets and etiquette books. A Late Retailer, *A Peep into Catherine Street* . . . (New York, 1846), the sagacious reflections of a businessman on the changes in selling and buying in what may have been New York's first ladies' mile, and Eliza Leslie, . . . *Manual for Ladies* . . . , 4th ed (Philadelphia, 1854), alerted me to new forms of behavior that reflected rising expectations about goods and services. Several articles in *Hunt's Merchant's Magazine* explained the larger economic setting. Another kind of perspective, derived from efforts to emancipate women's minds, came from Frances Trollope, *Domestic Manners* . . . , 2 vols. (London, 1832), as well as Elizabeth Cady Stanton, . . . *Reminiscences* . . . (New York, 1898).

The relative freedom of American women, compared with their European counterparts, appeared from the observations of many visitors to the United States. I grasped its significance more clearly when I read again

Emile Zola, *Au bonheur des dames* (Paris, 1883), that great novel of city
life seen through a department store, in connection with the thorough assessment of the operation of the Paris Bon Marché by Michael Barry
Miller, "The Department Store and Social Changes in Modern France:
The Case of the Bon Marché, 1869–1920" (Ph.D thesis, University of
Pennsylvania, 1976), and recognized the efforts to maintain the patronage
of a rather exclusive clientele in the first Paris department store. Analogous clues about trends in London, as well as about the English commitment to the small store, came from the writings of George Augustus Sala,
the tireless recorder of London life, particularly his newspaper articles and
*Twice Round the Clock* . . . (London, 1858), and *London Up to Date*
(London, 1894), as well as from the excellent study of William Whiteley,
*the* great shopkeeper, by Richard S. Lambert, *Universal Provider* . . .
(London, 1938).

Among other secondary materials, I benefited much from comments on
shopping and fashion by Hugh Dalziel Duncan, *Culture and Democracy*
. . . (Totowa, N.J., 1965), and Dorothy Davis, *History of Shopping* (London, 1966). The books on great stores or their founders range from entertaining reading—Lloydt Wendt and Herman Kogan, *Give the Lady* . . .
(Chicago, 1952)—to business biography—John H. Appel, . . . *John Wanamaker* . . . (New York, 1930)—and business history—Robert W. Twyman, . . . *Marshall Field* . . . (Philadelphia, 1954). Thoroughness places
Ralph M. Hower, . . . *Macy's* . . . (Cambridge, Mass., 1943), into a class
by itself. Among articles, a similar position is occupied by Harry E. Resseguie, ". . . A. T. Stewart," *Business History Review*, XXXVI (Autumn,
1962), 255–86, ". . . Department Store . . . ," *ibid.*, XXIX (Autumn,
1965), 301–22, and "Stewart's Marble Palace . . . ," *New York Historical
Society Quarterly*, XLVIII (April, 1964), 131–62. A broad perspective rec-
ommends H. Pasdermadjian, *Department Store* . . . (London, 1954),
among the general department-store histories.

The sporting press of nineteenth-century America contains many comments by early sports writers on baseball and other spectator sports. For
the middle of the century, I relied mostly on the New York *Spirit of the
Times*. The New York *Clipper* was launched in 1853; I followed that major
American sporting journal, which also covered the stage, from that date
until 1894 when it became exclusively a theatrical journal. I also kept an
eye on the popular New York *National Police Gazette*, which from the late
1870's on ran a column of sporting news and discussed baseball gossip
under the heading "Our National Game." Lastly, the sports page, the creation of the metropolitan press, became a source of information in the
closing decades of the century.

Several journalists provided leads. In particular Will Irving, "Baseball," *Collier's*, XLIII (May 8, 1909), 12–13, 32–34; May 15, 1909, 14–15, 26–30; June 5, 1909, 11–12, 25–26; June 12, 1909, 11, 31–33, sharpened my awareness about the relationship between the protective equipment of players and the kind of game the spectators wanted to see. Hugh Fullerton, "The Fellows . . . ," *Saturday Evening Post*, CC (April 21, 1928), 18–19, 184–88, directed me to the significance of the Chicago style of baseball reporting for American journalism and speech. His main theme, the essential role of journalists in spreading the gospel of baseball, is covered well by John Rickards Betts, "Sporting Journalism," *American Quarterly*, V (Spring, 1953), 39–56, for major nineteenth-century sports.

Henry Chadwick occupies a special position among early baseball writers. As reporter and statistician for the *Clipper* and editor of various baseball guides, he pretty much shaped the image of modern baseball as it appeared at the beginning of the twentieth century. The task absorbed him, and he never got around to writing the history of the game that some expected from his pen. Albert G. Spalding, one of the early ballplayers, who as promoter and sporting goods manufacturer actually managed to make the complicated transition to baseball mogul, used some of Chadwick's papers for *America's National Game* . . . (New York, 1911). As reminiscence and history, it is a book of lore and judgment, always insightful as well as monumental. Other accounts by early ballplayers are on a more intimate scale. Adrian C. Anson, *Ball Player's Career* . . . (Chicago, 1900), and Christy Mathewson, *Pitching in a Pinch* . . . (New York, 1912), recollect great plays, as did most others who followed them into print.

Good histories of the game are Harold Seymour, *Baseball: The Early Years* (New York, 1960), and *Baseball: The Golden Age* (New York, 1971), and David Quentin Voigt, *American Baseball: From Gentleman's Sport to the Commissioner System* (Norman, Okla., 1966), and *American Baseball: From the Commissioners to Continental Expansion* (Norman, Okla. 1970). There is no up-to-date general history of sports in the United States, but John Allan Krout, *Annals* . . . (New York, 1929), and Herbert Manchester, *Four Centuries* . . . (New York, 1931), furnish an outline. Foster R. Dulles, *History of Recreation: America Learns to Play*, 2d ed. (New York, 1965), also helps. John Rickards Betts died before he could complete this task. His well-informed . . . *Sporting Heritage* . . . (Reading, Mass., 1974), published posthumously, covers the century between 1850 and 1950. About twenty years earlier, his "Technological Revolution and . . . Sport," *Journal of American History*, XL (September, 1953), 231–56, had expanded upon a subject initially taken up by Frederic L. Paxson, "Rise of

Sport," *ibid.*, IV (September, 1917), 143–68. For the late eighteenth century and the early nineteenth, Jennie Holliman, *American Sports* . . .
(Durham, N.C., 1931), is still a good guide. The physical remnants of the
nineteenth-century ball park seem to have vanished, but Bill Shannon and
George Kalinsky, *Ballparks* (New York, 1975), collects some history and
pictures.

The rise of vaudeville is recorded in the columns of the metropolitan
press and the theatrical trade journals, particularly the *Clipper* and the
New York *Dramatic Mirror*. The latter, a leading source of information
about affairs of the stage at the turn of the century, established a regular
vaudeville department in 1895. Its Christmas number of December 24,
1898, presented "Twenty Years of Vaudeville," a kind of historical survey
that relied heavily on contributions from well-known impresarios. Walter
J. Kingsley, "Thirty Years . . . ," *ibid.*, November 26, 1913, pp. 4–5,
followed in these footsteps. In the early 1920's *Equity* collected the recollections of performers and arranged them into a general history that is
strong for the years after 1900. That material was published by Alfred
Bernheim, comp., "Facts of Vaudeville," *Equity*, VIII–IX (September,
1923), 9–13, 32–35, 37; October, 1923, 13–16, 35, 37; November, 1923,
33–40; December, 1923, 19–20, 34–43, 45, 47; January, 1924, 15–16,
40–43, 45–47; February, 1924, 19–20, 39–43, 45–47; March, 1924, 17–20,
37–39, 43–44. Together with the recollections of insiders, such as Michael
B. Leavitt, *Fifty Years* . . . (New York, 1912), or Robert Grau, *Business
Man in the Amusement World* (New York, 1910), it provides a good historical perspective.

Insights into the meaning of vaudeville for city people came from a variety of widely different sources. Rollin Lynde Hartt, *People at Play* . . .
(Boston, 1909), shrewdly assesses vaudeville in the context of other popular entertainments. Brett Page, *Writing for Vaudeville* . . . (Springfield,
Mass., 1915), goes beyond the mechanics of composition and carefully
delineates the impact of various kinds of sketches on the minds of spectators. William H. Birkmire, *Planning* . . . *of Theatres* (New York, 1901),
explains the visual effect of spectacular architecture on the audience.

These accounts by professionals helped most when I used them in conjunction with the perceptive comments by Caroline Caffin, *Vaudeville*
(New York, 1914). She outlines the logic behind the popular identification
with the show that sustained the successful entertainment. Her essays on
leading performers make their success seem plausible and even inevitable.
The strength of vaudeville's emotional appeal also speaks from various
songsters and collections of sheet music based on popular tunes sung in
the vaudeville house. Synopses of some 140 "Vaudeville Acts," collected

as a chapter in Kemp R. Niver, *Motion Pictures from the Library of Congress Paper Print Collection* . . . (Berkeley, 1967), 39–54, convey the staging and content of the variety show.

The literature of performers and reformers offered additional perspectives. George M. Cohan, "Mechanics of Emotion," *McClure's*, XLII (November, 1913), 69–77, systematically discussed the production of tears, laughs, and thrills. George Fuller Gordon, *My Lady Vaudeville* . . . (New York, 1909), documents the control of vaudevillians by booking agents and circuits. The exploitation of pleasure is the theme of reformers, forcefully reiterated by Michael M. Davis, Jr., *Exploitation* . . . (New York, 1912), and James Peyton Sizer, *Commercialization of Leisure* (Boston, 1917).

Among the general histories of vaudeville, Douglas Gilbert, *American Vaudeville* . . . (New York, 1940), and Joe Laurie, Jr., *Vaudeville* . . . (New York, 1953), excell because of their knowledge of performers. Bernard Sobel, *Pictorial History* . . . (New York, 1961), furnishes visual dimensions; John E. DiMeglio, *Vaudeville* . . . (Bowling Green, Ohio, 1973), adds the perspective of American popular culture. Albert F. McLean, Jr., has done much to deepen understanding of the variety show. . . . *Vaudeville as Ritual* (Lexington, Ky., 1965), and his publication of two B. F. Keith letters in *Theatre Survey*, I (1960), 82–95, are two examples of his contributions. A carefully researched and thoughtfully written biography of a great vaudevillian is Parker Zellers, *Tony Pastor* . . . (Ypsilanti, Mich., 1971). Robert C. Toll, *On With the Show* . . . (New York, 1976) is a good overview of theatrical entertainment in nineteenth-century America.

Many excellent general works on urbanization helped me to see the broad context of my story. Two monuments of scholarship tower over other works: Adna F. Webber, *Growth of Cities in the Nineteenth Century: A Study in Statistics* (New York, 1899), and Lewis Mumford, *City in History: Its Origins, Its Transformations, and Its Prospects* (New York, 1961). Blake McKelvey, *Urbanization of America, 1865–1915* (New Brunswick, N.J., 1963), and *Emergence of Metropolitan America, 1915–1966* (New Brunswick, N.J., 1968), were invaluable for their detailed coverage of complex features. Many of the books in the Urban Life in America Series (New York, 1967–78), Richard C. Wade, general editor, have inspired my search for answers. Good histories of individual cities contributed their share, such as Bessie L. Pierce, *History of Chicago*, 3 vols. (New York, 1937–57). Specific aspects of city life in the nineteenth and early twentieth centuries have received much attention in recent years, and I have profited from the debate whenever it touched my concerns.

# INDEX